INTEGRATING CHANGE

Change processes in organizations are time consuming, expensive, and often don't create the intended results. This book creates a new way for leaders to relate to change from a place of deeper understanding. Based on years of research, consulting, and teaching, the models and frameworks described in this book have been applied successfully in organizations such as Johnson & Johnson, AT&T, IBM, Facebook, Charles Schwab & Company, and Accenture.

The book provides breakthrough thinking to leaders who find themselves in the chaos of multiple, high amplitude changes that cannot be managed from an autocratic or even a participative mindset. The successful transformation of a human system does not require that people change who they are so much as it requires they become more of who they are—more like themselves. Change does not require new step-by-step models offered by an outside expert. It requires teaching people how to become model builders. As a result of this deeper transformation of mindset, not only will people in the organization be able to manage the particular change crisis facing them in the moment, they will develop a new relationship to change so that strategic thinking and breakthrough business outcomes become part of the organizational norm.

This book will primarily appeal to experienced leaders, senior managers, and change agents who have learned that the textbook recipes for initiating or responding to change don't work. It is also useful supplementary reading for students of organizational studies and leadership.

Mel Toomey is the Founder of The Center for Leadership Studies. Mel is an educator, executive advisor, and organizational consultant. He is the principal designer for one of the first Master of Arts in Organizational Leadership programs ever offered at a university.

Judi Neal received her Ph.D. from Yale University and is an author, scholar, and consultant in organizational transformation and workplace spirituality. She was the Academic Director of the Master of Arts in Organizational Leadership Program and is the President of Edgewalkers International.

INTEGRATING CHANGE

The Art, the Science and the Craft of Transforming Organizations

*Mel Toomey and
Judi Neal*

Routledge
Taylor & Francis Group

LONDON AND NEW YORK

First published 2022
by Routledge
2 Park Square, Milton Park, Abingdon, Oxon OX14 4RN

and by Routledge
605 Third Avenue, New York, NY 10158

Routledge is an imprint of the Taylor & Francis Group, an informa business

British Library Cataloguing-in-Publication Data
A catalogue record for this book is available from the British Library

Library of Congress Cataloging-in-Publication Data
Names: Toomey, Mel, 1939– author. | Neal, Judi, author.
Title: Integrating change : the art, the science and the craft of transforming organizations / Mel Toomey, Judi Neal.
Description: Abingdon, Oxon ; New York, NY : Routledge, 2021. | Includes bibliographical references and index. |
Identifiers: LCCN 2021010067 (print) | LCCN 2021010068 (ebook) |
ISBN 9780367675738 (hbk) | ISBN 9780367675752 (pbk) | ISBN 9781003131847 (ebk)
Subjects: LCSH: Organizational change. | Strategic planning. | Leadership.
Classification: LCC HD58.8 .T66 2021 (print) | LCC HD58.8 (ebook) |
DDC 658.4/06—dc23
LC record available at https://lccn.loc.gov/2021010067
LC ebook record available at https://lccn.loc.gov/2021010068

ISBN: 978-0-367-67573-8 (hbk)
ISBN: 978-0-367-67575-2 (pbk)
ISBN: 978-1-003-13184-7 (ebk)

DOI: 10.4324/9781003131847

Typeset in Joanna
by codeMantra

Imagine an organization
where people's visions and commitments
for the future are not compromised,
where they can work together aligned in
what they see and understand.
This book is an exploration of how such an
organization might become possible.

CONTENTS

FIGURES

TABLES

ACKNOWLEDGMENTS

Just like it takes a village to raise a child, it takes a community to write a book. The concepts, models, and practices in this book have been tested, modified, and extended by the organizational and leadership clients of the Generative Leadership Group, the Graduate Institute students in the Master of Arts and Organizational Leadership Program (MAOL), and the executives who attended the Integrating Change programs at the University of Arkansas and other venues.

We give special acknowledgment to Elisa Maselli who helped organize, and communicate many of the early versions of these ideas and who put in Herculean effort to manage details as we wrapped things up. Her understanding of the models and practices in this book are invaluable.

Alan Chapman and Brent Robertson are graduates of the Master of Arts in Organizational Leadership and Peter McGaugh worked as a Senior Consultant with Generative Leadership Group and also taught in the MAOL program. They each have made a deep commitment to the work of integrating change and organizational transformation. We are eternally grateful for the in-depth feedback they provided on this book and their mastery of this material and their feedback to us significantly increased the value and usability of this work. We are sure that they will be able to see the difference that they made.

Dana Toomey, Mel's wife, is a loving and thinking partner. She creates an environment full of beauty and creativity; an environment that has nurtured Mel during the writing of this book and throughout his life. She is a sculptress, an activist, a healer, an artist, and an educator. She carries this experience and knowledge with grace, all of which has had a major influence on any wisdom you find in this book.

Judi wishes to acknowledge Paul Kwiecinski for all the Friday morning calls dedicated to mutual writing support, and Marie Wolny for her lifetime of sisterly love. Ellis Ralph, Judi Neal's husband, generously read multiple versions of this manuscript and offered both insight and valuable editing, while at the same time cooking meals, doing laundry, tending the dogs, grocery shopping, and finding countless other ways to be supportive while Judi worked on this book. The difference he has made is in the quality of Judi's life, and the experience of being loved and fully supported.

PREFACE

Personal Statement – Mel Toomey

I've been a student of organizational life for many years. In my previous careers in real estate and software development, I noticed how organizations worked, what made them prosper, and what hindered success. I began to realize that "Organization" was not very well defined. (See Overview of This Book for why and when we capitalize "Organization"). We think of companies as their products and results, but there wasn't a concise way to talk about that amorphous thing, the higher idea of Organization itself.

This book is an attempt to clarify Organization. It is meant to give you ways to look at any organization, regardless of its industry or size, and see the mechanics or the architecture of it, and thus to be able to effect lasting change. There's nothing on the shelf currently to help leaders with that, or at least nothing that works consistently. The only tool we have is process – do this differently, or do more of it, do it smarter or better – but that's not the answer. We need a kind of X-ray vision into the workings of organizations, so we can see which levers to push to get lasting, impactful change.

I hope you get a sense that there is an alternative approach, not based in process, but in a kind of thinking that shifts reality. If we can see something differently, if our field of vision is altered so we can see behind the veil into the higher reality, then we can take entirely different actions and produce new and unprecedented results. But the value of this book, in large part, will depend upon your willingness to examine the information and observations expressed against the background of your own personal experience. I trust that the combination of these written words and your personal experience will combine in ways that provoke thinking and provide benefits to you and your organization.

This book is borne of five decades of reflection, research, and on-the-ground experience. To a large degree, what I have to say I learned with my colleagues and our clients. At the core of my learning over all this time, I have discovered that people at work are fundamentally committed to contributing and making a difference. *They want to know that what they do makes a difference.* And when people are present to and aware of their values, beliefs, commitments, purposes, and intentions, they are not only willing to stand for something, they have something on which to stand—a place from which to get their jobs done powerfully.

Writing about Organizations and change has been a challenging task. How does one present something that has "hard to say" or "un-say-able" dimensions? For me, Rainer Maria Rilke in *Letters To A Young Poet* expresses it well:

> *Things aren't all so tangible and sayable as people would usually have us believe; most experiences are unsayable, they happen in a space that no word has ever entered.*

I am very grateful for the partnership, genius, and persistence of my colleague and co-author Judi Neal. When we met, I was immediately impressed with her ability to really think, her willingness to explore areas within and outside her fields of expertise, and her commitment to spirituality in the workplace. In this book endeavor, she has provided academic rigor, curiosity, a willingness to stick with it even when the going got rough, and the ability to adopt and adapt to another person's perspective and have it make a difference for herself as well as the other. Without her, this book would never have been completed, and I am grateful for her partnership.

Mel Toomey
Goshen, CT
January 2021

Personal Statement: Judi Neal

I met Mel Toomey in 2006, on the day of the publication of my book *Edgewalkers*, a book about change leaders. Our conversation immediately focused on organizations and leadership and what it takes to be on the leading edge. We share a passion for understanding the processes that support healthy personal and organizational change and transformation.

We have been friends and colleagues ever since, and this book is our way of sharing Mel's powerful ideas with a broader audience than his clients and students. Mel is primarily a practitioner with academic credentials. I am primarily a scholar with practitioner experience. It is our hope that our different but complementary backgrounds enrich this exploration of what it takes to integrate successful transformation in organizations. The architecture of the thinking in this book is rooted in Mel's experience and his deep commitment to seeing the underlying patterns in what makes organizational transformation effective. I have done my best to support his work with my research in personal, organizational, and global systems transformation.

Mel perceives the world and communicates about what he sees in a nonlinear way. Like a wise sage, a conversation with Mel about integrating change can begin anywhere, with any issue, and is likely to lead to a sudden and unpredictable shift in the way you see things. This shift in your own seeing, can lead to new, emergent forms of action that you could not have anticipated before the conversation. Books are linear and are not interactive in the way that a conversation ought to be. My task has been to attempt to make this work appear linear and logical, in order to fit the constraints of a static piece of printed material, while attempting to keep the magic of Mel's wisdom alive. One way we do this is to keep revisiting certain topics, and relooking at them from different angles. It's like looking at different facets of a diamond. The central theme in this diamond is the intertwining of the three meta-disciplines of Organization: Managing, Leading, and Integrating Change. Every chapter revisits these relationships, but each time from a slightly different angle and with greater levels of distinctions.

In order for meaningful change to take place, people need to be willing to have some faith and trust that stepping into the unknown will result in positive outcomes for them personally and for the organization. It's like that moment in *Raiders of the Lost Ark* when Harrison Ford has reached the end of the trail and is standing at the edge of a large chasm. He knows he must take a leap of faith and he steps out into the empty space above the chasm, and a step appears under his feet. We invite you to take that leap of faith as you read this book.

On this Integrating Change journey, it is impossible to see exactly what the path is or where it will end up, and it requires a leap of faith into what we can sense but not yet see. This book provides an in-depth look at the underlying processes and structure of organizational change and transformation, with guidelines on how to think differently in order to achieve results beyond what could have been imagined or predicted.

Judi Neal
Fayetteville, AR
January 2021

OVERVIEW OF THIS BOOK

Mel Toomey

Judi Neal

Offer yourself to the world—your energies, your gifts, your visions, your heart—with open-hearted generosity. But understand that when you live that way you will soon learn how little you know and how easy it is to fail. To grow in love and service, you—I, all of us—must value ignorance as much as knowledge and failure as much as success ... Clinging to what you already know and do well is the path to an unlived life. So, cultivate beginner's mind, walk straight into your not-knowing, and take the risk of failing and falling again and again, then getting up again and again to learn—that's the path to a life lived large, in service of love, truth, and justice.

Parker Palmer

Introduction

Managing change was simple and effective in the days when life was relatively stable and predictable. Organizational leadership could plan for steady growth. You could plan for the introduction of a new product, and you could plan for the implementation of a new technology. There was time. Relationships with employees were straightforward and usually fairly autocratic, so you could order people to do what you wanted. Generally, only one change happened at a time, with long stable periods in between.

In today's world of *Black Swans* (Taleb 2001)—unpredictable crises with severe consequences—with multiple changes happening all at once, change cannot be easily managed and controlled. Chaos can lead either to integration or disintegration (Lorenz 1995). When chaos leads to integration, the organization evolves to a higher level of complexity, adaptability, and sustainability. When chaos leads to disintegration, the organization's viability is threatened. What is it about a successful response to unpredictable crises and chaos that makes the difference between evolution or disintegration? It begins with leadership. A leader's primary job is to initiate change. Change must first be initiated, then integrated, and only then can it be managed. This book provides a practical model that weaves these three relationships: The art of leadership, the craft of integration, and the science of management.

Based on years of research, consulting, and teaching, the models and frameworks described in this book have been applied successfully in organizations such as Johnson & Johnson, AT&T, IBM, Facebook, Charles Schwab & Company, and Accenture.

There are plenty of "how-to" books that provide a step-by-step plan for managing change. This book is different. Here you will learn new and innovative ways to relate to change through this radically new framework with proven measurable (and immeasurable) results in major organizations.

Change processes in organizations are time consuming, expensive, and often don't create the intended results. Our aim is to provide a more effective model of organizational transformation that will be useful to organizational leaders and those who are studying and implementing organizational change. Time and money are wasted in trying to "manage" change as if it were controllable. It is not controllable. Our hope is that this book will create a new way for leaders to relate to change from a place of deeper understanding. If you apply the concepts and approaches in this book, your organization will have much more energy and resources for productivity, for creating what has never been created before, and for making a positive difference in the world.

Our goal is to provide breakthrough thinking to leaders who find themselves in the chaos of multiple high amplitude changes that cannot be managed from an autocratic or even a participative mindset. The successful transformation of a human system does not require that people change who they are so much as it requires they become more of who they are—more like themselves. Change does not require people to change their thinking. It requires them to find new ways of thinking about thinking. Change does not require new step-by-step models offered by an outside expert. It requires teaching people how to become model builders. As a result of this deeper transformation of mindset, not only will people in the organization be able to manage the particular change crisis facing them in the moment, they will develop a new relationship to organizational transformation that integrates internal and external changes into the way the organization is led. This book provides a new model and new distinctions (easily recognized differences) that support breakthrough thinking and breakthrough projects in a chaotic and unpredictable world.

Other books about change conflate "management" and "leadership." Change begins with leadership. A leader's primary job is to initiate change. Change must first be initiated, then integrated, and only then can it be managed. *Integrating Change* provides a practical model that weaves these three relationships:

The Art of Leadership: When leading, the challenge is to create new possibilities for the organization, to focus on what does not yet exist, to lead organizational growth through new products, new services and new categories.

The Craft of Integration: When integrating, the challenge is to demonstrate feasibility and efficacy, to focus on what it takes to transform possibility into reality. To establish feasibility and efficacy requires concern not only for the reality of the marketplace, but also for the reality of an organization's capabilities and capacity (i.e., the headspace available to create, innovate, adapt and react).

The Science of Management: When managing, the challenge is to provide reliability, predictability and certainty to the business, to focus on taking care of what already exists, to work toward organic growth through stewardship.

Developing an effective organization includes going beyond the traditional work of increasing skills and competencies and going beyond the redesign of processes. It is also essential to develop the capacity to establish purposeful contexts in which strategic thinking and breakthrough organizational outcomes become part of the system's norm. "Context" is what leverages action. It is the source of meaning for work. Organizational environments that allow people to constantly learn, grow, and develop new ways to produce results are not necessarily predictable based on the past performance. This is what is meant by breakthrough.

Who Should Read This Book?

This book will primarily appeal to experienced leaders and change agents; people with work experience who have learned that the textbook recipes for initiating or responding to change don't work. It will appeal to deeper thinkers who are looking for an underlying framework to guide them in their thinking and action, and who are willing to look honestly enough at their assumptions, beliefs, and behavior in a way that opens up the possibility for personal transformation. Organizational transformation cannot occur without personal transformation (Neal 2018). *Integrating Change* will also be useful to those leaders who are courageous enough to take on challenges that can potentially make a huge contribution, even when they can't see where to start.

This book presupposes quite a bit of business or organizational knowledge and experience. It would not be a fit for an undergraduate student who is just getting his or her first job, for example. But it can be very useful and inspirational to someone who has been in the workforce and who has taken on informal or formal leadership challenges.

Organization of This Book

The first part of this book, Chapters 1 through 5, describe the basic elements of the Integrating Change model and the structure of the key elements of Organization. Chapters 6 through 13 delve more deeply into these relationships and structures, weaving in new concepts and practices to the process of integrating change.

Chapter 1: The Change Crisis

This chapter defines change integration and describes how people tend to react to change in organizational systems. It draws a distinction between risk and uncertainty. It makes the case that the craft of integrating change is equal to the disciplines of management and leadership.

Chapter 2: Organizational Integration

This chapter defines what is meant by "Organization" and distinguishes the three primary systems of Organization: Human Systems, Business Systems, and Development Systems. The three meta-disciplines with Organization are also described: Leadership (the domain of Human Systems), Management (the domain of Business Systems), and Integrating Change (the domain of Development Systems.

Chapter 3: Organizations and Reality

What if we could see organizations in dimensional rather than categorical terms? When we view something through a categorical lens, our understanding of it includes *prescribed meaning*. When we expand our observation of something to include its many dimensions, we also have the possibility of viewing *generated meaning*—the kind of meaning that is not, and perhaps cannot be, foretold or worked out in advance. One way of thinking about organizational reality emerges from the view that everything that communicates brings forth the organizational reality we inhabit, that is, what we see, sense, or know in the presence of communication. All Organization arises in language. This view of reality suggests the possibility that reality is a by-product of ongoing creativity.

Chapter 4: Organizations as Field Phenomena

Organizations can be seen fundamentally as field phenomena. As such, they are both complex and chaotic. When we view their *effect at a distance*, their complex nature is revealed. A three-circle model, presented below in this Overview is revisited for analyzing the elements of a field. Using this model, this chapter defines and distinguishes between leadership, development, and management as three organizational disciplines.

Chapter 5: Management, Leadership and Integration

People tend to collapse Management and Leadership into one and treat them as if they are interchangeable. However, they have very distinct roles to play in the midst of organizational change. An important key is to understand the differences between the ability to react and the ability to adapt. This chapter provides an analysis of integration at both the organizational level and the individual level and describes how vertical and horizontal integration apply to more than just the structure of the organization. Mastering integration is essential to innovation and breakthrough.

Chapter 6: The Art of Change Integration

Art is a process for change integration. In this process there are four catalysts (educate, develop, train, instruct), four capacities (create, innovate, adapt, react), and four types of action (disintermediate resource, intermediate possibility, mediate differences, and remediate problems). These are related to the distinctions of management, leadership and integration.

Chapter 7: Trust and Communication

Communication contributes to specialization and specialization inhibits communication. Integration is called for but is unrecognized in the roles of management and leadership and results in change that does not produce the intended results. Change must first be initiated, then integrated, and only then can it be managed. As we will see, trust in leadership does not stand by itself, it is part of a larger system of trust—a system that is manifest at many scales, such as individual, family, group, community, organization, and government. While trust is a global topic, it has compelling and real local effect. Leaders deal with this local effect on a daily basis. The absence of trust has a significant cost and its presence can be a strategic advantage. This chapter addresses trust at the scale of organization, and analyzes the relationship between trust, communication, and the integration of change.

Chapter 8: Integrating Breakthrough Change

Breakthroughs are desirable outcomes that go beyond our expectation for what's predictable. A breakdown is an outcome inconsistent with that which is intended. Breakthroughs can occur through circumstance or by intention. Breakthrough outcomes are not predictable, even with clear intention. But positive outcomes are more likely with intention.

Chapter 9: Toomey's Laws for Integrating Change

Based on years of consulting and teaching experience, Mel Toomey has derived these three laws for integrating change:

1. The longer a system survives, the less amenable it is to change.
2. The work needed to change is equal to the complexity of the system multiplied by the needed rate of change.

3. To every act of change integration there is an equal and opposite reaction directed at disintegrating the change.

This chapter provides several examples of organizational scale change integration.

Chapter 10: Breakthrough at the Scale of Your Own Experience

There are several underlying patterns and conditions for creating successful breakthroughs, regardless of the scale (team, department or total system). A detailed case study is presented as an example of the Four Design Steps of designing for breakthrough. This chapter revisits the importance of keeping risk and uncertainty distinct when undertaking breakthroughs. Specific guidance is provided on creating your own Breakthrough Initiative.

Chapter 11: Constraint and Creativity

A system optimized for efficiency will work under very limited conditions and is virtually useless outside a narrow range of conditions. A system optimized for effectiveness on the other hand will have broad application but will trade off efficiency for its flexibility. There are always constraints when optimizing a system and the basic trade-offs are between efficiency (rigidity) and effectiveness (flexibility). The Integrating Change model is consistent with what the researchers found regarding system optimization. The application of our organizational model has provided compelling evidence that optimization of Human Systems results from initiating "self-organizing processes" that are low in constraint and high in relationship.

Chapter 12: Calibration, Constraint and Leverage

Constraints are inherent in all systems. Constraints are necessary for creativity and innovation to occur, but it is helpful to understand how to calibrate constraints and to distinguish points of leverage for optimizing organizational transformation. This chapter draws on the systems analysis work of Donella Meadows and applies it to finding leverage where a small shift in one thing can thing can produce big changes in everything. Buckminster Fuller's concept of trimtabs is included as an example of working with and leveraging constraints.

Chapter 13: Source Code for an Integrated Organization

In order to understand Organization and to know how to create break-throughs, it is helpful to understand the underlying patterns and roles that make up the system. It is also helpful to know which roles to use under what circumstances. We present this as the Source Code of organizations built on the three sub-systems of the organizational system: Human Systems are the source of possibility; Development Systems are the source of efficacy; and Business Systems are the source of stewardship. This book concludes with suggestions for working with these ideas in your own organization.

The Call to Courage

When you are so daring as to envision a bold future—the realization of which changes what is understood, expands what is seen as possible, and honors the integrity of human interaction—then you appear dangerous to a world favoring stability, reliability, predictability and certainty.

In such a world, creating something new, something of value, calls for acts of existential courage. These acts are informed by, but not limited by, persisting norms. They are also acts shaped by designed futures—futures that call for breakthrough change; the kind of change that will not happen in the absence of community of educated leaders.

Three actions are essential for integrating change in organizations: (1) Honoring the past, (2) Empowering the future, and (3) Working in the present. Our goal is to provide you with the foundation and the "thinking about thinking" that support you in acting with courage.

Honoring the Past

The past provides a foundation on which you can stand. This foundation exists because those who manage existing affairs bring stewardship to resources at hand.

When stepping into a bold future, we need a place to stand—a place beyond what stewardship alone is designed to provide.

Empowering the Future

Fulfilling bold futures requires ways of working that are unfamiliar.

These new ways of working are not born solely of the past. They are forged by those willing to stand for possibility, doing so often in the face of no agreement, that is, "standing for what you see, even if no one else agrees." Studying the past, researching best practices, and consulting with experts are all necessary, but their combined contribution is insufficient for generating a breakthrough outcome. As leaders, it is easy to move towards the future when there is agreement. We define "agreement" as the shared perspective that an action is "right," meaning it will produce the intended results based on past evidence. Agreement resolves issues and maps processes through negotiation all before taking action. It is useful for situations where certainty and predictability are required from the start. It takes courage to envision and commit to a future where there is not yet any evidence or agreement of guaranteed results.

Working in the Present

To undertake the kind of actions that are guided by intention, informed by mistakes, and sustained by acts of courage, we must be prepared to be wrong—willing to make mistakes—and to remain steadfast to our stated intentions.

How to Use This Book

Our recommendation, as you read, is not to try to understand this material in a linear way, but instead to notice what concepts, relationships, or stories jump out at you that help you to see your organization from a new perspective. This is a way to engage in quantum thinking. Albert Einstein observed:

"The intellect has little to do on the road to discovery. There comes a leap in consciousness, call it intuition or what you will – the solution comes to you and you don't know how or why" (in Tsao & Laszlo 2019).

Levy advises, "Quantum reality requires that our either-or thinking be replaced by a more nuanced, layered, and fruitful integration of surface and depth, inside and outside, the part and the whole, the root and its branches." (Levy 2018: 58)

One of the goals of this book is to introduce a new language for working with organizations. We make the assertion that organizations originate in language, and language determines our perception of reality. These are two foundational concepts—"language" and "reality" that underlie the work we are presenting. We introduce a great deal of terminology and have provided a glossary at the back of the book to help your reading. Please feel free to refer to it regularly until terms feel familiar.

We have found that it also helps to share this material with organizational team members as you explore the relevance for your organization. To really get the most out of this book, we invite you to undertake a Breakthrough Initiative. This is a project that will make a significant difference to the organization's results and is something that has never been done before. This kind of breakthrough, as we said above, allows people to constantly learn, grow, and develop new ways to produce results are not necessarily predictable based on the past performance. More details and guidance are offered beginning with Chapter 8, but it helps to keep your Breakthrough Initiative in mind as you read through Chapters 1–7. When we say "breakthrough," we mean a result that is created under a very specific set of conditions, as follows:

1. Not predictable from past performance, even highly successful past performance; a quantum leap in results; one that is discontinuous with the past;

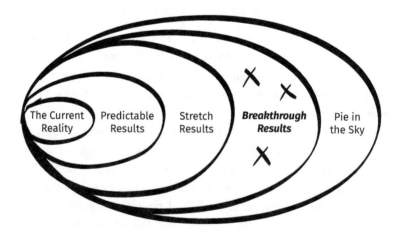

Figure 0.1 Locating Breakthrough Results

2. Produces significant value in terms of forwarding the organization's vision and/or goals;

3. Creates a new reality for the organization about what is possible;

4. Is committed to in advance, without knowing how.

The Attractor Model

Throughout this book you will see various versions of a three-circle model used to distinguish the key elements of organizational relationships. This is the Attractor Model and is what we refer to as a "machine tool," that is, "a tool that creates other tools." It is used to create a field of intention (more about this later). We call it the Attractor Model because it has the same properties as a strange attractor in chaos theory. This branch of physics describes the behavior of non-linear dynamic systems that are highly sensitive to initial conditions—popularly referred to as the "butterfly effect," in which the beating wings of a butterfly in Brazil can set off a tornado in Texas.

Chaotic systems often give rise to patterns that are attributed to strange attractors, which demonstrate a form of order distinct from that which comes from "cause and effect." Using the Attractor Model helps to distinguish the patterns and order in chaotic systems such as organizations. It helps us to distinguish all kinds of systems and outcomes by providing a framework, a way to think about them that brings clarity with velocity.

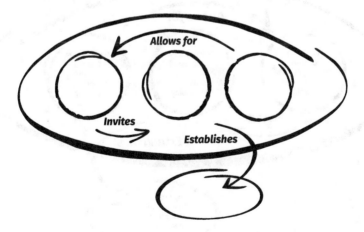

Figure 0.2 The Attractor Model Template

This Attractor Model has proved useful for distinguishing any number of individual and organizational relationships, including:

- Leadership, development and management (the basic systems of organization);
- Context, process and content (creating new realities);
- Recognition, rewards, and results (the components of incentive systems);
- Appreciation, acknowledgment, and accomplishment (creating employee engagement);
- Granting, developing, and earning trust (different forms of trust).

We encourage you to revisit this model whenever you want to be quantum or generative in your thinking rather than undertaking linear analysis. This is especially useful when you want to create something that is not just a modification of something in the past.

Creating the Playing Field

When undertaking any leadership undertaking such as a Breakthrough Initiative, it is important to design what we call "The Playing Field." The

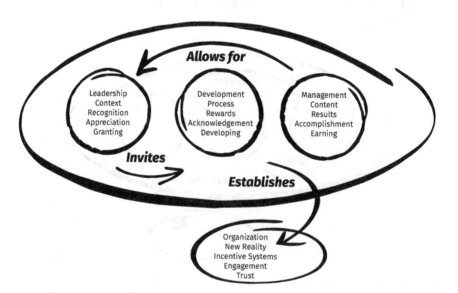

Figure 0.3 Attractor Model Applications

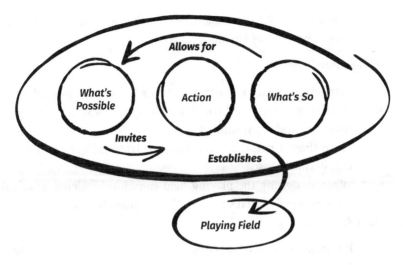

Figure 0.4 Creating the Playing Field

Attractor Model helps you do that. The traditional way to use this model is to begin your analysis in the right-hand circle titled "What's So," and enter a word or short phrase that describes the current situation. After brainstorming details about the current situation, you and your team then ask "What does this allow for?" You brainstorm possibilities that you and your team see available in the future and enter those in the left-hand circle titled "What's Possible." Those possibilities invite next actions. Enter your team's suggestions for next actions into the middle circle titled "Action." After this analysis, explore with the team what those actions establish in the world. What will be created that was not in existence before?

Here are a few more key points for working with creating the playing field:

1. **What's So?**

    •   Identify the current situation, including what's known, facts, interpretations, what is working/not working/missing/working but making no difference.

    •   Make these Critical Distinctions: fact/interpretation, breakdown vs. "something's wrong." Defining something as a breakdown allows for much more creativity and possibility than stating that "something's wrong," which creates blame and defensiveness.

- Elements of the dimension of "What's So?" are past-based — they exist or have already occurred.

2. **What's Possible?**

- Clarifying "what's so" allows for creating what is possible.
- Possibility is created through declaring a vision, mission, goal, mandate, and commitment.
- Make these Critical Distinctions: declaration, generous listening, granted trust.
- When designing the playing field consciously, elements of this dimension of "What's Possible?" are future-based.

3. **Next Actions:**

- Possibility invites next actions.
- This dimension focuses on action: promises, requests, proposals, invitations, offers.
- Elements of the dimension of "Next Actions" are present-based. You can only take action in the present.

Why is this important? In the absence of deliberate design of the playing field and possibility, the tendency is to have "What's So" shape "Next Actions." In other words, organizational culture tends to "pull" for the past shaping the view of the present, which in turn shapes our actions. "That's the way we've always done it." This can limit possible actions and, therefore, produce results within what is predictable. In order to produce breakthroughs, leaders must continually keep the possibility present so next actions can be shaped by the future *as well as* informed by the present. This keeps the playing field as expansive as possible.

Don't worry if some of this is confusing. This is a brief introduction to some of our language and models, and as we visit and revisit these ideas from different perspectives, you will experience increased clarity and ability to put these things into action.

In Chapter 1, we describe the "What's So?" or current situation of change in organizations, with the goal of helping you to see "What's Possible?" and building momentum towards "Next Actions" in order to achieve breakthrough results in your organizational transformation processes.

References

Levy, P. (2018) *Quantum Revelation: A Radical Synthesis of Science and Spirituality*. New York: SelectBooks.

Lorenz, E. (1995) *The Essence of Chaos*. Seattle, WA: University of Washington Press.

Neal, J. (2018) *The Handbook of Personal and Organizational Transformation*. New York: Springer.

Taleb, N. (2010) *The Black Swan: The Impact of the Highly Improbable*. New York: Random House.

Tsao, F. and Laszlo, C. (2019) *Quantum Leadership: New Consciousness in Business*. Stanford, CA: Stanford Business Books.

1

THE CHANGE CRISIS

Introduction

We each need only to look back at our direct experience to see how change is accelerating. When asked the question, "Will it stop?" most people answer, "Not likely." Change and the rate at which it is occurring can no longer be ignored. Research in combination with coaching senior leaders and facilitating large-scale change has contributed to our understanding of the pace of change (Conner 2006; Kelly, Hoopes, and Conner 2003). This book provides some insight to that understanding. The essence of what we have learned is fairly simple and, in retrospect, perhaps some of this is obvious.

1. Organizations have all the key attributes of societal formations and are therefore subject to the variability and unexpected changes that come with human interaction.
2. As the ease and speed of communication increases within and between organizational societies two direct correlations emerge:

   a. New specializations increase to exploit and manage the wealth of new information arising from increases in communication.

DOI: 10.4324/9781003131847-1

b.   The need to integrate change that comes with new information and expanding opportunities for growth also increases within organizations.

3.   As each established specialization deepens and new fields of specialization form there are two effects:

a.   Organizational reliability, predictability, and certainty increase.
b.   Specializations shift from being enablers of change to becoming major impediments to the integration of change.

While these statements are simple and perhaps obvious, their implications are complex and daunting. Our work with clients and students has led us to conclude that *success in business increasingly depends upon the capability to integrate change at ever increasing rates.*

Prior to the last few decades, most change could be integrated across generations of management. For example, consider that the computers we used to write this book can trace their ancestry back to a mechanical tabulator invented in 1880 for conducting the U.S. Census. As business grew more sophisticated, so did the tabulator. It transitioned through many forms into the multi-purpose electronic tool we rely upon today. We'll share the specifics of that story later in Chapter 9. Indeed, if you look back in history, it's not hard to identify numerous cases where changes from a single breakthrough hundreds of years ago are still undergoing integration.

The rate at which some change must be absorbed has increased along with the magnitude of changes. This is validated not just from our direct personal experience, but also by what other business leaders report. Our observation is certainly not a new idea. Almost 50 years ago, back in 1970, Alvin Toffler wrote in his runaway bestseller, *Future Shock:* "society for the past 300 years has been caught up in a fire storm of change. This storm, far from abating, now appears to be gathering force. Change sweeps through the highly industrialized countries with waves of ever accelerating speed" (Toffler 1970: 1). Our concern is that the storm has reached global proportions, now, and yet most businesses and organizations continue to operate as though the storm has yet to arrive (Aburdene 2005).

Exactly What Is Change Integration?

Business cannot change on its own. It is the people in an organization— *human systems*— who change the business of the organization—*business*

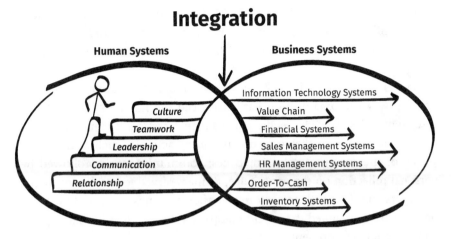

Figure 1.1 Integration of Human Systems and Business Systems

systems. When change is needed, change integration takes place between the people in a company and the business of a company. You might call it the "give and take" work done to align human systems and business systems around change. Integration takes the changes that emerge from human systems and translates them into workable solutions for business systems (see Figure 1.1).

In every instance of change in any organization there will be winners and losers. From the human systems point of view, the successfully integrated change will end up with most folks feeling like winners. We have seen, however, that more often, when change initiatives are undertaken, integrations are focused on the concerns of business systems such as IT, Value Chain Management, Financial Systems, HR, Sales, and so forth. Little attention is placed on human systems during integration. Most work with human systems involves sorting out reassignments, promotions, changes in accountabilities, plus amelioration and placation for those who are unhappy about how it turned out for them. This is certainly necessary work, but not sufficient for the integration of change at the scale of an entire organization.

Dr. J-Robert Ouimet was the Chairman of Ouimet Cordon Bleu, the largest frozen food producer in Canada. He wrestled with this dilemma of his organization's over-emphasis on business systems, or what he referred to as "economic systems." Ouimet Cordon Bleu is an example of an organization that intentionally designed a balance between the human systems and the economic systems (Ouimet 2010). In his model, there are two pillars in an organization: the economic pillar and the human pillar. Each pillar is an "Integrated System of Management Activities" (ISMA).

Several case studies have been written about Dr. Ouimet's company and the way the organization has rebalanced the human systems. These case studies describe 14 specific management practices designed to create greater integration in the company, including activities such as the sponsoring or mentoring of new employees; community service followed by personal reflection on the experience; dinners served to employees by the managers; and inner silence before and after meetings. Each of these practices has been designed to support company values such as human dignity and personal development at work.

In Chapter 5 we will look deeper into this liminal space between human systems and business systems that we are calling change integration, but for now let's examine how organizations, like people, tend to react to change.

Change, Risk, and Uncertainty

Risk and uncertainty are two terms that most of us freely use interchangeably. In actuality, although experiencing risk and uncertainty may feel the same to us—the same excitement and even nervous jitters—we are reacting to two different stimuli. This is certainly the case in the world of business and organizations.

When you take a personal risk, you face the potential for loss of something you already possess. You can risk your life or risk money in a volatile stock. In organizations, risk is usually a financial term associated with loss of money. Whether at a personal or at an organizational level, it's possible to manage risk. For instance, you can reduce risk through preemptive planning.

Uncertainty, on the other hand, applies to what you don't yet have but intend to acquire or achieve. You cannot risk what you don't yet own, because there's nothing to lose. Any new challenge we undertake always introduces uncertainty and sometimes a degree of risk, but if we all approached change exclusively as risk and halted out of fear of failure, little new of value would ever be accomplished. We can deal better with uncertainty by being open to surprise and willing to adjust our expectations in favor of outcomes that were not previously imagined. That queasiness in the pit of your stomach is simply fear of the unknown, and you can master that. Taleb writes:

> Indeed, in some domains – such as scientific discovery and venture capital investments – there is a disproportionate payoff from the unknown, since you typically have little to lose and plenty to gain from a rare event. We will see that, contrary to social science wisdom, almost no discovery, no technologies of note, came from design and planning – they were just Black Swans. The strategy for the discoverers and entrepreneurs is to rely less on top-down planning and focus on maximum tinkering and recognizing opportunities when they present themselves.
>
> (Taleb 2010: xxv)

Any organization, because it is created by and comprised of people, experiences uncertainty, too. Organizations, just like people, need to address the correlation between change, risk, and uncertainty. For any organization, changes will always be accompanied by increased risk—usually financial risk—and greater uncertainty. The bigger the change, the higher the risk and the greater the uncertainty. But change is also the life of organization. Anticipating changes in the mood of the public and jumping upon new opportunities is what keeps a business prosperous. It can be deadly to the well-being and growth of the organization if uncertainty around change is misidentified and treated like risk.

One of our favorite reminders about embracing uncertainty as opportunity is probably sitting right on your desk—the handy Post-it® Notes from 3M. (More about 3M and Post-it Notes in Chapter 7.) These little lifesavers originated in 1968 when 3M scientist Dr. Spencer Silver was trying to formulate a new type of glue. He created a substance that was not tacky enough to permanently bond (a "failure!"!) but it did have a remarkably resilient quality. You could lightly attach small items, then easily pull them apart, and then reuse the glue to attach other items. He showed it to other scientists but, when no one could identify a problem that it could solve, he put it on the back burner. Six years later, in 1974, Dr. Silver's colleague Art Fry was tired of losing his place in his hymnal at church choir, each time his bookmark fell out. Art remembered that strange adhesive, saw a possibility, and 3M gave him permission to experiment until he created repositionable notes that would safely adhere to paper (History Timeline: Post-it Notes, 2019).

3M has been so successful because 3M people focus upon the surprise of uncertainty, not the risk of change. They are masters of the process of change integration. In our work at we have found that mastering the *craft of change integration* is a highly effective means for organizations to mitigate risk and to increase certainty, particularly when organizations undertake large-scale change. *Integration is an organizational metadiscipline*—one with standing equal to that of *management and leadership*. If you, the reader, have ever led or worked on change initiatives in your organization, you may see that the preponderance of validity for the case will come from your own direct experience. Nevertheless, we will share additional evidence from our own clients and research, as well.

Perhaps the most compelling reason for raising integration to a stature equal to that of leadership and management is expressed in a series of IBM studies, where they found that the number of companies that could not demonstrate success with major change initiatives had tripled in the years intervening between studies.

The IBM Global CEO Studies and the Challenge of Change

In 2015 IBM published its eighteenth Global C-Suite Study about change in business, based upon conversations with more than 1,500 business leaders from 21 industries in more than 70 countries (IBM Institute for Business Value, 2015).

This report identified that the thing that makes most executives cringe is the "Uber syndrome." One executive said that this is "where a competitor with a completely different business model enters your industry and flattens you" (IBM Institute for Business Value, 2015: 1).

> Management guru Clayton Christensen coined the term "disruptive innovation" to describe how new entrants target the bottom of a market and then relentlessly move up market, eventually ousting established providers. But what was once a relatively rare phenomenon has now become a regular occurrence. Innovations that harness new technologies or business models, or exploit old technologies in new ways, are

emerging on an almost daily basis. And the most disruptive enterprises don't gradually displace the incumbents; they reshape entire industries, swiftly obliterating whatever stands in their way.

(IBM Institute for Business Value 2015: 1)

In the IBM 2008 Global CEO Study (Jorgensen, Owen, and Neus 2008) they reported that the percentage of CEOs expecting substantial change in their business had climbed from 65 percent to 83 percent in just two years. However, in 2008, those who reported that they had successfully managed change rose only 4 points, up from 57 percent in 2006 to 61 percent in 2008. The disparity between expecting change and feeling able to manage it—what they call the "Change Gap"—nearly tripled between 2006 and 2008.

More recently, the 2018 IBM Global C-Suite Study found that disruption from start-ups was nowhere near as impactful as expected. Instead, business leaders report that 72 percent of the disruption in their industries come from innovative industry incumbents. What happened, according to the report, is that dominant incumbents "honed their skills to acquire nascent disruptors, along with their digital skills and innovator talent" (IBM Institute for Business Value, 2018: 7). So even the source of change and disruption has become unpredictable!

These findings point to the critical importance of integrating change. When the rate of change increases sufficiently, managing that change becomes difficult or impossible if it has not first been integrated into the organization. Said another way, it is not possible to manage what has not been integrated.

Put the Horse Before the Cart

Another finding in the IBM 2008 study highlights that we need to first integrate the organization before we make any attempts to integrate change.

Nearly all CEOs are adapting their business models—two-thirds are implementing extensive innovations. More than 40 percent are changing their enterprise models to be more collaborative.

(IBM Institute for Business Value, 2008)

A company generates the internal changes of business models, implementing innovations and changing enterprise. The purpose of these kinds of adaptations is to prepare an organization to respond to external conditions—such as demand for change from customers, collaborators, governments, and global enterprise. All indications point to this trend continuing.

> CEOs are moving aggressively toward global business designs, deeply changing capabilities and partnering more extensively. CEOs have moved beyond the cliché of globalization, and organizations of all sizes are reconfiguring to take advantage of global integration opportunities.
>
> (IBM Institute for Business Value, 2008)

The Nine Change Drivers

The three IBM Global CEO studies looked at nine "change drivers." As the research continued, the report eventually compared data from eight years, from 2004–2017, as shown in the graph below (see Table 1.1). Of the nine change drivers, CEOs considered Market Factors—external/organizational factors—to be the leading concern up until 2012 and leading again in 2017. People Skills—internal/individual factors—was second until the recession in 2010, with ups and downs since then. Technological skills, on the other hand, has made a steady climb as a driver of change, and was in first place in the 2018 report.

This IBM study of CEOs' viewpoints is one of the largest ever undertaken. More than half of the 1,000+ CEOs polled said they expected to make major change initiatives in their organizations. The study is replete with remarks about the need for geographic integration, cultural integration, employee-to-customer integration, and many inexplicit forms of

Table 1.1 IBM's Nine Change Drivers Over Time

2004	2006	2008	2010	2012	2013	2015	2017		
								#1: Market factors	69%
								#2: Technological factors	63%
								#3: People skills	61%
								#4: Regulatory concerns	
								Macro-economic factors	
								Socio-economic factors	
								Environmental issues	
								Globalization	
								Geopolitical factors	

(IBM Institute for Business Value, 2018:3)

"change integration." One CEO put it this way: "we need to move away from an operational focus to a client interface focus ... this requires new skills and a new skill mix for the corporation" (IBM Institute for Business Value, 2008: 37).

The Search for People Skills

The last part of the quote bears a secondary discussion. Do we really think that corporations possess "skills?" Of course not. A corporation is populated with people and it is people who have skills, not the corporation. But the CEO, though well meaning, is yet defaulting to an operational focus that perceives "the corporation" as a non-human set of "tools" that can be re-machined for new uses, when the need for change arises. Too many organizational leaders unwittingly continue to subscribe to this Machine Age approach to business. Scientific management approaches make similar errors, training employees for repetition and reliability, and then registering surprise and disappointment when the unexpected occurs (Morgan 2006).

Back to these new skills for integrating change—where are they going to come from? Yes, training will provide some level of what is needed. But what about those more subtle abilities that come only with experience—the kind of experience that is traditionally garnered over a decade or more by moving a promising candidate through several job assignments? In most organizations, experienced people are stretched to their capacities, due to layoffs and downsizing schemes. Hiring part-timers, temps, and the under-skilled to cut expenses is not a future-centric, long-term growth strategy. Before long, increased demand will force companies to face the need for experienced leaders. We still hear some executives say that "when the time comes" they will get experienced leaders much like they might acquire any other asset. Where will they find them? In a People Store with an inventory of experienced leaders? Not according to surveys on talent acquisition, as we will see shortly.

We have found that people skills encompass a range of interpersonal and intrapersonal communication competencies. In organizational human relations, the emphasis for people skills is on social-emotional awareness, self-presentation, self-management, getting along with others, negotiating differences, resolving interpersonal and intrapersonal conflict, decision-making and getting agreement. In the book *Essential People Skills for Project*

Managers, Flannes and Levin (2005) propose that handling people problems is the most challenging part of the manager's job. As they see it, resolving difficult issues between people, particularly when leading a strong-willed project team, is critical to defusing problems before they build to an impasse. Dale Carnegie Training (2005) in the book, *The 5 Essential People Skills*, claims that nine decades of insight into human relations tell us that five skills—*building rapport, being curious, communicating, having ambition,* and *resolving conflicts*—are key to "people skills."

Applying people skills has limits and these limits are seldom taught along with the skills. There is plenty of skill building done around *reaching agreement* and *resolving conflicts* in order to reach agreement. The deep background assumption is that conflict is not productive—it's better to work in harmony and go along to get along. Yet many of us know from personal experience that any agreement reached in order to avoid conflict often leads to a phenomenon known as the *Abilene Paradox* (Harvey 1988), in which the group agrees on a decision that every individual member knows is ill-advised, because each one remains silent rather than voice their objection, assuming the other members are all in favor, and not wanting to disappoint or upset them.

To avoid conflict, people stick to the safe path. They do things they know will make no difference and fail to do things that they know will make a difference. Since organizations have relied in the last several decades on training programs, the people skills that employees have mastered best are all associated with the ability to adapt. If it were only this simple and adaptation were sufficient! Look into your own organization. How is conflict managed? How are those who raise challenging questions treated? Is respectful conflict welcomed and encouraged? Or is everyone just trying to fit in?

Language Barriers

Our research and related findings indicate that most senior leaders lack adequate language to tackle the challenges of change their companies face. They've been educated and trained in the deeply ingrained, traditional approach to change in organization. The notion has persisted that we can figure out how to manage what has never been done before, if we just apply the same step-by-step, continuous improvement logic we've always used to understand how to work with repetitive tasks on the production line. In the past we had the luxury of more time to test, refine, and improve—to get the bugs out through extended trial and error. But now change occurs so fast that there is precious little time to integrate today's big change before tomorrow's is already breathing down our necks. Companies are struggling, in part because they keep trying to retrofit to new products and processes the same standards of performance that you apply to those that have been proven over time. They are also struggling because they try to adapt to external forces as if they are linear and predictable when all too frequently they are discontinuous and the result of disruptive change, as we saw in the IBM study.

Now we have a tough new game in place, played in the name of technological innovation and beating the competition into the marketplace at any cost. The stakes are global. The challenge is exacerbated by another old habit entrenched among players at the top—a dangerous intolerance for any reports of bad news.

In 2009 to 2011 America glimpsed the "good news only" culture at Toyota, when over 9 million cars were recalled (Haq 2010). Akio Toyoda appeared before a house committee on February 24, 2010, to apologize for 39 deaths due to runaway Toyotas. Although public hearings before Congress will never fully expose what transpired behind closed corporate doors, apparently errors had been hidden from senior management since at least 2004. In 2010 the company was still not sure where all the problems lay, but meanwhile a corporate memo circulated at Toyota bragged that over $100 million was being saved with shortcuts on car production. Akio Toyoda declared that Toyota would correct a culture of arrogance and secrecy (Conley, Rhee, and Ross 2009).

Certainly Mr. Toyoda and other leaders at high levels do care deeply about corporate responsibility and they want to know what's going on, both the good news and the bad news. Did employees at Toyota deliberately hide bad news or were they just caught up in the old daily game of adapting to obstacles? We will never know for sure. But we do know from our own experience that if senior executives really get the new game, they seldom communicate downward their openness to the truth. Are they skilled translators? Indeed, as the rate of change rises, are better people skills and translation skills sufficient for successful change integration at the scale of organization? We don't think so.

Summary

Change integration is the alignment of the human systems with the business systems of the organization. In the past, when the rate of change was much slower, there was time to adapt to internal and external changes without having to think about it much. Those days are gone. We need new frameworks for thinking about change so that it can be quickly and effectively integrated into the organization. This enables the organization to more readily focus on the service and products that are provided to customers, as well as to focus on effective relationships with other stakeholders, instead of feeling distracted by disruptive changes. You can't manage change, but you can integrate it through aligning the human and business systems.

The IBM studies reported in this chapter demonstrate that CEOs are grappling with change at an unprecedented rate and are responding with major redesign of their business systems and business models. At the same time, they also recognize the need for increased people skills, but they may be focusing more on adaptation skills rather than innovation skills that lead to business breakthroughs.

The next chapter describes greater distinctions between the three metadisciplines—Management, Leadership, and Integration—with a more in-depth focus on the metadiscipline of Integration.

References

Aburdene, P. (2005) *Megatrends 2010: The Rise of Conscious Capitalism.* Newburyport, MA: Hampton Roads Publishing.

Conley, M., Rhee, J., and Ross, B. (2009) Top Executive Denies "Cover up" in Probe of Runaway Cars. Retrieved from https://abcnews.go.com/Blotter/toyota-cover-runaway-car-concerns/story?id=9007163 on February 10, 2019.

Conner, D. (2006) *Managing at the Speed of Change: How Resilient Managers Succeed and Prosper Where Others Fail.* New York: Random House.

Dale Carnegie Training (2005) *The 5 Essential People Skills: How to Assert Yourself, Listen to Others, and Resolve Conflicts.* New York: Simon & Schuster.

Flannes, S. W. and Levin, G. (2005) *Essential People Skills for Project Managers.* San Francisco, CA: Berrett-Koehler.

Haq, H. (2010) Toyota Recall Update: Dealers Face Full Lots, Anxious Customers. *The Christian Science Monitor.* Retrieved from https://web.archive.org/web/20100202035132/http://www.csmonitor.com/USA/2010/0129/Toyota-recall-update-dealers-face-full-lots-anxious-customers on February 10, 2019

Harvey, J. B. (1988) *The Abilene Paradox and Other Meditations on Management.* San Francisco, CA: Jossey-Bass.

History Timeline: Post-it Notes (2019) Retrieved from www.3m.com/us/office/postit/pastpresent/history_ws.html on January 13, 2019.

IBM Institute for Business Value. (2018) Incumbents Strike Back: Insights from the Global C-Suite Study. Retrieved from www.ibm.com/downloads/cas/Y9JBRJ8A on January 13, 2019.

IBM Institute for Business Value. (2015) Redefining Boundaries: Insights from the Global C-suite Study. Retrieved from www.ibm.com/downloads/cas/VJEP6Z9D on January 13, 2019.

IBM Global CEO Study (2008) Enterprise of the future. Retrieved from www.ibm.com/downloads/cas/XDWLBNZ2 on February 18, 2020.

Jorgensen, H. H., Owen, L., and Neus, A. (2008) Making Change Work. IBM Institute for Business Value.

Kelly, M., Hoopes, L., and Conner, D. (2003) *Managing Change with Personal Resilience: 21 Keys for Bouncing Back and Staying on Top in Turbulent Organizations.* Raleigh, NC: Mark Kelly Books.

Morgan, G. (2006) *Images of Organizations.* Los Angeles: Sage Publishing.

Notre Projet (2019) *Integrated System of Management Activities.* Retrieved from www.notreprojet.org/?page_id=3936&lang=en on August 2, 2019.

Ouimet, J. R. (2010) *Everything Has Been Loaned to You: Autobiography of a Transformational Leader.* Montreal, Canada: To God Go Foundation.

Taleb, N. (2010) *The Black Swan: The Impact of the Highly Improbable.* New York: Random House.

Toffler, A. (1970) *Future Shock.* New York: Random House.

2

ORGANIZATIONAL INTEGRATION

Introduction

In order to understand organizational integration, we must first understand what we mean by "Organization." In this introduction to the field, we begin our delineation of what we mean by organization from the view of complex chaotic systems. We provide a foundational description of the three primary systems that are essential to an organization, and explore the distinction between theory and theoretical. Throughout this book we will revisit these three primary systems, each time with finer and finer distinctions. In a way, it's like learning a new language. First you are taught a few simple words and some basic structure of the language. With each lesson you learn new vocabulary, new grammatical rules, and a few practical phrases you can put into action in simple conversation. As you gain mastery of the language, you are able to think and act in new ways in a culture that used to seem a mystery to you.

To begin our understanding of organizational integration, it is helpful to understand what an organization is, to be able to view organizations as systems, and to delve into the concept of organizational leadership.

DOI: 10.4324/9781003131847-2

Don't worry about understanding everything that's in these pages. Over time, as each chapter revisits some key ideas in new ways, you will begin to get comfortable with this new way of seeing and working with organizational systems to bring about positive transformation.

What Is an Organization?

While we talk about organizations all the time, we seldom stop to ask: What is an organization? Why do organizations exist? How are they designed? We might assume that we already know the answers, and perhaps we do. There is compelling evidence in our society that our implicit answers are no longer sufficient to handle the challenges people working in organizations face today. Every day, we see the evidence for this in the news and in our own organizations. What follows is a theory of organizations based on over 50 years of Mel Toomey's personal observation, with the last 20 years spent formulating the theory of integrating change and checking the theory against observations in organizational practice. The elements of this theory that will be discussed in the material that follows include:

- Human systems, business systems, and developmental systems as the three primary subsystems of organizations.
- The three metadisciplines within organizations: leadership, management, and development; and their functions.
- Organizations as systems.
- The two classes of reality.
- Organizational reality.
- Language and reality.
- A language for non-physical reality.
- Organizations as field phenomena.
- Modes and strategies for thinking about organization.
- A taxonomy for organizations.

Two of the Three Primary Subsystems of Complex, Chaotic Systems

Organizations are complex, chaotic systems comprised of three essential subsystems: human systems, business systems, and developmental systems. The day-to-day business of any organization is structured by its business systems and conducted by its human systems. While business and human systems are distinct, they are also closely interrelated. It is the interface between them—developmental systems—that constitutes an organization. An important distinction: an organization's business systems derive from its human systems, but the reverse is never true. While business systems are very important and impact on human systems to a degree, they are the overarching concern of only a small fraction of an organization's population. The majority of people working within an organization are concerned with its human systems—what people are committed to, how they work together, and what they need to get their jobs done. Too often, these things are not recognized within an organization's business systems.

Not having a clear distinction between business systems and human systems can also lead to waste in the application of human resources. We can witness such waste in any number of circumstances, for example, when moments of extraordinary creativity are followed by unpredictable results. A dubious form of "cleansing" usually follows, along with a squashing of the very means through which the creativity had emerged. The justification often used by management is that people went outside the established rules of engagement to produce the results. They are told: "This is not the way we do things around here." Sometimes when extraordinary results are produced people are told: "We expect this of our people." Or "Compared with our competition we still have a long way to go." Neither response is empowering. Even when the results justify the means, if the rules get broken to produce the results, it is considered the worst possible offense. If we are totally honest about it, most of us frequently break the rules of our organizations. Sometimes rule-breaking is actually systemic and includes unwritten rules for engagement around breaking the rules for engagement.

Corvette Story

One of our favorite examples of rule-breaking that ultimately paid off is the survival of GM's Corvette. Back in the early 1950s, Harley Earl, GM's famous head of design, wanted to build a roadster for college students that would sell for about $1800. Right from the start, his brainchild faced extraordinary challenges to its existence.

This incredible story that appeared March 18, 1997, in the money section on the front page of USA Today:

Covert Activity Saved Sports Car

The 1997 Chevrolet Corvette is an amazing car, mostly because it exists at all. A cadre of Corvette lovers inside General Motors lied, cheated and stole to keep the legendary sports car from being eliminated during GM's management turmoil and near bankruptcy in the late 1980's and early '90s.

In fact, GM's auditors and security staff wound up probing Chevrolet for suspected embezzlement because more than $1 million had been secretly diverted to unauthorized Corvette test vehicles. Chevy General Manager Jim Perkins, now retired, told GM sleuths he did it: "We needed the cars. It was that important. And if I have to resign my job and find a way to pay you back out of my own pocket, I'll do it." That ended the inquiry.

The article later continues:

"Were they doing something outside the system?" GM spokesman William O'Neill asked rhetorically, answering. "At the time, the system was broken and needed to be fixed. Today's system has been fixed, not completely, but enough that people wouldn't be put in that same position again."

(Healey 1997: 1B)

The story goes on to relate how the team broke rules, laws, and traditions, such as forcing designers and engineers to cooperate and work together as a team, to bring the car to market. The full story is recounted in *All Corvettes Are Red*, by James Schefter (1997). This is a classic example of how we risk destroying creative thinking in an organization when we don't fully understand how business, human, and developmental systems work and how they are interrelated. The question is: how can we respect the rules for engagement on one hand, that is, "the ways we do things here," while on the other, honor creativity and the willingness to break with conventions and norms to forward the purpose of our organizations?

One view is to change people—that's the answer. While this is a valid statement, this view does not provide the greatest leverage for change. A better understanding of organization may have far more leverage. To better understand the concept of "Organization" we need new ways to think about organizations. If we can see the inner workings of "Organization," find the levers for systemic change, and understand the design of the interface between business, people, and organization, then there is considerable leverage available.

In this book we use Organization with a capital "O" to distinguish when we are talking about the abstract concept of Organization as a field. We describe Organization as a field phenomenon more thoroughly in Chapter 3. In other places we use the more standard use of "organizations" with an "s" to distinguish types of organizations or a specific group of organizations such as "manufacturing organizations" or "financial organizations."

Overview of Organization as Systems

Organization can be thought of as systems comprised of three overarching organizational metadisciplines: leadership, development, and management. In organizations where the nature of systems is neither appreciated nor understood, these three metadisciplines collapse into an indistinguishable blur. When these metadisciplines are appropriately defined, leadership is concerned primarily with human systems, management with business systems, and development with the interface between the two. Development focuses on developmental issues at the scale of the entire organization. These three metadisciplines form the backbone of this book and will be revisited over and over again, each time with new distinctions so that the reader will gain greater mastery of understanding the nature of organizations as systems.

Management

Of the three metadisciplines, management has the most visibility. As the steward of organizations, it is concerned with continuous improvement of business systems. If we assume that the fundamental objectives of management are the creation and maintenance of reliability, predictability, and certainty for the business, then management's preeminence is appropriate.

Leadership

Leadership gets a lot of airtime, and most people agree that it's important to organizations, but many organizations give little or no formal attention to its role or quality. Its "seat at the table" is seldom equal to that of management. Discussions about leadership usually lead to people telling stories about their favorite leaders or sharing what they think leadership really is, citing books and programs to reinforce their views. Odds are good that a conversation about leadership will move from discussion to debate, since books and programs take very diverse approaches on the subject. After a few rounds, debate usually devolves into an agreement to disagree, after which people become less inclined to share what they're really thinking. "Been there, done that, not worth it," they rationalize, until they locate others who agree with them. Then private conversations follow which satisfy individuals and make little difference to the organization. In many organizations, this seemingly endless set of conversations serves only to neutralize the development of their leaders.

What is the function of leadership? Topping the list of the most important things leadership provides is *new possibilities* for an organization's business. Possibilities arise when people are in communication and communication is understood to be a cornerstone for human systems. Possibilities are more than ideas about new or different ways of doing things. They are distinct in that they not only alter the future of the organization, but they also reach back into the organization's history to re-contextualize it, bring new meaning to its history, and empower the work done so far.

From our research and consulting work, we have found that most views about leadership and approaches to developing leaders share related roots. While some views appear to be opposing, when held in the appropriate context, they are actually complementary.

Unlike management, the field of leadership is not highly codified, with a consistent body of knowledge about what constitutes leadership. From a linguistics point of view, codification is the process of *standardizing a language* that was not previously crystallized in *writing*. While a lot has been written *about* leadership, it has not been treated as a language and codified to nearly the same extent as management. So that leaves leadership open to a much wider range of views, interpretations, and opinions. Perhaps the nature of leadership does not allow for the same levels of codification as does management. In fact, a good case can be made that attempts to codify leadership actually disempower our relationship with it. That leads us to inquire: What if our understanding of leadership would benefit from an approach that is distinct from codification?

Understanding the distinctions between management and leadership is fundamental to understanding organizations. These disciplines are neither differing levels of the same thing nor interchangeable disciplines. Rather, they operate interdependently with developmental systems serving as an inter-mediator between them. When we understand this, we can begin to apprehend organizations as systems comprised of systems. It is then possible to find key points from which to leverage systemic change.

Development

Development serves as the inter-mediator between management and leadership, building bridges between the possibilities accessed by leadership and the realities handled by management. The goal of development is to bring *efficacy* to possibility, thus grounding it into a manageable reality. This process of transformation takes place across a spectrum of *feasibility* that begins with possibility and concludes with a manifest new reality— literally, a transforming of possibility into reality. With many missteps and failures along the way, it is seldom a smooth ride.

Because most organizations have limited tolerance for anything beyond what can be shown to be reliable, predictable, and certain, the metadiscipline of development is generally under-regarded. Yet, the more an organization resists recognizing and distinguishing this discipline, the more likely that sub-rosa groups will emerge which are engaged in development activities. Even when they have no management agreement or support, these groups carve out a space for development. Some become so well organized that they can take on the appearance of secret societies. Knowing that their work is not sanctioned, they stay out of sight, working for a perceived "common organizational good." As shown above in the Corvette story, in some cases, their work actually contradicts specific management decisions. They stay below the radar, work hard, and trust the results they produce are sufficient to gain forgiveness later for transgressing the established norms.

Creative Development

While they may not always be hidden, integrating change activities frequently are not actively revealed. For example, Mel's company, Generative Leadership Group, was asked by the newly hired divisional head of HR, we'll call her Mary, to consult with a large processing service division of a major financial institution. The division employed a few thousand people, most of whom were earning between $10 and $15 per hour. Our assignment was to work with the division's senior management to develop their leadership abilities. We discussed her expectations and agreed that we could fulfill them. We had worked with Mary previously, when she was head of HR for a large division of a major drug company. Because she had established her jurisdiction in the drug company, her request to fund our program there had been granted without much question. But at the financial institution, her request was denied and attempts to overcome the denial were politely, but firmly, rebuffed.

Mary asked us to wait until she could find a way to move forward with our assignment. True to her word, she called several months later and reported, "I have the funding now." She had applied for a grant from a state fund set aside to develop leadership that would impact people living in inner cities—as did most of this division's employees. So, we launched the leadership development program, along with other work for which she had received grant money. The results proved to Mary's superiors that funding her requests for developing leadership was a good investment. She was then able to procure a budget for training and development in her division that did not require grants.

However, Mary did not stop there. When she learned that her company would pay 80 percent of the tuition for any accredited degree program, she made a deal with a local university to provide a two-year associate degree for some of the division's hourly workers at a reduced cost in exchange for making sure that their program registration was filled. Mary set up internal support for those interested in pursuing an associate degree. She helped people fill out applications and arranged for temporary funding of tuition until the company reimbursements were processed. She found that many of her people had attended a university in their homeland and welcomed the opportunity to continue their education. In time, workers in Mary's division filled two programs at the university, and she began negotiating for a similar arrangement on a four-year degree program.

Mary did not operate outside the policies of her organization. She came up with creative ways to work within constraints and to find approaches to her development objectives that were consistent with the objectives of her company's management. She says she is fairly certain that if she had asked permission to do these things, she would have been denied. This is a good example of how development can work when an individual takes initiative and is able to make a difference. To be effective in her efforts at development, Mary had to think creatively about how to meet her objective.

Viewpoints

Throughout this book we talk about scale and viewing Organization from different viewpoints. We highlight four different categories of viewpoints that are important to understand in organizational integration: (1) Scale, (2) Point of view, (3) Fact and interpretation, and (4) What's obvious, isn't.

Scale

An organization is comprised of many different layers and functions, and issues can be seen from many different viewpoints depending on one's perspective or position. For example, CEOs look at the strategy and activity of their organization from the perspective of the whole organization, in the context of the world outside the company. A salesperson will see the organization from the perspective of quotas, products, territory, competition, and so on.

Each of these is an example of viewing the organization, or one's responsibilities, from a different scale. There are endless examples of scale. You can also consider the different perspectives that a telescope and a microscope provide—each allows us to see our world at a different scale. Why is it important to consider scale? Being able to consider diverse perspectives gives us a more rounded view of a situation or concern. It also helps us communicate more effectively when we are aware of and value the scale or perspective from which another person is talking.

The point is that it is beneficial to listen to others with an appreciation of the perspective from which they originate. Leaders must look at issues from many scales (organization, departments, groups, teams, individuals) and from different functional perspectives (executive, sales, marketing, finance, etc.) in order to make effective and efficient decisions.

It is also helpful to consider the scale from which another person may be listening, when you are designing your own communication. You likely do this naturally already: you probably wouldn't bring every single little detail of your project or initiative to your CEO, because he/she likely listens from a much broader scale than that. It is very helpful to consciously include the listener's scale, regardless of who it is, when you are creating a communication of any kind, whether a memo, debrief, presentation, status update, verbal or written report, and so on. You may have to use your knowledge of the listener's accountabilities to determine the appropriate scale, or you

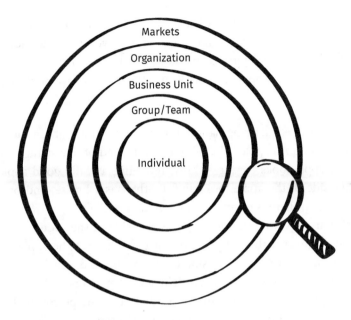

Figure 2.1 The Viewpoint of Scale

could ask, "At what scale do you want the details? The 10,000-foot view, or a worm's eye view—or something in between?"

We offer this hint: when a problem appears unsolvable, look for the solution at the next larger scale. Here's a real-life example from the Oscar-winning documentary, "Man on Wire." Philip Petit, the high-wire walker, strung a cable between the twin towers of the World Trade Center in 1974 and walked between them, 104 stories above the ground, one morning. When he was planning his illegal caper, he hired a helicopter to fly him over the towers to get a better perspective on the structures, how to string a rope between them, and where he might attach his cable. Being able to see the tops of the towers from above them gave him information he could not get from walking on the roofs of the buildings. Conversely, when you need clarity or finer resolution on something, look at it from a lower scale.

Point of View

When you are creating something new—a new project, a new team or working toward a new outcome that hasn't been produced before—it is very important to seek out different perspectives. By understanding the point of view of people who sit in different parts of the organization, or who bring different functional backgrounds and different expertise to a project or desired outcome, you can get a more well-rounded view of the situation, the potential pitfalls, possible concerns and maybe even new and different ways to approach it. We use the story below to illustrate the point.

> Imagine there is a string hanging from the ceiling, right in the middle of the room. An apple is hanging from the end of that string. One side of the apple looks terrific—shiny, red—like a really good apple. The other side of the apple looks awful—there is a bruise, and on closer inspection, there is even a worm crawling out of it!
>
> If you are sitting on the "good apple" side of the room, and you're hungry, a reasonable proposal might be: "Let's eat the apple!" If you are sitting on the "worm" side of the room, and you hear someone propose eating the apple, you might say: "You're crazy! I'm not eating that apple!" (Unless, of course, you don't like the person making the proposal, in which case you might say, "Go right ahead!")

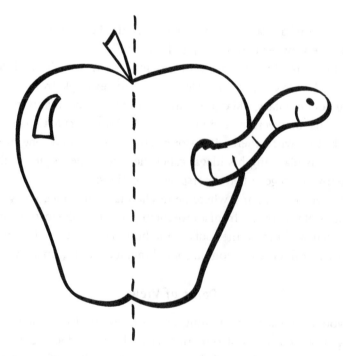

Figure 2.2 Point of View

The question is, "Who has the right point of view?" Everybody! Everyone has a point of view, and from where they are sitting, it is a valid point of view.

In organizations, most people probably won't be straightforward enough to tell others that they're crazy (especially if your boss or the leader is making the proposal). People say things like: "Let me think about it," or "I'll get back to you," or "Let's form a committee and study it," and so forth. So, if you are the one making the proposal, particularly if you are the boss or the leader, and you notice some reticence in people's responses, a very useful question to ask is: "What do you see?" That is not only a productive question, it is also respectful, since it shows that you have a serious interest in other people's points of view.

You want to solicit diverse points of view, because they will give you information about the project or initiative that you don't currently have, sitting where you sit and looking from your own unique—but limited—perspective. You get those diverse points of view by asking people "What do you see?" and listening generously to their responses.

Fact and Interpretation

An important distinction in many work situations is the ability to distinguish the difference between facts and interpretations. First, some definitions.

Facts are observable and measurable phenomena. The term "fact" may apply to physical things like rocks, forks, or machinery (things with size, weight, location, etc.). It may also apply to non-physical things such as mathematics, where it is a fact that $2 + 2 = 4$ and it is a fact that $2 \times 3 = 6$. To test for a fact, you can ask, "Is this true or false?" For example, "Is this an oak tree?" implies "Is it true that this is an oak tree?"

Interpretations belong to the non-physical world of reality and therefore depend on language for their existence. More about the non-physical world of reality later. Because there is no physical reality to an interpretation, no physical object or measurable outcome, their existence is mutable, depending on how we talk about them.

For example, the statement "This machine works well" is an interpretation. There are many possible definitions for the word "well"—it may run without breaking down for long periods of time, it may not need a lot of

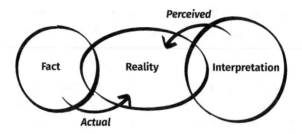

Figure 2.3 Fact and Interpretation

fuel, it may produce the desired number of widgets every hour. How you interpret the word "well" determines the actual meaning of the sentence. On the other hand, "This machine produces 3,000 widgets an hour" is a fact. If someone says such a machine works well, that interpretation is based on the machine's productivity and on measurable standards for that productivity. "The Mona Lisa is a beautiful painting" is another interpretation. Some may consider it beautiful, while others may not.

Consider this situation: two employees call in sick. Someone says, "Oh no, Bill and Janet have called in sick. That means the project they are working on will be delayed. They just can't be counted on. They probably weren't even that committed to start with." Where are the facts in these statements? The only fact is that Bob and Janet called in sick. It is not a fact that they aren't committed to the results of their projects, or that they can't be counted on, or that the project will now be delayed—these are all interpretations. Interpretations may have a basis in fact but are not themselves facts.

To test for an interpretation, you ask, "Is this interpretation *valid* or *invalid?*" An interpretation is valid if, on its face, it accounts for the known facts. If it does not, in whole or part, then it is invalid. Validity is not absolute. An interpretation may be more or less valid or invalid. Any set of facts can have many valid interpretations (see the Mona Lisa example above!).

Because of this, we find that another question is useful: "Does the interpretation empower what the team is committed to?" If it does not, we recommend that you create or invent a different interpretation. For example, say you are attending a yoga class, and the instructor does not give you any feedback about your positions. One interpretation might be: "This instructor is ignoring me. She must not like me for some reason." Another, more empowering interpretation might be: "I must be doing my poses really well, so she doesn't feel the need to correct me!" The second interpretation is probably more empowering! And you can always get the facts by asking the instructor for feedback on your poses.

The same goes for a work situation—if your boss disagrees with you, you might think, "Wow, I am really messing up here, she must think I'm an idiot." Or you might reinterpret that to: "I wonder what she sees that I don't see? Maybe I can learn something from this. Or ... maybe I see something that's obvious to me, that I haven't communicated fully." The first, disempowering interpretation might lead you to clam up and stop contributing. The second, more empowering one might lead you to ask for or offer clarification, and eventually to a more fruitful discussion and possibly even a better solution.

One useful technique is called the MRI—"Most Respectful Interpretation." In this technique, when you find yourself upset by a situation or a person, brainstorm a list of at least five reasons why this happened, or what motivated this person to act that way. Then choose the most empowering, the most positive, or the most respectful interpretation and act upon that. All too often our default is to assume the worst about others, and this process gives us a healthier way to act when we don't have all the facts (Scherer and Shook 1993).

We have found that people and groups sometimes relate to interpretations as if they were facts and waste time arguing about which is true. What's important about interpretations is that they shape action. When interpretations don't empower our commitments, then action is not shaped in favor of our commitments. When interpretations do empower our commitments, then action is shaped in favor of the commitments.

Much of what is considered "fact" in organizations is agreed-upon interpretation, and therefore it does not appear to be susceptible to change. Experimenting with other possible interpretations can open up entirely new avenues for action and change (Scherer and Shook 1993). Relating to the facts, distinct from interpretations, and resolving issues based on grounded facts and empowering interpretations is possible when we can see that facts and interpretations are distinct and related, not separate and different. This makes it possible to commit to interpretations that empower the fulfillment of commitments and projects and invite communication.

What's Obvious, Isn't

The title here is intended as shorthand for "What's Obvious Doesn't Get Communicated." Because what's obvious to us, isn't necessarily obvious to everyone else! We tend to not communicate things that are obvious to us—because we assume they are obvious to everyone else. Remember the apple story, and that we often think that our point of view is the right one—so of course we think that others should share it. It's so "obviously" right—at least to us.

Sometimes when we get into conversations where people don't agree with us, or "see things our way," we are inclined to defend our point of view, explain it more, sell it, try to convince, persuade, argue ... without noticing that we haven't asked them what they see. Something else may be "obvious" to them!

In most situations, the best course of action is to pay attention to things that may be obvious to you, and make sure you communicate them to others. One of our clients said that whenever he was convinced everyone around him was an idiot, that was a wake-up call to see what was obvious to him that he hadn't communicated! Do this even when it seems unnecessary and make sure others understand precisely what you mean.

If you are working with someone and you do not understand the rationale for what he or she is doing or asking you to do, it is likely that there is something obvious to one of you that is un-communicated. Stay in the conversation until what is obvious is fully revealed.

Figure 2.4 What's Obvious Doesn't Get Communicated

Organizational Leadership: Is it Theory or Theoretical?

At this point, it's important to understand the distinction between a theory and what is theoretical. A while ago, a friend and colleagues of Mel's, who heads a small New England university specializing in Master's degrees for new fields of study, reviewed this material. He commented: "What you are saying here has the makings of a compelling theory." In recounting the conversation over the next few weeks, Mel realized that his friend uses language in a very deliberate, specific way. He had used the word *theory*, not *theoretical*. As Mel brushed up on the distinction between the two terms, he saw something that influenced how he was thinking about organizations and about leadership:

The word *theory* derives from the Greek *theorein*, which means "to look at." Theories are based on *what has been observed*. In science, a theory is called a *hypothesis*. While the terms *theory* and *theoretical* are related in derivation, *theoretical* is once removed from its origin. What is considered *theoretical* is based on *something that has not yet been observed*. In science, this is called *conjecture*. For example, black holes were *theoretical* (based on conjecture) before they were observed, and now that they are observable, we have an emerging theory of black holes.

With this in mind, we conclude that what is presented in this book is a theory about organizations based on the critical observations of participating observers. Therefore, it is more of a hypothesis than a conjecture. Readers working inside of organizations, as well as scholars studying organizational phenomena, can judge for themselves just how much this theory helps them understand their own experiences and observations.

References

Healey, J. (1997) Covert Activity Saved Sports Car, *USA Today* (March 19, 1997): 1B.

Schefter, J. (1997) *All Corvettes Are Red: The Rebirth of an American Legend*. New York: Simon & Schuster.

Scherer, J. with L. Shook. (1993) *Work and the Human Spirit*. Spokane, WA: John Scherer & Associates.

3

ORGANIZATIONS AND REALITY

Introduction

While modern organizations have been examined extensively in case studies, they remain largely unexplained in terms that give us direct access to the potential of this domain. There is no unified theory for organizations, one that accounts for all possible manifestations. Perhaps the realm of organizations, like leadership, does not lend itself to codification. Therefore, we will need a theory to deal with it.

At this time, we have myriad models for organizations, most of which are valid but seem to place organizations in categories, such as pharmaceutical, consumer products, financial services, community base, profit, not for profit, and so on. This categorical approach even reaches down to individual organizations, such as Ford, IBM, Citibank, and Microsoft, which have been observed and modeled in case studies that are useful for people who work within each organization and somewhat useful for others in their industries as well. Yet, a foundational examination of Organization has yet to be undertaken—one that would account for the fundamental nature of most, if not all, organizations. Such an examination would provide an

DOI: 10.4324/9781003131847-3

understanding of organizations of all types—community, and enterprise, governmental and military. To accomplish this, we must first make a shift in thinking that changes our view of organizations and the way we think about them. Today, we view organizations categorically, classifying them according to type, industry, and function. What if we could see organizations in dimensional rather than categorical terms? When we view something through a categorical lens, our understanding of it includes prescribed meaning. When we expand our observation of something to include its many dimensions, we also have the possibility of viewing generated meaning—the kind of meaning that is not, and perhaps cannot be foretold or worked out in advance. This chapter explores the development of such a dimensional view—a view in which holographic representations become possible. We are using the term "holographic" here to mean "existing simultaneously at every scale of organization." With this understanding, we can then begin to examine the processes of integrating change and transformation.

We begin this chapter by exploring the traditional view of defining and codifying organizations, and then move into a deeper discussion about the nature of organizational reality.

Organization Theory

A Traditional View for Defining an Organization

When we speak of organizations, what do we mean? The topic is a broad one, but generally, an organization is defined as a group of people with one or more shared goals operating in a formal structure. It is useful to note that a broad, well done definition does not constitute a theory, unified or categorical. However, defining the subject provides a useful starting point for us. The following is the Business Dictionary definition of an organization (2020):

or·gan·i·za·tion (plural or·gan·i·za·tions) noun

Organization—a social unit of people that is structured and managed to meet a need or to pursue collective goals. All organizations have a management structure that determines relationships between the different activities and the members, and sub-divides and assigns roles, responsibilities, and authority to carry out different tasks. Organizations are open systems—they affect and are affected by their environment.

Each aspect of this definition is in concert with our experience and observations. Yet, while each seems to point to what organizations are, none provides access to their basic nature. Before we begin to look more closely at the underlying nature of organizations, we will broaden the work of defining them categorically. Management science provides a more specific look into organizations by categorizing them into five types (Peter and Hull 1976; Coase 1990; Handy 2005; Scott 2016):

- Pyramids or Hierarchies
- Committees or Juries
- Matrix Organizations
- Ecologies
- Composite Organizations.

Management science is often used synonymously with **operations research** because the underlying thinking for both disciplines is similar, yet there are specific distinctions in the way the terms are used. As defined below, operations research is concerned with the problems of industrial engineering. Management science is concerned with the problems of business management.

Operations research is a field which addresses industrial engineering challenges and provides aids for decision-making around complex real-world (physical) systems to improve performance.

Management science is a field which addresses business management challenges and provides aids for decision-making around complex business (non-physical) systems to improve performance.

Here, as in many other attempts to address problems within organizational systems, we find a physical world model used as the precursor for addressing non-physical world challenges. What solves physical world problems may well serve as a good means for understanding non-physical world problems and for creating and applying variations of the "cause and effect" model of Newtonian physics to non-physical world business problems. Business systems seem to respond well to this approach, while human systems appear at first to respond to this approach for solving problems, but then in only very limited ways.

As detailed later, it is possible to expand our thinking about organizations beyond the limits of traditional thinking without defeating this approach, but rather by picking up where it leaves off.

Organizational Structures

Thinking, in general, requires some type of language, be it words, gestures, images or the like. Hence, the way we think about organizations is defined, even limited, by the language we use. The definitions that follow are examples of the language we typically use today to envision and give shape to organizations.

Pyramids and Hierarchies

A hierarchical structure allows an authority to direct others who have lesser authority. This is the classic bureaucracy. One "rises" through a hierarchy by seniority or by acquiring authority over more people. Pyramidal structures within hierarchies are used to achieve repeatable results because they are believed to provide the shortest path connecting the authority or standard-setter to the worker. Because this structure is only as good as its weakest link, it suffers from poor communication and for supervisory faults, and is lacking in creativity and the opportunity to innovate.

The classic fix for the communication problem is a company newsletter. In another solution, people email their bosses about what has been done, what is planned, including an outline of current problems. Each boss makes a summary for his group and sends it up the chain of command. Then all the bosses send their summaries downward, appended to the summaries from their bosses. Each version represents a shift in context, agenda, and meaning, so the information does not necessarily communicate once it leaves its originating context and gets escalated and interpreted by the next level of context.

Context is the source of meaning for the content of communication, and the context in which a communication originates is often distinct from the one in which it is subsequently received. As a result, the meaning of the content tends to morph. Because meaning is a significant shaper of action, the results of communications are too often inconsistent with the actions and results that are intended or needed. For simple, straightforward solutions, hierarchies have their place.

The pitfalls of hierarchies are satirized in The Peter Principle (Peter and Hull 1976), a book that introduced the term hierarchiology and the axiom, "In a hierarchy every employee tends to rise to their level of incompetence."

Committees and Juries

Committees and juries make group decisions as peers, sometimes by casting votes. Whereas committees are usually assigned to perform or direct further actions after making initial decisions, juries are charged only with reaching a particular decision. In common law countries, legal juries render decisions of guilt and liability, and quantify damages.

Sometimes a selection committee functions like a jury. In the Middle Ages, juries in continental Europe were used to determine the law according to consensus among local notables. When committees lack structure, they can flounder aimlessly without making decisions. To help prevent floundering, they can use such methods as Parliamentary Procedure as described in *Robert's Rules of Order* (Robert and Patnode 1989), the more user-friendly *Interaction Method* (Doyle and Strauss 1992) of meeting design and facilitation, or its recent interpretation in *Roberta's Rules of Order* (Cochran 2004). Many groups designed as teams function more like committees or juries than teams. Sometimes a group starts out as a team and from there devolves into a committee or jury.

Staff Organization or Cross-functional Team

An expert's staff helps him get his work done. To this end, a "chief of staff" decides whether an assignment or problem is routine or unique. If it's routine, it's assigned to a staff member who is a junior expert. The chief of staff schedules the routine tasks and checks on their progress and completion.

If a task is not routine but is critical, the chief of staff passes it on to the expert, who solves the problem and educates the staff, thereby converting the unique problem into a routine problem.

A staff has the capacity to make decisions quickly, and to carry out assignments efficiently, though less reliably than committees or matrices. For this reason, businesses often prefer to work through a staff. However, a staff can break down easily, usually because of issues between people.

An executive committee can be a staff with special expertise in choosing people. This is how General Electric succeeded under Jack Welch. As with an executive committee, the boss of a "cross-functional team" has to be a non-expert, because so many arenas of knowledge are required.

Matrix Organization

On the face of it, this is the perfect organization. As illustrated below, the horizontal dimension is "functional," assuring that each type of expert in the organization is well trained and measured by a boss who is a super-expert in the same field. We can think of this as the professional services part of an organization. The vertical dimension is the "executive" branch of the organization in which the boss has a broad understanding of many areas of expertise. Operating together, these dimensions of the matrix initiate and complete projects through experts led by generalists or through experts led by experts interfacing with generalists. In any case, each intersection is a potential field for initiative.

Matrix organizations can consistently create complex technical products like airplanes, engines, or software. Even so, it can take time to go through channels. Getting to the point of actually *doing* something can require the approval of each type of expert, and each expert's boss! One way to speed up this procedure is to practice alignment. This is a way of moving things forward on the premise that it is more important to put the game in play than it is to get the game perfect before play (Carse 2011; Pinchot and Pellman 1999).

Ecologies

Based on the principle of "survival of the fittest," ecologies are good metaphors for organizations in which the culture encourages intense

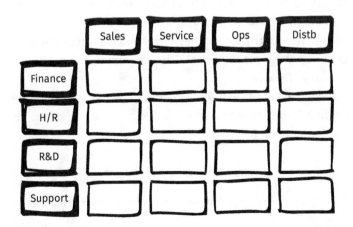

Figure 3.1 Matrix Organization

competition. Meritocracies, in which ability leads to position and authority, are a type of ecology, as is the ranking system used in the military.
One could make a case that the Internet and other open source and free
software projects are also run as forms of meritocracy that operate like
ecologies.

Ineffective groups in such an organization will starve and eventually
"die," and effective groups will receive more resources. Every group is
paid through budget allocation for what they actually do, and, in effect,
runs a tiny "intrapreneurial" business that has to show consistent returns
measured by results.

Ecologies can be very effective organizations, but they can also be waste-
ful. While an ineffective group may have valuable training, it is very hard
to recycle its people into other parts of the business if what was worked on
is seen as a failure or the group is seen as ineffective. This can lead to bit-
terness, followed by reorganization and downsizing.

At the 1997 World Future Society conference, Tachi Kiuchi, Former
Chairman and CEO of Mitsubishi Electric America and Chairman of the
Future 500, gave an address entitled "What I Learned from the Rainforest."
In it, he illustrated how his experiences in the ecologies of the natural
world influenced his approach to leading his company (Shireman and
Kiuchi 2001).

Composite Organizations

A composite organization attempts to apply each of the above types of
structures appropriately within the various functions of the organization.
Very occasionally, a true organizational genius can make this work for a
while, but not necessarily for the long term. Success can outgrow the ability
of the genius, and so many special cases can emerge that handling them
becomes unmanageable.

One golden exception may be a hierarchy of staffs, where every staff
above the first level works to find or develop the right people. This is the
model used at General Electric.

Chaordic Organizations

An emerging model of organizing human endeavors, based on a blending of chaos and order (hence "chaordic"), comes from the work of Dee
Hock (1999), founding CEO of Visa International, and his early creation

of this multi-faceted financial network. Blending democracy, complex systems, consensus decision-making, cooperation, and competition, the chaordic approach attempts to encourage organizations to evolve beyond the increasingly nonviable hierarchical, command-and-control models.

Having reviewed some means of categorizing organizational types, we can recognize the reality of these categories, particularly the ones we have experienced. When we see something as being "real" we seldom ask ourselves what are the implications of applying this term.

What Is Reality?

The term *reality* is used in many ways and has many meanings. In common colloquial usage, *reality* means our individual "perceptions, beliefs, and attitudes" as in: "Well, that may be your reality, but it's not mine!" Some philosophers have contrasted *reality* with nonexistence. For example, a house made of pure silver is a possibility, but it's not real. Other philosophers theorize about reality by saying what it is, rather than what it is not.

How we interpret reality can also depend to a large extent on what we *say* it is not.

In ethics, the arts, and political theory, reality is distinguished by contrasting *the ideal and the real*. In ethics, *ethical perfectionism* suggests that we have an obligation to be perfect human beings, which is *the ideal*. This is contrasted with our notions about human nature, which, combined with our experience of one another, forms our *reality*. As illustrated in the examples that follow, how we view human nature shapes our actions.

During the Romantic period, artistic portrayals represented *the ideal*. This was followed by the Realism movement in the 19th century, which evolved into naturalism, where visual portrayals represented *the reality*.

In U.S. politics, we have theories that fall generally into two broad camps—liberal and conservative. The reality of liberalism includes *the ideal* that it is possible for human nature to change. In direct contrast, conservative reality holds that human nature is not likely to change in any meaningful way. We actually live in a multi-verse of realities with ample evidence that both views are true. What if our organizations not only exist in a multi-verse but are themselves multi-verses? What would this suggest?

As these examples illustrate, when the context shifts (ethics, art, politics), so does the meaning of reality. This suggests that *reality is context-dependent*, and that we can't take our relationship to it for granted. This is a key point in our exploration and begs the questions: "Do we spend enough time creating a context for projects and initiatives (intended future realities). Do we build context into our communications?" If we do, are we also considering the context in which the communication will land?

While all the above models for structuring organizations are valid and provide contrast, they do not address the elements that constitute organizational reality. So we will not be drawing from them directly in our exploration. Rather, we are inviting you to think of organizational reality in several other ways.

What Constitutes Organizational Reality?

One way of thinking about organizational reality emerges from the view that everything that communicates brings forth the organizational reality we inhabit, that is, what we see, sense, or know in the presence of communication. This view of reality suggests the possibility that reality is a by-product of ongoing creativity.

Another way assumes that everything already exists but may not as yet have been fully represented in language. So our job is to more accurately represent what is already there. In the first case we are creating, and in the second case we are representing. What if both are true for an organization? This suggests that *everything that actually exists* is only part of the *reality of* organization.

The implications of considering *reality* as "what is real" can be tricky. "Reality" can include what actually exists, as well as what does not exist yet seems feasible. Perhaps the things we say, see, sense, and know all contribute to creating a given reality.

Both these modes of thinking about organizational reality view it through the lens of what can or could be observed, apprehended, or understood inside the language and container of a given systems-of-analysis, such as philosophy, psychology, mathematics, or science.

A third viewpoint from which to consider organizational reality is *possibility*, which lies outside the scope of most current systems-of-analysis, but is an important aspect of our exploration. At times, the reality of *possibility* goes beyond our individual and collective imaginations. As we become aware of how our own view impacts the way in which reality emerges, we open the door to inhabiting possibility. This means that, to live in the realm of possibility, we must become more responsible for knowing, seeing, and sensing what we believed previously was not available to us. This will require us to transform our relationship with language.

The Johari Window

A good tool to bring to this part of our exploration is The Johari Window, created by Joseph Luft and Harry Ingham (1969). As illustrated below, it can be used to clarify the nature of interpersonal communications by using four quadrants that represent two dimensions: whether information is or is not known by each of the two parties.

The Four Quadrants of the Johari Window

- In the first quadrant, called The Arena, both parties know all the relevant information. Open communication is based on common assumptions and knowledge about how the first person acts. A key adjective to describe information in The Arena is "open."

Johari Window	Known To Self	Not Known To Self
Known To Others	Open The Arena	Blind The Facade
Not Known To Others	Hidden The Blind Spot	Unknown The Unknown

Figure 3.2 The Johari Window

- In the second quadrant, called "The Facade," the first person knows information about himself of which the second person is unaware. The first person can choose to bring the information into the open (self-disclosure) or use it surreptitiously to his own advantage.
- In the third quadrant, called "The Blind Spot," the first person is unaware of information about himself of which the second is aware. The question for the second person is whether or not and how to inform the first person about his blind spot.
- The fourth quadrant is called "The Unknown." This represents information unknown to both parties.

As presented in our exploration so far, when viewing the concerns of organizations, we can look through a lens that includes three dimensions of reality: the aspects of reality that exist and can be seen, the aspects that do not exist but are imaginable, and those aspects that are unimaginable, yet possible, if we knew how to look for them. When we look through this lens, we create a *context* for generating *reality*. In the *context of organizations*, that *reality* has a unique meaning. Therefore, as a concept, *reality* is contrasted to what is not reality.

What Is "Possibility"?

In thinking about organizational reality, we can also go beyond *what it is* or *is not*, and view it in terms of *possibility*. Consider that *what it is* implies that something is present and *what is not* implies that something is missing. Interestingly, the condition of *is not* is dependent upon the condition of *is*. Implicit in the condition *is*, is the condition *is not*. Said another way, *is* and *is not* are interdependent conditions.

Interdependent conditions can form a spectrum. Let's look at these two conditions that way and see what we find. Depending on which side of the center point, we find something is more or less real. Another way to think of this is that a non-physical reality is subject to a mutable existence.

Figure 3.3 Spectrum of *is* and *is not*

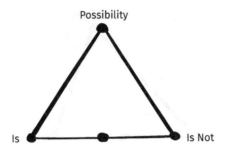

Figure 3.4 Interdependent Spectrum of *is* and *is not*

Let's imagine we are walking through a village market in Europe in the mid-17th century. The question "Where are all the taxi cabs?" will never be heard because taxi cabs do not exist at this time. So the question would have made no sense and would be meaningless. For taxi cabs to not exist they first must exist. Only from our current perspective in time can we say sensibly that taxicabs were missing in the mid-17th century. However, placing ourselves back in that timeframe, we can imagine that "self-propelled" transportation might exist in the mind of a genius inventor. Given the mental constraints of that time, such a person would want to be careful of such conjecture lest he find himself confined to the local "mad house."

Numerous studies have concluded that *adverse circumstances* can be *precursors* to new and better realties (Nayak and Ketteringham 1986). Similarly, we can hypothesize that *created possibility* can act as a *precursor* to new and better realities.

If we add possibility of the spectrum of existence above, a fundamental shift occurs in what can be imagined. Now, rather than an infinite number of points on a spectrum, we have an infinite number of points on a field. The spectrum allows for categorization, the field allows for dimensionality.

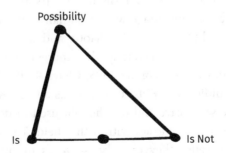

Figure 3.5 Bi-directional *is* and *is not*

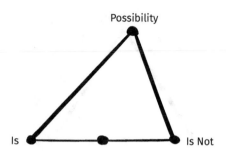

Figure 3.6 Possibility Changes the Shape

Now consider that possibility is multi-directional and Is-Is Not are bi-directional. This suggests that *possibility* changes the shape of a field and therefore alters dimensionality.

Even though circumstance and possibility are events that create a disturbance in the status quo, *circumstance* and *possibility* are fundamentally different types of *precursors*. With circumstance, if the event is sufficient to *provoke reaction* we must work after the event has occurred or behind the curve, in response to an unexpected outcome. With *possibility*, the event *stimulates action not reaction*, and we can work in front of the curve to influence the creation of the future and mediate outcomes that are desirable.

We can think of *possibility* as a field phenomenon that argues for the existence of certain patterns, but not for others. This deserves a lengthy discussion that would go beyond what is appropriate at this point. For this examination, consider *possibility* as a product of *design*, not of a fortuitous epiphany. While epiphanies are interesting, we can't count on having them. But we can count on designing *possibility* as a matter of choice. When we design possibility in the context of an organization, we can take into account the *patterns* we want to emphasize. Sometimes thought of as organizational behaviors, these patterns are precursors to the various social actions that we want to encourage within human systems.

A field of possibility is naturally chaotic and does not lend itself to imposed order. One way to encourage the emergence of patterns of possibility is to design *attractors* (Lorenz 1995; Gleick 1998). In organizations, key performance indicators (KPIs) can serve as attractors. When they are designed with the same care and forethought used in designing the field of *possibility*, KPIs become *attractors* within that field. The careful design of KPIs is essential because they can also serve as unintended detractors.

In addition, KPIs used as attractors in a field of possibility are quite different than those used to account for what is already there, or the *current reality*, because they do not lend themselves to *methods of* quantitative *analysis*. Their real value is mined through methods of qualitative evaluation.

Qualitative evaluation is an assessment process that answers the question, "How well did we do?" Here are some examples from a qualitative evaluation of a school literacy program:

- Content, quality, and relevance of a program
  What was learned?
  Are the learners using their new knowledge? If so, how?
- Attitudes and achievements of the learners
  What do the learners think about the classes, the teachers, and the materials?
  Do they think the literacy classes made a difference in their lives? If yes, what kind of difference?
- Selection, training, attitude, and ability of teachers and other literacy personnel
  Did the teachers do a good job of communicating the new information?
  Did they respect and support the learners?

In contrast, quantitative analysis breaks down a subject into its constituent parts in order to describe the parts and their relationship to the whole. It can also be used to derive information, such as using the analysis of financial information to establish financial ratios, the cost of capital, asset valuation, and sales and earnings trends and ratios.

Two Classes of Reality

To better understand organizational reality, it is helpful to explore the principles that inform its existence. In the exploration that follows, we propose that there are two broad classes of reality, Class I and II, and that organizations belong to Class II Reality. To understand their fundamental nature, I propose we step back from organizations and explore the class of reality to which they belong. We'll begin by looking at the basics of both classes of reality, then focus on Class II Reality and the principles that govern organizations. As we uncover these principles, we will begin to see how organizations are synthesized.

Class I Reality is the tangible, physical world, which can be measured directly and consistently, such as the weight of a cinder block or a volume of water. Class II Reality is the non-physical world that either is not measurable, or is measurable indirectly. It is also inconsistent across events of measuring, yet forms recurring patterns when viewed through the proper perspective. Class I Reality is what we can observe and engage with most directly, such as inert matter and living matter. While Class I Reality has many rich languages for dealing with its existence, it does not require those languages to exist. *Class I Reality exists independent of language.*

In contrast, Class II Reality exists only in language, and *depends entirely on language for its existence.* Organizations belong to this class of reality, which is intangible and exists nowhere else but in language. While this reality often manifests physical artifacts—products, for example—it is non-physical at its essence, and its artifacts represent realized possibility and a means for measuring indirectly an organization's existence and performance.

Language is the basis for how people and organizations perceive themselves. Language can lock us into the past or it can open up new potential through the use of "future-based language" or "generative language" to declare what is important. In this way we can rewrite the future (Zaffron and Logan 2009).

So your desk, the coffee cup on your desk, the building you work in all exist in Class I Reality. Even though Class II Reality has artifacts that mark its existence, Class II Reality itself lives only in language. A nation exists in a Class II Reality. Even though nations have people, products, and natural resources (all Class I Reality) that *represent* the nation, they are not

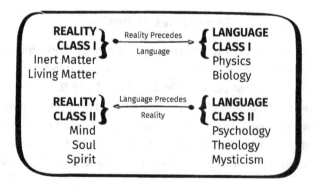

Figure 3.7 Reality and Language

the nation. Where is the United States? Of course, it is in North America, but that's a landmass, mountains, rivers, and so on. The nation itself exists only in language. Moreover, there are Class II Realities that come together to form other Class II Realities. States or provinces, currencies, languages, and borders are all Class II Realities that combine to define the existence of a nation. Organizations are similar in that they have headquarters, logos, products, advertising, but organizations are not located within these things. They are located in language.

Language and Class II Reality

The challenge in examining the phenomenon of organizations lies in the nature of language itself and in the basics of definition. Any attempt to define something presupposes two things: that it exists and that it lends itself to a language of reference and description. Consider describing a simple physical object. Descriptions, no matter how elaborate, may be useful, but they are reductions of what is observed and can never render a faithful representation of the object itself.

Consider the challenge of describing a work of art. Such attempts are difficult for two reasons:

1) Descriptive language is reductionistic.
2) Descriptive language does not capture the originating experience, but only its memory.

Imagine you are in Rome in the church of San Pietro in Vincoli. In the nave of the church, you encounter Michelangelo's "Moses." The statue is overwhelming in its dimensionality. Never standing in one place, you move to capture all aspects of the statue. After a time, details emerge that were not apparent in your first or even second viewing. You become aware of the lighting, the church itself, the sounds, and the smells. Soon you become aware of your own responses to the work.

Now try to imagine describing the physical object, your experience of the surroundings, and your own responses to the work. Even the most exhaustive description will not fully integrate the experience. The most careful detailing of the statue itself will not capture its majesty, much less the religious, political, or emotional overtones.

When we consider physical reality, there is no question that we include and can relate to physical objects. There is another class of reality represented by non-physical objects that we do not necessarily think of as reality, at least not in the same way we think of physical objects. So, in the case of something that is not there in a non-physical form, such as the organization in which we work, how much more difficult is the challenge of using language to describe it?

A Language for Non-physical Reality

One of the challenges in interpreting organizations is that they are in a state of constant change. Because we do not have a rigorous language for change, we are relegated to descriptive-reductionistic language when we attempt a description of organizational processes and systems as a means for change. Thinking of organizations as quantum phenomena is a way to enrich what we can know about them and serves as a foundation for creating a language for change (Tsao and Laszlo 2019). In their work exploring the connection between organizational development and quantum organizations, Tasdelen and Polat (2015) contrast Newtonian or mechanistic organizational structures with quantum organizational structures. According to their research, a major shift in consciousness is needed for an organization to evolve from Newtonian to Quantum and that this shift is necessary in order to adapt and respond to the multiple changes in the environment affecting organizations. From a Newtonian viewpoint, the world is stable and calls for structures that support certainty, absoluteness, and simplicity. In contrast, from a quantum viewpoint, organizational structures need to allow for "uncertainty, contextuality and multiple possibilities in organizations" (Tasdelen and Polat 2015: 573).

David Bohm, a well-respected quantum physicist and philosopher writes eloquently about the fundamental nature of reality and the new quantum view of the universe.

> [The]inseparable quantum interconnectedness of the whole universe is the fundamental reality ... the classical idea of the separability of the world into distinct but interacting parts is no longer valid or relevant. Rather, we have to regard the universe as *an undivided and unbroken whole*. Division in particles, or into particles and fields, is only a crude abstraction and approximation. Thus we come [through quantum theory] to an order that is radically different from that of Galileo and Newton— the order of *undivided wholeness*.
>
> (Bohm 1975:158) [italics are in the original]

We typically think of organizations in terms of their "distinct but interacting parts." A quantum view of Organization sees the "undivided wholeness."

What if we were able to use a combination of both languages, descriptive-reductionistic language and a language for change? By adding to our more familiar descriptive-reductionistic language a way to think of or to apply language to organizations in change, we could apprehend concurrently the location-in-time, direction, and velocity (Heisenberg 1927) of a given organization; to see its undivided wholeness.

Descriptive-reductionistic language is critical. It provides us with a snap-shot of a "state-in-time." It allows us to isolate variables, identify constants, and understand where an organization is at a particular point in time. Descriptive-reductionistic language "nails" *location-in-time* but does not give us *direction and velocity*. This is where a language for *organizations in change* could make a significant difference in our ability to lead change efforts. It would be like working from a motion picture instead of just a snapshot.

When both descriptive-reductionistic language and a language for change are available, we can ask the question: "Given the current situation, do we need to better understand how things work together (*relationship*), or do we need to better understand each thing in greater detail (*resolution*)?" We could also ask "Do we need to better understand what it means (*relationship*) or how it works (*resolution*)?"

To increase resolution, we must also increase the number of *constants* and reduce the number of *variables*, thus moving toward Class I Reality. To increase relationship, we must do just the opposite as we move toward Class II Reality. So, in any given situation it is useful to assess in which direction to begin working. Move to the right to better understand the relationship between things, or move to the left to better understand the details of the things. No matter which direction we move first, it follows logically that a move in the other direction is also needed to bring a more complete understanding of the situation. The following diagram (Figure 3.8) and Table 3.1 provide some of key corresponding attributes of Class I and Class II Realities.

Language, for the purpose of this exploration, doesn't mean only spoken or written language, such as English, French, or German. In our use of it here, the term has a broader definition that includes math, psychology, physics, theology, geology, dance, and music as languages, as well. This is important because we *think in language*, and what we can think is limited by the language we use choose to think in. Consider this question: "In what language can you think of the whole of your organization?"

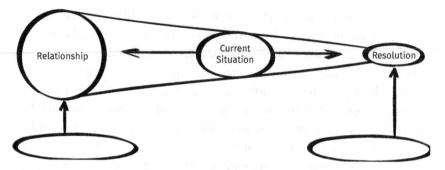

Figure 3.8 Relationship—Resolution Continuum

Table 3.1 Key Corresponding Attributes of Class I and Class II Realities

CLASS II REALITY	CLASS I REALITY
Subjective	Objective
Conjecture	Prediction
Evolving Norms	Fixed Norms
High Deviation from Norms	Low Deviation from Norms
Lower Frequency	Higher Frequency
Higher Amplitude	Lower Amplitude
Lower Resolution	Higher Resolution
Relationship Dependence	Relationship Independence
Scale: Macro	Scale: Micro
Inquiry	Reductionistic Thinking

When we look closely, it is not hard to see that *there is no language in which we can think about organizations*, let alone a language for an *organization in change*. We do, however, have languages for parts of organizations. Finance, Operations, Sales, Marketing, and Research and Development, for example, all have their own languages. While these are also the names of departments, each has a language of its own—an artful language designed to use in thinking about the problems and challenges peculiar to its sphere. When we deal with systemic issues in an organization, meetings with groups of the various stakeholders can sometimes seem like a Tower of Babble. We leave them confused and feeling that we've neither understood others nor been understood. If others tell us they don't understand, we often give them more details because we assume that more facts will bring them more clarity.

Just as different organizational languages need translating for those unfamiliar with them, the same is also true for "concepts." We often have to *translate* what we say about concepts in our fields of organizational expertise into terms that are understandable by others who have different sets of expertise. Translation always diminishes what we see and, at best, leaves others with some skeletal outline of the concept. Because areas of specialization call for special languages, there will always be a need for translation.

We propose that we also need a *language for change*. That is, we need a language to use in thinking about change that addresses an organization as a whole. The whole organization cannot be apprehended through the sum of its parts alone or even by bringing the parts into greater resolution. It also cannot be apprehended through the descriptive lens of any one discipline. Therefore, we need a new language that allows us to talk about the organization as a whole progressing through change. Change occurs in time and over time. Grasping change in relationship to temporality is fundamental for changing Class II Reality.

Time, the Present, and Class II Reality

In the Western world, Class II Reality existence occurs inside a temporal paradigm that is so old and so pervasive that we no longer see it or notice its implications. About 1600 years ago, St. Augustine made a compelling observation about temporality. He wrote:

> The PRESENT of past things is the <u>memory</u>, the PRESENT of present things is <u>direct perception</u>, and the PRESENT of future things is <u>expectation</u>. (Emphasis added)

This quote from *Confessions* (1998) was written around 400 A.D., 30 years before St. Augustine's death at the age of 76. It articulates the temporal paradigm that is the foundation of Class II Reality. It also points to a pervasive and unexamined background that shapes our contemporary world. There are powerful insights in what St. Augustine suggested. He saw *everything* as existing in the present, including the past and future. Even 1600 years after his compelling insight, we do not think this way. In our world, we have been taught to believe:

- There is the present, preceded by the past and followed by the future.
- There is the past, followed by the present and the future.
- There is the future, preceded by the past and the present.

This suggests that we think of past, present, and future as sequential attributes of time, not as related and distinct phenomena of temporality. What if time and temporality are related, but are not the same thing? Suppose time is categorical and processional—future into present and present into past. Then what is temporality? Consider this possibility: temporality is dimensional not categorical and it is about the present (the now framed by the past and the future), in a non-processional relationship in which the past informs the now, and the future shapes the now, and the now establishes the present. Temporality is dimensional-relational and time is categorical-processional. While this is correctly said (at least we hope so) it is not easy to understand. Language is a limitation and we are challenged by this limitation not the idea being put forth.

Because language is basically linear, writing about this construct of the present must also be linear. Can you imagine the present happening all at once, something like the scene in a photograph? This way of looking at the present allows us to see it more like a snapshot than as a sequential construct like watching a film. Think of it this way: time is about measurement (categorizing) and temporality is about relationship (bringing together).

When we place a snapshot in time along with a series of properly related and sequenced snapshots, something more than a picture or series of pictures forms. We literally begin to see patterns of change-in-relationship that are not available looking at the snapshots separately. How much and what is revealed depends on perspective, frequency, amplitude, frame, and depth-of-field.

Taking this idea a little further, we do not think or say there is "now" and there is "the present" or that the present exists only when now is framed by the past and the future. It does not occur to us that the past and the future, as temporal phenomena, are in the present, and that the present is formed by the now in relationship with the past and future. In taking this view, we must also consider depth and centricity. That is to say, there is "temporal-depth" or a certain amount of past and future in the present.

There is also temporal-centricity, a certain relative weighing of past and future in the present.

Another way to think about this idea is to overlay on the terms past, present, and future the terms memory, perception, and expectation. This formulation of the model has these three elements in a new relationship where memory allows for expectation, expectation shapes direct perception, and direct perception establishes Class II (non-physical) Reality. Here memory and past arise together. Expectation and future arise together.

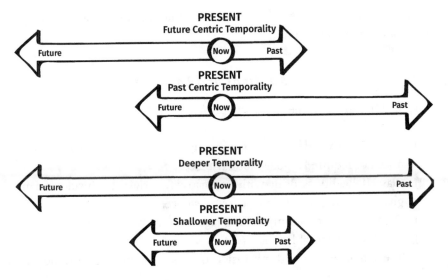

Figure 3.9 Temporal Depth

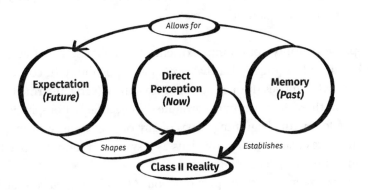

Figure 3.10 Temporal Centricity

Direct perception and now arise together. Memory, Direct Perception and Expectation form a framework we call present. This construct is one way of accounting for the way we conceptualize the present. These relationships suggest that our memory of the past gives rise to our expectations for the future, and that our perceptions in the moment (now) are colored or shaped by a remembered past and an expected future. This also suggests that without memory, there is no past, and without past, there is no future.

Scaling this model from the memories, expectations, and perceptions of an individual to those of an entire organization provides useful insights into the nature of non-physical realities and new possibilities for dealing with them more effectively. The following material presents and develops some of these possibilities.

Organizations and Language

This section builds on the following principles:

1) Class I Reality is dealt with in time, originates outside of language, and does not require language for existence.
2) Class II Reality is dealt with in temporality, originates inside of language, and requires language for existence.
3) Organizations exist only in language and in Class II Reality.
4) We think inside of language(s).
5) The language(s) we think inside of create boundaries around our thinking.
6) Communication occurs through the medium of language, and, therefore, shapes organizational reality.

Non-physical reality comes into existence through a series of events that can begin with a simple idea that occurs as a possibility in conversation. The possibility moves through stages of feasibility (early, intermediate and late). From there, it moves into a grounded (objectified), non-physical reality. If we follow the beginning stages of any organization, we can account for what takes place through this lens as a system in motion—one that is dynamic and always changing.

An organization is a *system* phenomenon. As such, it is interactive and *auto-forming*. It lives beyond the boundaries of Class I Reality, of descriptive-reductionistic language, objective reality, and its parts. The singular term "Organization" refers to the abstract conceptual field of the dynamics that create and maintain individual organizational entities.

Summary

In order to understand how to integrate change in an organization, it is essential to have an expanded awareness of what constitutes the field of Organization; that "conceptual field of the dynamics that create and maintain individual organizational entities." Our traditional view of codifying organizations by various typologies does not provide us the rich view of the dynamics and dimensions of organizations and their relationship to internal and external change forces.

This chapter offered a more fundamental view of Organization by examining the nature of reality and the distinctions between Class I and Class II Realities. Within these two realities, we also examined the nature of time and temporality as we begin to create the building blocks of a *language of change*.

You may find yourself wondering what all this has to do with transforming your organization, or from a scholarly perspective being able to understand theories of change and transformation. But we ask you to grant us your trust and we unfold the elements of this new language.

To better see into Organization, we will use quantum physics in Chapter 4 as an analogy for organizational systems. Thinking of organizations as quantum phenomena—as fields of energy—is not sufficient to explain the whole reality of organizations but can help to clarify organizational performance and to formulate ways to influence it. Organizations exist only in language and the medium for language is communication. If we think of communication as *energy*, then the nature of communication might well be informed by the thinking of quantum physics, and in particular, the field theory of quantum mechanics (cf. Gleick 1998; Lorenz 1995; Tsao and Laszlo 2019).

In the next chapter we will introduce the concept of organizations as field phenomena and will continue to build on this discussion of Class I and Class II Reality.

References

Business Dictionary (2020) Organization. Retrieved from http://www.businessdictionary.com/definition/organization.html on May 24, 2020

Carse, J. (2011) *Finite and Infinite Games: A Vision of Life as Play and Possibility.* New York: Free Press.

Coase, R. (1990) *The Firm, the Market, and the Law.* Chicago, IL: University of Chicago Press.

Cochran, A.C. (2004) *Roberta's Rules of Order: Sail Through Meetings for Stellar Results without the Gavel.* San Francisco, CA: Jossey-Bass.

Doyle, M. and Strauss, D. (1992) *How to Make Meetings Work: The New Interaction Method.* New York: Jove Books.

Gleick, J. (1998) *Chaos: Making a New Science.* New York: Viking Penguin.

Handy, C. (2005) *Understanding Organizations*. New York: Penguin Business Library.

Heisenberg, W. (1927) Über den anschaulichen Inhalt der quantentheoretischen Kinematik und Mechanik. *Z. Phys.* 43, 172–198.

Hock, D. (1999) *Birth of the Chaordic Organization*. San Francisco, CA: Berrett-Koehler.

Lorenz, E. (1995) *The Essence of Chaos*. Seattle, WA: University of Washington Press.

Luft, J. and Ingham, H. (1969) *Of Human Interaction*, Palo Alto, CA: National Press.

Nayak, P.R. and Ketteringham, J. (1986) *Breakthroughs! How the Vision and Drive of Innovators in Sixteen Companies Created Commercial Breakthroughs that Swept the World*. New York: Rawson Associates.

Peter, L. and Hull, R. (1976) *The Peter Principle: Why Things Always Go Wrong*. New York: Bantam Books.

Pinchot, G. and Pellman, R. (1999) *Intrapreneuring in Action: A Handbook for Business Innovation*. San Francisco, CA: Berrett-Koehler.

Robert, H. and Patnode, D. (1989) *Robert's Rules of Order* (original 1876 edition revised). New York: Berkeley Books.

Scott, R. (2016) *Organizations and Organizing: Rational, Natural and Open Systems Perspectives*. New York: Routledge.

Shireman, B. and Kiuchi, T. (2001) *What We Learned in the Rainforest: Business Lessons from Nature*. San Francisco, CA: Berrett-Koehler.

St. Augustine. *The Confessions*. Bibliothèque de La Pléiade; Paris, France: 1998. [(accessed on February 22, 2013)]. English version. Available online: www.ourladyswarriors.org/saints/augcon10.htm

Tasdelen, T. and Polat, M. (2015) Organizational Development and Quantum Organizations, *International Journal of Social Science and Education* 5(4): 570–579.

Tsao, F. and Laszlo, C. (2019) *Quantum Leadership: New Consciousness in Business*. Stanford, CA: Stanford Business Books.

Zaffron, S. and Logan, D. (2009) *The Three Laws of Performance: Rewriting the Future of Your Organization and Your Life*. San Francisco, CA: Jossey-Bass.

4

ORGANIZATIONS AS FIELD PHENOMENA

Introduction

A new way to perceive and think about organizations is to see them as field phenomena. We can think of a field in several ways:

- As a complex set of forces that serve as causative agents in human behavior.
- As a region or space in which a given effect exists.
- As an area of reality where some things are more likely and/or others are less likely to happen than others.

Communication is a field phenomenon. Once this principle is accepted, it can then be leveraged not only by individuals but also by organizations.

This chapter presents a three-circle model that can be useful in understanding the elements of any field phenomena, in this case, organizations. It is also extremely useful for both linear and non-linear analysis of various organizational challenges and opportunities.

DOI: 10.4324/9781003131847-4

Class I and Class II Reality as Field Phenomena

Early in the 19th century, there was revolution in the then nascent field of physics. An English scientist named Michael Faraday (1791–1867) proposed a reversal of conventional thinking. A modern physicist described that reversal as follows:

> According to Faraday, rather than looking upon the potential field of force that could be exerted by a bit of matter on other matter (should the latter be located at any of the continuum of spatial points) as a secondary derivative property of that matter, one should rather consider the continuous field of potential force as the elementary feature.
>
> He then viewed the "discrete particle" aspect as a secondary, derivative property. *According to the field theory proposed, the real stuff of the material world is the abstract (i.e. not directly observable) aspect associated with the potential field of force of matter.* (emphasis added)
>
> This view challenged a prevailing philosophic stand, presently known as "naive realism," which asserts that only that which we human beings directly perceive to be there, outside of us, is the reality from which a true description must follow. Faraday's abstract approach, on the other hand, took the fundamental reality to be at a level underlying that of human precepts.
>
> (Sachs 1974: 21)

It took over 100 years for the genius of Faraday's view to be appreciated. Not until the development of quantum field theory, in the 1930s and 1940s, was the view that fields might be the "real stuff of the world" accepted among physicists, and then only to a limited degree. As reported by Gary Zukav in his groundbreaking book, *The Dancing Wu Li Masters* (1979), today's quantum physicists have shown that

According to quantum field theory, fields alone are real. They are the substance of the universe and not "matter." Matter (particles) is simply the momentary manifestation of interacting fields which, intangible and insubstantial as they are, are the only real things in the universe.

> (Zukav 1979: 200)

So, what are these elusive phenomena called fields? We cannot observe them directly. We recognize them only by their effects. When observing an apple falling from a tree, Newton introduced the first field, gravitation.

As defined by Faraday, gravity is a secondary derivative property of matter. Einstein later postulated that the gravitational field was not a property of matter at all, but the result of space-time curving in response to matter. Thus, gravity for Einstein was not a force, but a medium—an agency through which something is accomplished.

The other field with which we are most familiar is magnetism. We can infer its presence from, for example, iron filings lining up in rows instead of scattering randomly.

The dictionary defines a field as:

- An area or division of an activity.
- The sphere of practical operation outside a base.
- A space on which something is drawn or projected.
- A region or space in which a given effect exists.
- A complex of forces that serve as causative agents in human behavior.
- A particular area in which the same type of information is regularly recorded.

Michael Talbot, a prominent modern physicist, has said:

> Although we know a great deal about the way fields affect the world as we perceive it, the truth is no one really knows what a field is. The closest we can come to describing what they are is to say that they are spatial structures in the fabric of space itself.
>
> (Talbot 1986, cited in Wheatley 1994: 46)

For purposes of our work in communication, we can take a probability-based definition of a field as "an area of the world where some things are more likely to happen and/or others are less likely to happen." Thus, when iron filings are within a magnetic field, they are more likely to line up than in the absence of such a field. The stronger the magnetic field, the greater the probability of the filing lining up. In the gravitational field of earth, objects are more likely to fall down and less likely to float than they are in outer space, where the gravitational field is weak or non-existent.

Recent thinking in quantum physics and chaos theory has hypothesized that fields are far more pervasive than was previously thought. Field theory may account for the effect of intention in human behavior, as well as for non-linear physical phenomenon such as cause-at-a-distance (Schafer 2013; Tsao and Laszlo 2019).

Perception and Reality

While listening to the president of a large mining company explain why his organization was not like others, Mel realized something. After reviewing of a list of GLG's clients, the president said his company was unlike companies from other industries such as pharmaceutical, consumer goods, manufacturing, high-tech, and so on. For that matter, it was even unlike other companies in the mining industry. He made it clear that he saw his organization as unique, and everything he said to support this claim made sense. Then he began to describe the challenges his organization faced. As Mel listened, he realized that what the president was saying about his company's challenges actually did apply to the majority of GLG's clients. In most cases, the challenges were categorically the same. Mel also noticed that he was describing the challenges in terms of what his organization *was not*, and it dawned on him: "What if we perceived organizations in light of *what they are not?*" It didn't take long to see the validity of this observation.

This led to two other questions: "What is common across every organization? And, what is an organization anyway?" Mel sensed the importance of this realization, given the recurring patterns of challenges faced by all varieties of organizations. These initial realizations have evolved into an inquiry about new ways to perceive the reality of organizations and to inform alternative approaches to fostering organizational integration.

Organizations are fundamentally field phenomena. As such, they are not only complicated and complex, they are also chaotic, quantum, socialistic, and cultural in nature. When we view their *effect at a distance*, the nature of complexity is revealed through emerging patterns. Sometimes, when something curious happens, we may be moved to ask: "Why did that happen?" or to say: "Wow! That came out of left field." We are pretty sure that somewhere, there's a *cause*, and, given the complexity of the system, finding it seems almost impossible. When we can begin to see the patterns of application that precede the emerging patterns in results, we have seen into Organization as a complex system.

There is also the chaotic nature of organizations, which means they are *starting-conditions sensitive*. This condition is easy to observe. We can repeat a process in exactly the same way it was done previously and then notice that the outcome, compared to the last time, often falls into a range between noticeably different to completely and inexplicably different. What we don't always observe is that the state of the system has changed between the applications of the process. This uncertainty of outcome exists because different parts of the system are subject to variable rates of change. Predicting rates of change is more likely in those parts of the system that lend themselves to continuous improvement, and is least likely where discontinuities are desirable.

Leadership Requires Mastery

Leadership requires mastery not only of content and process but also context. For organizations to grow and flourish in ever-changing business climates requires new leadership competencies that cannot be developed just through additional knowledge (*content*), or by applying new ways and means to work (*processes*). What is required is mastery of a third domain—the domain of meaning (*context*). With this mastery comes the power to design, influence and create at the level of *field*, where peoples' actions are shaped. Mastery of all three domains—content, process, context—allows us to design and implement at the scale of the whole system, as well as to tune applications to the specific needs of subsystems, and to conduct tactical execution that is consistent with an organization's business objectives.

This means that developing an effective organization includes going beyond the traditional work of increasing skills and competencies and going beyond the redesign of processes. It is also essential to develop the capacity to establish purposeful contexts in which strategic thinking and breakthrough business outcomes become part of the organizational norm. Such environments allow people to constantly learn, grow, and develop new ways to produce results that are not necessarily predictable based on past performance.

Elements of an Organizational Field

What creates an organizational field? The most honest answer to this question is: "It depends," or even "We just don't know." When we look into to this question carefully, we find many possible and valid answers to it, and there is no one *right* answer. There are answers that may be useful, depending upon one's objective. In the material that follows, we'll focus on the objective of *systemic change* to discover a new way of answering this question, one that has proven very helpful in thinking about how to foster systemic change in large-scale systems.

Creating a Field

We'll start by applying the Attractor Model we use for understanding fields. (The Attractor Model was introduced in our Overview at the beginning of this book.) In the Attractor Model, the existence of a field is dependent on the presence of three members: *content, process,* and *context.* The model is also dependent upon these three members being in a particular relationship, along with multiple relationships. For a field to exist, the base flow of relationship is: Content *allows for* context, context *invites* or shapes process, and process *establishes* field.

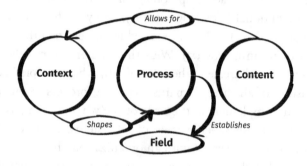

Figure 4.1 What Constitutes a Field?

Content is the facts of the situation, the "What's so?"

Organizational States

What makes organizations unique as fields is that they exist in two states at the same time: a *default state,* where the organization works to *maintain continuity,* and a *generated state,* where it works to *create and integrate the resulting discontinuities.* The dominant norm for most organizations most of the time is the default state. On occasion an exception to the norm appears, one that does not displace the norm, yet can cause considerable disruption. This is a *generated state* in which something outside of the norm becomes real for the organization. That something may be seen as good (a breakthrough), or as not good (a breakdown). In either case, something is present that is a major deviation from the norm and is unexpected. When discontinuity is seen as a breakthrough or breakdown, the view is misleading because a breakthrough is a breakdown in continuity. We can't have one without the other; they are mutually arising phenomena.

Achieving Continuity

Organizational continuity is achieved by a closed system that improves business processes. Figure 4.2 is a simplification of the relationship that keeps the system closed. Business systems tend to validate results registers—the practice of documenting or "registering" results—and results registers, in turn, tend to reinforce business systems. And so it goes.

They can interact as either virtuous circles (positive feedback loops) or as vicious circles (negative feedback loops). Both interactions function as closed systems.

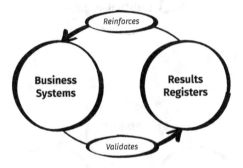

Figure 4.2 Closed System

Virtuous Circle

A company invests it its employees' ability to provide services to customers by training employees and creating a corporate culture in which they are empowered. This leads to increased employee satisfaction and competence, and results in superior service delivery and customer satisfaction. In turn, this creates customer loyalty, and improves sales and profit margins. Some profits are reinvested in employee development, thereby initiating another iteration of a virtuous cycle—systemic improvement.

Vicious Circle

A company decides to harvest their investment in people and culture by reducing costs to increase earnings. This reduces budgets for wages, training, product development, and understanding of customer needs. This increases employee dissatisfaction, lowers competence, and increases turnover, and results in poor service, customer dissatisfaction, increased

Figure 4.3 Virtuous Circle

Figure 4.4 Vicious Circle

customer turnover, and loss of market share. Reduced sales and margin lead to further reduction of investment, thereby initiating another iteration of the vicious cycle—*compartmental improvement*.

The preceding are examples of continuity and improvement. The models exemplify the way change is thought through in most organizations: the first being a positive feedback loop that produces a systemic improvement and the second a negative feedback loop that produces a compartmental improvement.

One does not have to do more than scratch the surface to see that a vicious circle is almost always initiated by individual concerns for personal survival, a need to look good, and a commitment to get the monkey off my back and on to the back of someone else. This is usually accomplished through authoritative mandate. Such approaches always set up negative feedback loops.

On the other hand, an individual concern for organizational survival can set up positive feedback loops and engender virtuous circles—both serving to benefit the organization. However, doing this in the face of inappropriate demands for short-term results requires real leadership. It takes someone who will take a stand for the organization, who will face facts— all the facts not just a selected set—and finally someone who can enroll those concerned with near-term results in the value to the organization of taking an intermediate view. (See "Call to Courage" in Chapter 1.)

Establishing Norms

Best practices are a good example of organizational norms that lead to positive change. Identifying best practices requires an examination of business systems (process) and organizational knowledge (content). By providing new content and new processes, garnered from an examination of best practices in a large number of organizations, advisory consultants (Bain, McKinsey, PWC, etc.) help companies increase their overall efficiency. Sometimes the magnitude of the changes our organization needs will exceed the tolerance for change inherent in the current prevailing norm, also referred to as, "The way it is around here." The basic reinforcing-validating loop of process and content has evolved in organizations over the last few hundred years to ensure consistency. This means there is only room for change that does not threaten the established norms. However, when there is a need for change includes upsetting the established norm, new content (knowledge and information) and new processes (ways and means) fall flat because those who must apply them do not embrace them. These are the people who have been rewarded for their adherence to the prevailing norm. This, coupled with people's natural attachment to the status quo, means that what it takes to integrate change in an organization is often underestimated (see Figure 4.5).

Figure 4.5 Prevailing Norm

Norms Solidify in an Unexamined Context

Context is the second thing needed to establish an organization initially—the first is people. No people, no organization. When people organize, context emerges. Both people and context must be dealt with when making and integrating significant changes in an organization. Unexamined context is what fixes (solidifies) the prevailing norm. In turn, the prevailing norm organizes peoples' actions. Together, context and prevailing norms not only establish Organization, but they are its binding elements. In most organizations, context goes unexamined and therefore some changes, no matter how hard they are worked on, never take hold. We must find ways to understand the context for Organization at large and our particular version of our organization. Cultural surveys and 360-degree evaluations are valuable, but they are insufficient for revealing context. These are examples of appliqués and they are only one part of a systemic examination of context. We will look further into context and norms.

Prevailing norms provide a lot of value. They are an important part of what maintains our organization. In examining "the way things are around here," all but the most superficial aspects of prevailing norms have been entrenched for a long time and are fixed by context. "The way it is" includes deeply embedded cultural and societal characteristics, which have stood the test of time.

In our model, organizational culture and society are located within unexamined context (the far left circle in Figure 4.6). If proposed changes

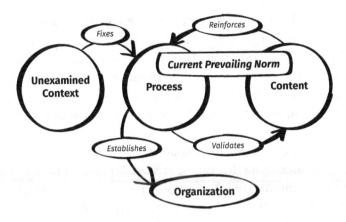

Figure 4.6 Unexamined Context

don't violate the prevailing norm too much and if enough effort is applied, then change can take hold. That is to say, change will integrate. Adoption is the test for integration. If there is no adoption, then change will not occur. It is worth noting that changes to process and content do not have much, if any, effect on context. So the unexamined context either accommodates the intended change or not. If not, then we need to look into changing context. Or do we? When we talk about changing culture in our organization, what we may really be up to has to do with context. Culture clearly manifests in context, but it is not itself context. Another way to think of culture is as one expression of organizational context.

Generating Context by Looking the Other Way

We can look into the "unexamined context" of Organization—get to the roots of what already is, and break it down into its component parts. This is useful and helps us understand why things work the way they do. But the "iconoclastic" approach has us looking inward. We can also look the other way—that is, we can look outward to what is not yet—to the possibilities—to what might be. For such outward-looking exploration to gain traction, it must be put into context—a context that brings relevant meaning to the possibilities.

Context provides meaning and purpose for the processes and content of our organization. It helps us to know why we are doing something. It tells us something about value of our work. Therefore, when working outside of the existing norms (outside the box), context must be created for the undertaking. The pre-work is to use context in a way that ultimately will bring forth new norms. We will never get to do this on a blank slate in our organization. There is no such thing as a context free organization. The context for our organization is always already there, unexamined—it is inherited—it is a legacy passed on from one generation of management to the next. We might say "It comes with the territory" we call organization.

There is some good news about context. And that is, it lives in language. It is therefore something that can be created. To grasp this idea, we must be willing to grant that language is more than spoken and written word—the stories we tell—the myths we unwittingly perpetuate. In the sense that we intend it here, language also includes gestures, impressions, demonstrations, and other visible and audible expressions. What this would mean to us is that when the existing context in our organization is insufficient to allow for the level of change needed in the organization, then it is possible for us to generate context. It is possible for you to generate context! In fact, you do it all the time ... mostly you don't know you're doing it so you can't be fully responsible for the meaning that is conveyed in what you say.

A generated context is one that goes beyond the preexisting, oft unexamined, context. It is a step or two out of bounds. When developed properly, it does not challenge the existing context. It in fact will honor it—appreciate and validate it, and then move beyond it with the recognition that moving beyond is only possible because of what has gone before.

When we include the preexisting context inside of the new context, it has the effect of empowering all that it has taken to bring our organization to its current state. A well-designed generated context helps those who work in our organization to understand why they are doing something, and to see the difference what they do is making. When we examine context in the foreground of Organization with the same attention we might give operations, manufacturing, or distribution, we begin to see the implications of treating it as "the soft stuff." The idea that context, or for that matter culture or leadership, is the "soft stuff" has to rank among the top ten most uninformed views about Organization that one could imagine. If they are so soft, why do organizations have such a devil of a time making changes around them?

A well-developed context increases the probability that people will take actions consistent with the needed change, even those actions that have previously seemed "outside the box." Context helps us think differently about the challenges we face, and amplifies the application of new processes and content. The presence of a generated context changes the relationships between all elements within its field and sets up a dynamic that allows for our organization to maintain norms for consistency on one hand, and benefit from *planned discontinuities*, on the other hand.

When context is generated, then meaning is created, and many norms become possible within the organization. Instead of trying to resolve the unending conflicts that arise between sales and marketing or manufacturing and packaging or "fill in the blank," what if we could begin to see and appreciate that the norms for each of these areas are distinct? A "qualified lead" from marketing does not equal a qualified lead as far as sales is concerned. Sales staff complain that marketing does not produce qualified leads. Marketing says it does. Neither recognizes that the norms for qualified leads are different in each organization.

Generated context can transform context, process, and content as well as how they are related. In the foreground of Organization, *meaning* now shapes *action*. *Action* validates *results*. *Results* reinforce *action*. *Action* and *results* in relationship one with the other bring forth many *norms*. *Norms* inform *meaning* and establish the *organization*. We wish there were a better way to say this, but we have come to the limits of written language, because written language is sequential. What we are pointing at is not sequential. It is holographic … it's all happening all at once. Even the graphic is insufficient. It fails to represent the recursive nature of the holographic nature of Organization.

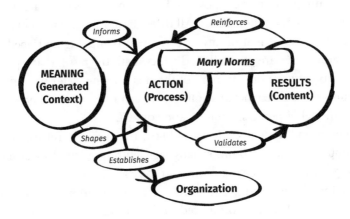

Figure 4.7 Generated Context

Because *action* and *results* reinforce and validate one another, they energize the organizational field for change in that they have the potential to bring forth new norms. Norms *inform* meaning which *shapes* action. This shaping of action through meaning shifts the field of organization from being a closed system to being an open one. An open system is more amenable to change, more available for contribution, and less likely to be lost to orthodoxy. More than one executive has followed the orthodoxy rather than challenge it, only to have their organization come to ruin. It is possible to challenge something with a deep respect and regard for what it provides. It is possible to honor those who believe in it, and at the same time bring forth facts and interpretations that make a compelling case for action outside of the established orthodoxy. In most cases, an organizational orthodoxy is nothing more than a *moldy norm* that has been around so long that it has become "the right way."

Leadership, Development, and Management as Organizational Metadisciplines

Taking this model one step further, we can access another "window" into organizations. As we touched on earlier, in most business literature, *leadership* is indistinct from *management*. The model that follows makes explicit distinctions between leadership and management and identifies a third discipline called *development*. These three metadisciplines constitute the primary subsystems of Organization; Human Systems, Business Systems, and Development Systems. When they are in proper relationship to each other, these metadisciplines make it possible for organizations to create new, sustainable, and compelling realities. All three disciplines are present in every organization. It's not that of any one of them is missing and needs to be added. Rather, they are generally indistinct, with the result that a powerful relationship between one or more of them is missing. After we define and distinguish these three metadisciplines, we can then examine how they fit into our model of process, content, and context.

To understand these disciplines and how they are interrelated, we need to continue to build a common language with consistent meaning. The following summation draws from our observations in our work with organizations to this point. These are working definitions and a model in development, and we are committed to their remaining so. Because every engagement both confirms and expands this exploration, it remains in the mode of open inquiry while it continues to grow into a new theory that can be applied and tested for validity over time.

- Leadership *is about creating possibility for futures that do not currently exist.* Leadership is the discipline of creating and communicating new futures that are beyond an extension or continuation of the past. Because effective leadership requires a powerful relationship with possibility, it is an essential ingredient of breakthrough change in organization.
- Development *is about efficacy.* Efficacy is the fostering and nurturing of the new possibilities that leadership creates. Efficacy is the test for demonstrating feasibility, or the kind of demonstration that brings definition and resolution to possibility at levels sufficient for management to do its part. Development works on a spectrum that begins with an early stage of refining a possibility so it can be seen as feasible and continues to a late stage of designing the systems that allow possibility to become the reality required for it to be passed along to management. The focus of development is effectiveness. A powerful relationship with development leads to the socialization of discontinuities (breakthroughs), while preserving reliability, predictability, and certainty during periods of change.
- Management *is about stewardship.* It brings predictability, reliability, and certainty to the day-to-day affairs of the business. Management focuses on efficiency, along with preserving and improving the current reality through the use of incremental change processes such as continuous improvement. Management of the current reality allows for the time, money, and permission to create new futures. In a well-managed business, the current reality is not a limitation, but rather a way to inform leadership about the foundation on which possibility can be created. Hence, leadership is only possible to the degree that the current reality is succeeding.

When we map *leadership, development,* and *management* onto the model that demonstrates the relationship between *context, process,* and *content, possibility* becomes the overarching *context, efficacy* is the overarching *process,* and *stewardship* becomes the overarching *content* in organization.

Newtonian physics and cause-and-effect give us the understanding we need to change the world of Class I Reality (physical). Because organizations

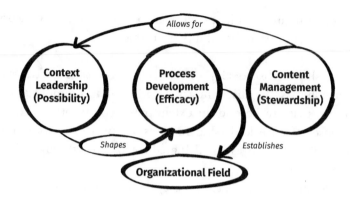

Figure 4.8 Organization as Field

are a Class II Reality (non-physical), bringing about changes in this reality requires a different approach.

Summary: Sorting Out the Chaos of Organizations

As we discussed earlier, fundamentally, an organization is a chaotic system. All organizations generate recurring, fractal-like patterns at the *scale of the entire organization* or the whole system. Most of these patterns are not unique to an organization and only a few are unique to an industry. These patterns arise from entanglements between these three subsystems:

- *Human systems* which are the concern of *leadership*.
- *Development systems* which are the concern of *development*.
- *Business systems* which are the concern of *management*.

The three-circle model presented in this chapter provides an important way to look at these subsystem patterns in order to more effectively integrate change in the organization, particularly in times of chaos.

Chaos can lead either to integration or disintegration (Lorenz 1995). When chaos leads to integration, the organization has evolved to a higher level of complexity, adaptability, and sustainability. When chaos leads to disintegration, the organization's viability is threatened. Trust is one of the key variables that makes the difference.

Because trust is such a critical variable in change integration, we will visit this topic in more depth in Chapter 7. Meanwhile, in Chapter 5 we will go more into depth about the interrelatedness and interdependence of the three metadisciplines of management, leadership and integration.

References

Lorenz, E. (1995) *The Essence of Chaos*. Seattle, WA: University of Washington Press.

Meadows, D. and Wright, D. (2014) *Thinking in Systems: A Primer*. White River Junction, VT: Chelsea Green Publishing.

Sachs, M. (1974) *Ideas of the Theory of Relativity: General Implications from Physics to Problems of Society*. New York: Wiley.

Schafer, L. (2013) *Infinite Potential: What Quantum Physics Reveals about How We Should Live*. New York: Deepak Chopra Books.

Talbot, M. (1986) *Beyond the Quantum*. New York: Bantam Books.

Tsao, F. and Laszlo, C. (2019) *Quantum Leadership: New Consciousness in Business*. Stanford, CA: Stanford Business Books.

Wheatley, M. (1994) *Leadership and the New Science*. San Francisco, CA: Berrett-Koehler.

Zukav, G. (1979) *The Dancing Wu Li Masters*. New York: William Morrow and Company.

5

MANAGEMENT, LEADERSHIP, AND INTEGRATION

Introduction

People tend to treat the two concepts of management and leadership as if they are interchangeable. However, they have very distinct roles to play in the midst of organizational change. An important key is to understand the differences between the ability to react and the ability to adapt. In this chapter we will provide a historical background on the origins of the management theory to explain how management and leadership concepts have become misunderstood. We will then describe the important meta-discipline of integration (development systems) of management (business systems) and leadership (human systems) in creating organizational transformation.

Developing a New Organizational-Scale Discipline

In many organizations, whether for profit or non-profit, the terms *specializations* and *disciplines* are used interchangeably. However, we do want to clarify up front that there is a difference. A discipline is a branch of instruction or

DOI: 10.4324/9781003131847-5

learning, like science or economics. A specialization is a subset of a discipline. For example, marketing and sales are specializations that fall under the discipline of business management. Specializations often have titles associated with them, like Director of Graphic Arts or VP of Regulatory Compliance.

Both disciplines and specializations can be *scaled*. Some familiar examples of specializations at the scale of organization are Chief Operating Officer, Chief Financial Officer, and Chief Executive Officer. The disciplines they serve are respectively operations, finance and management. As organizational needs evolve, other more recent examples include Chief Brand Officer, Chief Analytics Officer, Chief Compliance Officer, and Chief Strategy Officer, to name but a few of many.

When we say "organizational-scale discipline," we are suggesting that leadership and management are two *metadisciplines* that overarch other disciplines and their specializations. The third metadiscipline of integration of change has actually always been here, too, but up until now has been overshadowed by leadership and management.

A condition common to virtually all organizational disciplines is that their existence depends upon: (1) The presence of identifiable need, and (2) The recognition that this need is relevant to the organization's future. The three metadisciplines require an additional condition in order to operate: the willingness of people in specializations and disciplines to build capability in one or more of the three areas. Beyond that, integration is an evolving metadiscipline and it has its own unique needs: people willing to fill emerging roles, plus help of the discipline.

A Brief History of Management Theory

In physics, "work" is defined as a transfer of energy. In human terms, there are four kinds of energy: (1) physical, (2) emotional, (3) intellectual, and (4) spiritual. As management theory has evolved, it has come to integrate more of the kinds of human energy available. This evolution has emerged out of an increasing holistic view of the relationship between the human being and the workplace. Ken Wilber (2001) describes the underlying dynamic of evolution as a process of transcending what has gone before while also including the previous level of development – "transcend and include." This is evident in the evolution of management theory.

Following is a history of the different management schools of thought from the beginning of the twentieth century until now. The major schools of thought are scientific management, human relations, operations research, employee involvement, and workplace spirituality (Neal 2013, 15–17).

Scientific Management

Frederick Taylor (1911) is considered the first management theorist and the founder of management science. He was an industrial engineer and his focus was on the efficiency of production. He developed time and motion studies as a way of analyzing where there might be excess effort that could be eliminated. In the late 19th and early 20th centuries, many of the factory workers were immigrants who spoke little English, so it made sense to break the jobs up into small, discrete actions that could be easily explained or demonstrated. Taylor's belief was that workers were primarily motivated by money, so he created a compensation system based on the more you produce, the more you are paid. This is the concept of "Economic Man." He saw the human being as simply an extension of the machine, and the goal was to harness the physical energy of the human being as efficiently as possible. He saw scientific management as a way to create increased productivity while at the same time making physical work a little easier for the working man. Taylor's scientific management was very effective and was soon the prevailing paradigm of management. His concepts and methods continue to be an essential part of the metadiscipline of management today.

Human Relations

In the 1920s, a group of researchers (Mayo 1945) conducted a scientific management study at Hawthorne Works, a Western Electric plant in Cicero, Illinois, near Chicago. The company wanted to know what level of illumination levels in the plant would lead to the highest level of productivity. The researchers found that when the lighting was turned up incrementally, productivity would also increase incrementally. Confoundingly, when they turned the lighting back down to its original level, productivity continued to increase. It also continued to increase when the lighting was turned down to a level similar to moonlight. Mayo hypothesized productivity must have increased because of the relationship with the researchers. During the study, researchers were continually asking the workers about how the lighting levels affected their well-being and motivation. These demonstrations of care during the experiments, and the granting of more freedom and control to the workers, led the researchers to explore the idea that human relationships and workers' emotions might be just as important as—or even more important than—the physical environment of the work. This is a great example of integrating the Human Systems and the Development Systems.

The Hawthorne studies led to the development of the human relations school of thought, with a focus on such topics as motivation, conflict resolution, team building and group dynamics, and communication skills. These topics are still taught in business schools today, and there are many case studies that demonstrate that paying attention to the emotional energy of human beings at work is of great benefit. In recent times, Daniel Goleman's (1994, 2006) popular work on emotional and social intelligence exemplifies current thinking and practice in the school of human relations.

Operations Research

Operations Research (OR) emerged during World War II. It is based on the premise that human beings are not just physical beings and emotional beings—they are also intelligent beings.

OR employs mathematical modeling, statistics, and algorithms to arrive at optimal or near-optimal solutions to complex logistical problems. War is such a complex problem. To help deal with this complexity the Allied Forces recruited scientists to assist with military operations. Technology and resources were limited, so to make the most of them, the scientists applied simple mathematical models (simple by today's standards). By the end of the war, the most successful models were already embraced within the corporate sector and quickly grew to became known as the management sciences. Over the last 70 years the OR models upon which the management sciences are based have become increasingly sophisticated. Managing is a complicated process within the complex system of organization. Today we find the management sciences firmly embedded in university programs. Many of these are required capabilities for the overarching roles found in manufacturing, operations, finance, marketing, sales, information technology, research and development, human resources; each is a specialization in its own right. The examples below provide a mind-boggling peek into organizational complexity and specialization.

Specializations that use Decision Analysis include:

- Engineering
- Forecasting

- Game theory
- Industrial engineering
- Logistics
- Mathematical modeling
- Optimization
- Probability and statistics
- Project management
- Simulation
- Social network/transportation forecasting models
- Supply chain management.

Business uses the management sciences for problem solving in such areas as:

- Identifying processes in a complex project which affect the overall duration of the project;
- Designing the layout of a factory for efficient flow of materials;
- Constructing telecommunication networks at low cost that have quality of service (QoS);
- Assessing the quality of experience (QoE) if connections become busy or get damaged;
- Allocation problems like road traffic management and "one way" streets;
- Determining bus service routes that require the least number of buses to maintain service;
- Designing the layout of a computer chip to reduce manufacturing time and cost;
- Managing a supply chain based upon uncertain demand for the finished products;
- Efficient messaging and customer response tactics;
- Robotizing or automating human-driven operations processes;
- Globalizing processes to take advantage of cheaper materials, labor, land, etc.;
- Managing freight transportation and delivery systems;
- Scheduling: personnel staffing, manufacturing steps, project tasks;
- Blending raw materials in oil refineries;
- Pricing science to determine optimal prices in retail and B2B;
- Developing evidence-based policy.

Employee Involvement

Building on OR techniques and approaches, the next breakthrough in management thought was Employee Involvement (EI). This school of thought was based on the realization that experts at the top of the organization were not the only ones who could bring their intelligence to bear on the complexity of organizational challenges and opportunities. In the 1970s, W. Edwards Deming (1993) and Joseph Juran (1974) each had developed new approaches to quality management that involved putting people in teams and teaching them statistical process control methods along with team problem solving techniques. Their methods were a unique integration of the human relations school and operations management, pushed down to the level of those actually doing the work. This EI approach is based on the premise that each employee is the expert on his or her job. With EI, employees can apply their intellectual energy, as well as their physical and emotional energy. Before the EI movement, it was common to hear employees say of management: "They want us to check our brains in at the door" when coming to work.

Quality Circles and EI Teams were two of the most common structures that were put into place in order to tap into the knowledge employees had of the best ways to do their work. It also required training managers to let go of some of their control; to listen to and to value employee input; and to respond as positively as possible to employee suggestions.

Workplace Spirituality

It used to be that three topics were taboo in organizations: politics, sex, and religion. Each of these topics has the potential to create friction among employees and could also create a hostile environment that could cause someone to sue the company for harassment or discrimination. However, a number of organizations in the 1990s broke one of those taboos and declared that faith and spirituality were important parts of being a human being, and they encouraged people to bring their whole selves to work (Neal 2013). Some of these organizations include the Body Shop, Medtronics, Tom's of Maine, McKinsey, and Ford Motor Company. Research also demonstrates that an organizational culture that supports workplace spirituality can lead to increased job satisfaction, organizational commitment, and a greater sense of meaning and purpose among employees (Harris et al. 2019).

The primary focus of workplace spirituality is to support all members of the organization in clarifying and deepening their sense of meaning and purpose. This school of thought encourages individual and contemplative practices in the workplace, such as shared silence before meetings begin, employee resource groups for different religious affiliations, prayer breakfasts, and the creation of sacred space such as silence or meditation rooms. More recently, many organizations such as Google, Aetna, and Target have adopted programs of mindfulness meditation to encourage creativity, stress reduction, and better decision making (Tan 2012).

In each of these five schools of management thought—(1) Management Science, (2) Human Relations, (3) Operations Research, (4) EI, and (5) Workplace Spirituality—no theoretical distinctions have been made between the three meta-systems of management: (1) Managing, (2) Leading, and (3) Integrating. As management theory has evolved over the past, it has encompassed an expanded definition of what it is to be human, and the potential for bringing the whole self to work in terms of the four human energies—physical, emotional, intellectual, and spiritual. That's wonderful progress, but what has still been missing from our management theories and practice is a systemic understanding of how change and transformation come about in organizations, and the role of the metadiscipline of integration.

Management and Leadership: Collapsed Distinctions

We believe that the gaps pointed out in the IBM Global CEO studies in Chapter 1, which suggest that there's a significant decrease in the ability of companies to integrate change, are indicative of the kind of thinking which comes from having *collapsed distinctions between management and leadership*. Senior executives speak of creativity and innovation—the artful domain of leadership—but then set specific expectations and narrowly defined goals—the scientific domain of management. Is it any wonder that people respond with actions suited to problem solving, and not with the expansive thinking needed to bring new things into existence? Actions generated from a "problem-solution" management model are of little or no value in creative and innovative pursuits (Gershon and Straub 1989). The challenge of doing what has not been done before is the metadiscipline of leadership.

Integration

Integration is the third organizational metadiscipline. We offer four approaches to integration and describe various ways to categorize the discipline of integration.

With Change You Can't Fit a New Idea into an Old Notion

IBM discovered in their "Enterprise of the Future" study (2008) that most CEOs take four approaches to integration. More than 60 percent implement a globally oriented strategy. These are the "extensive globalizers" and "globalizers." The roughly 40 percent remaining use either a local or a blended approach.

To achieve these levels of change integration, the study suggests that the organization of the future will place increasing importance on social connections within and across organizations. Real-time collaboration using social networking will close the distance between people, allowing good ideas to develop more quickly and problems to be solved faster. These companies of the future, the study suggests, will have *management development*

Table 5.1 The Enterprise of the Future Study

CEOs' responses fall into four distinct clusters.
The two most common approaches are more global. One focuses locally. And the fourth falls in the middle between both extremes.

	Globally oriented	Equally important	Locally focused	
Deeply change the mix of capabilities, knowledge and assets	◆	● □	❖	Maintain current mix
Partner extensively	◆ ●	□	❖	Do everything in-house
Actively enter new markets	◆ ●	□	❖	Defend your core
Globalize brands/products	◆ ●	□	❖	Localize brands/products
Optimize operations globally	◆ ●	□	❖	Optimize operations locally
Grow through mergers and acquisitions	◆ ●	□ ❖		Grow organically
Drive multiple cultures	◆ □		● ❖	Strive for one culture

Key:

◆ Extensive globalizers

● Globalizers

□ Blended thinkers

❖ Localizers

programs and ways to identify *high-potential candidates* throughout the company, not just from headquarters. These programs will step the *future leaders* of organizations through multiple global experiences, exposing them to a variety of cultures and markets. Do you notice the unexamined assumption behind these statements: "management development programs," "high-potential candidates," and "future leaders"?

Lurking in the background is the premise that identifying high-potential candidates and then putting them through a management development program—most likely an MBA program—will automatically result in accomplished leaders of change integration sometime in the future. There is little question that competency in management is one prerequisite for leadership. But it's only one. Developing management capability cannot confer a guarantee for successful leadership. To design a car requires understanding how cars work, but to know how cars work is insufficient to take on designing one. And so it is with leadership and management in organization. Managers keep the organization working smoothly. Leaders design the organization's future. An admittedly simplistic statement, and there is, of course, significant nuance not accounted for, but it's important to see that leaders don't just pop up like mushrooms in the damp, shady soil of management; leaders are not a naturally occurring phenomenon.

However, over the years our experience has strongly suggested that anyone who has mastered management and chooses to learn to lead does have a *capacity* to lead that can grow. If you choose to lead, you must be willing to take on your own development, not only the skills that apply to managing business systems, but also the personal and spiritual growth that is needed to lead human systems. Leadership is not an aspect of management; leadership is a distinct field of study. Managers must master the management sciences, while leaders must master the leadership arts. Managing and leading are two distinct organizational-scale disciplines. The management sciences are a well-established field of study while the leadership arts are an emerging field plagued by often-repeated myth and superstition—"Leaders are born, not made." "You have to be in control to lead." "Good leaders are charismatic."

Attracting and Retaining Talent

In the days of unpredictable pandemics, protests against racism, climate crises, and economic uncertainty, business leaders find it more critical than ever to attract and retain talent, even as they must furlough non-essential workers. Now, more than ever, organizations need people who have the vision to lead, the skills to manage, and the ability to integrate ongoing, relentless change.

Mercer concluded in their *Global Talent Trends 2020 Report* (Mercer 2020) that there is a significant difference of opinion between employees and human resources about what skills are relevant today and what will be in demand in 2025.

The Mercer report conclusions align with our view that organizations are very effective at management development, but tend not to pay enough attention to leadership development (i.e., soft skills) and are not even aware of the existence of the metadiscipline of integration. The report states: "The risk for everyone is that, if we place a premium on quantifiable techni-cal skills, we may neglect to nurture the necessary skills for tomorrow" (Mercer 2020: 39).

One of the Mercer recommendations for attracting and retaining talent is in alignment with the human relations and the workplace spirituality schools of thought. While a significant portion of their report highlights the need for artificial intelligence and data analytics in attracting and retaining talent, they also emphasize the need to honor human intuition and empa-thy, and the value of creating organizations that inspire employees.

Mercer's research shows organizations that lead with empathy are more energizing to work for. Empathetic organizations are tuned into the expe-riences of their workforce and continuously improve them—simplifying and digitizing repetitive tasks while increasing the meaningful moments that people crave. They are bravely and radically redesigning their people

Table 5.2 In-Demand Skills

2020: *In-demand skills according to employees*	2020: *In-demand skills according to HR*
<ul><li>Innovation</li><li>Complex problem solving</li><li>Interpersonal skills</li><li>**2025: In-demand skills according to employees**</li><li>Innovation</li><li>Global mindset</li><li>Digital leadership</li></ul>	<ul><li>Digital marketing</li><li>Data visualization</li><li>UX design</li><li>**2025: In-demand skills according to HR**</li><li>Agile transformation</li><li>Design thinking</li><li>Entrepreneurship</li></ul>

(Adapted from Mercer 2020: 39)

processes, work operations, and HR design to deliver what employees and colleagues truly want out of work (Mercer 2020: 50).

While the IBM studies mentioned in Chapter 1 emphasize the need for organizations to take a more global and strategic mindset (emphasis on management), this Mercer study begins to show movement in organizational leaders towards more integration of management and leadership disciplines.

Talking Apples and Oranges? Context and Perspective

Messages from the top regarding change can be confusing or misleading, because they don't come with the context or perspective afforded the speaker. The President and CEO of West Japan Railway Company was in quoted the 2008 IBM study is as saying:

> The key to successful transformation is changing our mind-set. For large companies, it is easy to be complacent—we have to change this. Our company culture must have a built-in change mechanism.
>
> (Yamazaki 2008)

Two words in this CEO's statement have potential for mischief—*transformation* and *mechanism*. In the first place, they have nothing to do with each other. Putting them in the same statement is at best a domain error, and more likely oxymoronic. There is nothing wrong with changing by transforming mind set, but there is a disconnect for the workforce when leaders perceive change to be *mechanistic*. The car you drive is a mechanism—an assemblage of parts that move in a predictable pattern; it will never have a transformation and it's going to change in one way only. It will fall into pieces over time. But people are not mechanisms; we are organisms, the smartest of all organisms on this planet. In the face of change, we can choose to support the new company culture or to walk away. No built-in change mechanism can "drive" us, because no two people are alike and all people are changing daily.

"Transformation" is language that brings some unpleasant baggage. In many company-wide change initiatives, transformation has been used as a code word for reengineering the company through major downsizing. Use it gingerly; this term could be a bit reactivating for the workforce. If you think we're being overly cautious, wait to see what happened when the CEO of British Petroleum (BP) made a well-intended declaration that had unintended consequences, because the context in which the statement was spoken and the context in which it was heard were not aligned. This story is told in more detail in Chapter 9.

Setting context is not enough; context must also be aligned. Both responsibilities belong to the speaker. Communicating context is a delicate leadership skill and the higher the speaker's position, the less room there is for error.

Language Reflects Thinking

The words we speak reflect not only *what we think*, but also *how we think*. To use the word "mechanism"—"the arrangement of connected parts in a machine"—points to the machine-world, Newtonian view that leaves the work of integration indistinct in companies undergoing change. We are not going to see the day of "built-in change," that is unless one considers "stuff happens" as built-in change. This notion arises from a common and largely unexamined view that organizations are systems or organisms. But organizations are, in fact, fields and how change occurs on a field (see Chapter 4) is quite different from that of changing a system or an organism.

To attempt any "built-in change mechanism" can provide only a portion of the power to integrate change. In many companies, capability to *react* and *adapt* is considered to be the mechanism. This mechanism is born of necessity, well developed and fine-tuned over time. Because they have minimal headroom (remaining capacity) for improvement, we refer to *react* and *adapt* as two highly realized capacities. Organizations that are weak in either of these two capabilities lack the flexibility to survive, while those that thrive are masters of both. Management invests in training and instruction to maintain the ability to adapt and react, but improvement is hard won because there is so little headroom. When we react or adapt, we're trailing behind the curve of change and not calling the shots.

React and adapt aren't bad; they're just not the whole picture when an organization needs to integrate change. Organization, when viewed from a systems perspective, is designed for survival, with survival meaning "to maintain existence in a recognizable form." Change that is sourced externally occurs as a threat to stability and the organization responds defensively, even when the change is desirable. A well-developed organizational mechanism to react and adapt promotes continuity and avoids discontinuity. "Built-in change mechanisms" do allow companies to survive by reacting and adapting. However, two additional capacities are required if companies are to thrive in a world engulfed in change—the capacities to *create* and to *innovate*. Neither is mechanistic; each must be generated continually through education and development; both offer limitless capacity.

For a more updated and research-based view of transformation, see *The Handbook of Personal and Organizational Transformation* (Neal 2018).

Categories of Integration

Leadership and management roles provide relatively clear career path opportunities. Not so with integration of change. Those who work on integration usually have their "day jobs" and integrating change is an added assignment. It may be a learning experience, but it's not likely to add a chevron on the uniform of your career path.

As a starting place, think of *integration* as falling into two broad categories, *organizational* and *individual*. Within each category there are two additional sub-categories that we can best describe in the following general activities.

Organizational Integration

The two sub-categories of organizational integration are (1) Intra-organizational integration and (2) Inter-organizational integration.

Intra-organizational Integration (within a single organization)

Essentially the quality of intra-organizational integration is the limiting factor for how much externally generated change an organization can integrate and make operationally reliable. It is also a determining factor in how an organization is viewed by suppliers, customers, governing agencies, investors and the marketplace. For high-quality intra-organizational integration to occur, leadership must continually articulate organizational purpose, empower organizational commitments, and generate context. Active involvement of leadership embodies communication—not just sending messages but also receiving messages from employees. It generates the experience employees have of working in organization. Leadership's communication is emblematic of the organization—it can form a powerful reason for "being-at-work" beyond getting a paycheck for just being at work. The work of intra-organizational integration includes...

(1)   Facilitating breakthroughs:

This is the work of leading and supporting teams that have been charged with producing breakthrough outcomes.

(2)   Integrating breakthroughs:

This work is more a process of discovery than it is the product of research. It's about working out the new rules for engagement so they can actually be implemented and are appropriate for their intended purpose. Done well, this work can ensure that the change has efficacy and is feasible in the context of the people and the business.

(3)   Integrating organization:

This is the work of refitting and restructuring the relationship between human systems and business systems within the organization. It includes insuring that operating groups are aware of the implications of impending breakthroughs. Sponsors and change agents are key players (Conner 1998, 2006).

- Sponsors must understand the kind of changes that will be required at the scale of organization.
- Change agents, who report to sponsors, must know how to facilitate the inter-group or inter-departmental alignment needed to sustain breakthrough results until the new levels of performance become predictable through the day-to-day management processes.

Inter-organizational Integration (across two or more organizations)

The nature of inter-organizational integration varies widely and can include relationships with suppliers, customers, governing agencies, and sometimes even with competitors. Relationships may be brief or extend over long periods. They arise from and endure as long as there is mutual need—with need being either tactical (supplier on demand) or strategic (alliance partner). The tactical relationships are largely shaped by formal agreements. Strategic relationships, in addition to formal agreement, may also rely on shared commitments and voluntary alignment on matters not governed by agreements. These inter-organizational relationships are the fabric of industry and they influence the health of economies. The quality of inter-organizational relationships is found in transactional equity—the more equity, the healthier the relationship.

Individual Integration

At this point, we'd like to pause again to repeat something about Organization that is fundamental, yet too often overlooked in a changing world. Organizations are created by people, and if the people leave or choose not to act, an organization will fail. As humans, we organize ourselves around work. No organization exists without people and at the root of every change in organization, there are people who both effect the change and are affected by it. Thus individual integration, though it seems to be digressing from a discussion of change, is actually where it all starts. There are two sub-categories of individual integration: (1) Intrapersonal integration and (2) Interpersonal integration.

Intrapersonal Integration (within an individual in organization)

Essentially the quality of intrapersonal integration sets the outer limits for what is possible in interpersonal relationships. Healthy intrapersonal integration is an internal process that involves how we experience ourselves. We each have ongoing articulation of an individuated "self" that empowers or disempowers our commitments. Experiencing "self" is actively generated by our ongoing internal symbolic processing of messages for which we are both sender and receiver. Said less formally, how we see ourselves is emblematic in how others see us—it's the "badge of being" that we wear. It manifests in our attitude, prevailing mood and, what some would call, our style.

Interpersonal integration (across individuals within organization)

The quality of interpersonal integration, fleeting or enduring, is found in regular business interactions between two or more people. The relationship is shaped by shared commitments, mutual agreements, voluntary alignment, organizational policy, and guidance from superiors. These interpersonal relationships are the basis of the social fabric for organization and they are foundational to the formation of human systems, where the work of Organization is performed. The health of interpersonal relationships is largely determined by the presence of interactions that can be seen as consistent with the purposes of the organization.

In addition to two broad categories of integration just discussed—organizational and individual—we have two overarching aspects of integration. One is external change, while the other is internal. Both categories—organizational and individual—are needed to refit and restructure an organization into which change is being introduced. At any given time, an organization will have a certain capacity to absorb change. When its capacity is too limited to accommodate the level and rate of change needed, then preparatory work within the organization itself must take place first. An important part of the preparatory work is intra-organizational integration.

Vertical and Horizontal Integration

A facet of change understood by leaders but not well accepted by managers is that creativity and innovation lead to organizational discontinuity. This is part of organization's built-in paradox regarding change. Companies need to have reliability, predictability, and certainty to survive, but, at the same time, they need flexibility and discontinuities (breaks with established norms) to thrive. But even though there is a need for discontinuity, some parts of an organization—for instance, groups shouldered with responsibilities for production—will *react* quickly to "contain" and suppress anything associated with discontinuity and then *adapt* to prevent similar disruptions in the future. This phenomenon may account for the comparative lack of investment by organizations in creativity and innovation.

A second contributing factor in resistance to change has its roots in corporate tradition. Both management and leadership are most comfortable with *vertical change integration* within hierarchical spans of control. Neither has a good understanding of *horizontal change integration*, the kind that must transcend spans of control within an organization or across several companies.

Traditionally, the terms *vertical* and *horizontal integration* are concerned with structuring ownership and control of companies.

Vertical integration describes a structure that unites companies through a hierarchy, usually leading to common ownership. Each member is product focused or service focused by market segment. Steel tycoon Andrew Carnegie introduced the idea and his thinking led to others using the approach to promote financial growth and operational efficiencies.

Horizontal integration describes a structure commonly used in marketing to sell a product in numerous markets. It also describes the takeover or merger of firms within the same industry that are at the same stage of production. Thus a car manufacturer might merge with another car manufacturer.

In our work with clients, we use the terms *vertical* and *horizontal change integration* to describe approaches to integrating change that are directed at establishing new norms—ones that go beyond continuous improvement.

Vertical integration establishes new norms within a span of control confined to a single organization, such as IT, marketing, operations, sales, or manufacturing. The introduction of an ERP (Enterprise Resource Planning) system within a company would be an example.

A horizontal change integration will establish new norms *across* vertical spans of control within the same company or across vertically integrated companies. For instance, a single discipline such as IT may be found in different organizations. The standardization of hardware platforms and software applications across several vertically integrated companies would be another example.

Unreliable horizontal integration is all too common. We believe it's partially attributable to a lack of formal, high-quality leadership education and development. Both leadership education and development are weak verticals in most companies. The abysmal success rate for large-scale change for the last several decades reveals that the strong verticals for management are not enough to get the job done in most cases.

Because management and leadership are strongest in vertical change integration, they come prepared to *mediate* horizontal change integration from conflicting perspectives. Out of habit, they actually find it easiest to

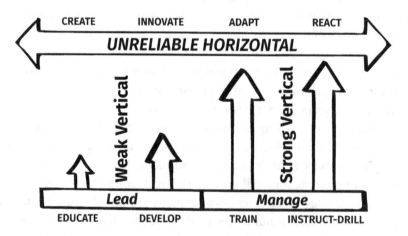

Figure 5.1 Unreliable Horizontal Integration

identify their points of disagreement and to agree upon subjects to be mediated. Yet even when a workable agenda is negotiated, leadership's approach to mediation will promote innovation, while management's approach will remain adaptive. Indeed, leadership's context is creative and management's context is reactive, so communication is inhibited. All too often, conflicts around priorities and actions result with breakdowns being resolved by the intervention of authority.

Summary: Bridging the Innovation Gap

Mastering horizontal and vertical change integration is a necessary first step before breakthrough change can start. The second, less obvious, step is also needed—focusing on establishing the new organizational discipline of integration, so that it carries the same stature as the organizational disciplines of leadership and management. Integration as a metadiscipline is a means of moderating the natural clash between leadership and management approaches to change. This new organizational discipline nurtures the integration of change, while it spares the organization from unproductive conflict or compromise.

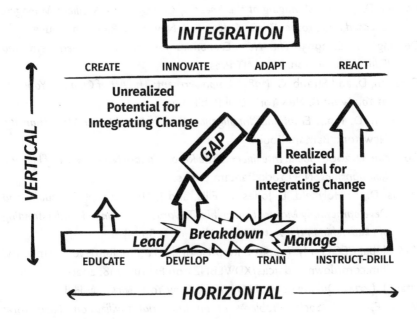

Figure 5.2 Vertical and Horizontal Integration

In summary, there are three metadisciplines necessary for healthy organization functioning and for adaptive and innovative response to internal and external changes—managing, leading, and integrating. Historically, business schools and business publications have used the terms "managing" and "leading" interchangeably, but these are two very different but interconnected disciplines. In academia, management is considered a discipline and a field of study, and unfortunately, leadership has been considered a subset of the discipline of management. We contend that leadership and integration are both significant factors in organizational success and worthy of their own fields of study and practice. This chapter concludes with a delineation of the different aspects of integration at the organization and individual level. Understanding and utilizing these distinctions are essential if you are to have mastery of organization change and transformation. In the next chapter we will explain the four catalysts for integrating change and their relationship to the metadisciplines of leadership and management.

References

Conner, D. (1998) *Leading at the Edge of Chaos.* New York: John Wiley & Sons.

Conner, D. (2006) *Managing at the Speed of Change: How Resilient Managers Succeed and Prosper Where Others Fail.* New York: Random House.

Deming, W. E. 1993. *The New Economics for Industry, Government and Education.* Boston, MA: MIT Press.

Gershon, D. and Straub, G. (1989) *Empowerment: The Art of Creating Your Life as You Want It.* New York: Dell Publishing.

Goleman, D. 1994. *Emotional Intelligence: Why it Can Matter More than IQ.* New York: Bantam Books.

Goleman, D. 2006. *Social Intelligence: The Revolutionary New Science of Human Relationships.* New York: Bantam Books.

Harris, D., L. Holyfield, L. Jones, R. Ellis, and J. Neal (2019). *Spiritually and Developmentally Mature Leadership: Towards an Expanded Understanding of Leadership in the 21st Century.* New York: Springer.

IBM Global CEO Study. (2008) Enterprise of the Future. Retrieved from www.ibm.com/downloads/cas/XDWLBNZ2 on February 18, 2020.

Juran, J. (1974). *Quality Control Handbook.* New York: McGraw-Hill.

Mayo, E. (1945) *Social Problems of an Industrial Civilization.* New York: McMillan.

Mercer (2020) *Global Talent Trends 2020 Report: The Future of Work*. Retrieved from www.mercer.com/our-thinking/career/global-talent-hr-trends.html on July 19, 2020.

Neal, J. (2013) *The Handbook of Faith and Spirituality in the Workplace*. New York: Springer.

Neal, J. (2018) *The Handbook of Personal and Organizational Transformation*. New York: Springer.

Tan, C.-M. 2012. *Search Inside Yourself: The Unexpected Path to Achieving Success, Happiness (and World Peace)*. New York: HarperCollins.

Taylor, F. (1911) *The Principles of Scientific Management*. New York: Harper & Brothers.

Wilber, Ken. (2001) *A Theory of Everything: An Integral Vision for Business, Politics, Science and Spirituality*. Boston, MA: Shambhala Press.

Yamazaki, M. 2008. Quoted in IBM Global CEO Study. (2008) Enterprise of the future. Retrieved from www.ibm.com/downloads/cas/XDWLBNZ2 on February 18, 2020.

6

THE ART OF CHANGE INTEGRATION

Introduction

This chapter provides an analysis of integration at the organizational level and the individual level and describes how vertical and horizontal integration apply to more than just the structure of the organization. Mastering integration is essential to innovation and breakthrough. We begin this chapter by looking at integration through the lens of art and creativity as the basis for different categories of the process of taking action in service of breakthrough transformation.

Art is a process for change integration. In this process there are four catalysts (educate, develop, train, instruct), four capacities (create, innovate, adapt, react), and four types of action (disintermediate resource, intermediate possibility, mediate differences, and remediate problems). These are related to the three metadisciplines of management, leadership, and integration.

Art is a Verb!

In 1997 a professional actor and educator, Eric Booth, published a volume intended for artists exploring what he had learned about creativity during

DOI: 10.4324/9781003131847-6

his years of experience in the theater. To everyone's surprise, *The Everyday Work of Art* would soon have an extraordinary cross-over effect upon leaders in all walks of life and organizations. In that book, he reconnected the association between our creative selves and our jobs, an association that we had lost when the Industrial Revolution and Machine Age coaxed us away from our agrarian roots. The *Everyday Work of Art* is a hopeful and inspiring work, whether you feel like a cog in the machinery or a like hamster on a treadmill … and especially if you plan to embark on breakthrough change integration! It begins by setting forth the "old" definition of art, which is "new" again to us.

> Contrary to conventional wisdom, art has not always been a noun, a valuable object relegated to a museum or a ticketed event in a performance hall. At the birth of the word "art" it was a verb that meant "to put things together." It was not a product, but a process. If we can reclaim that view of art—as a way of looking at and doing things, as a series of experiences and experiments—all of us gain a fresh grasp on the proven, practical ways to construct the quality of our lives.
>
> (Booth 1997: 5)

Let's take a moment before digging deeper and let's set agreed-upon context for some of the "terms of art" in this book. Note that there are 15 important verbs in this chapter and all are about *process*. They are ongoing and one doesn't just stop before another can begin. Process is the context when we "put things together" in breakthrough change integration. As we "art" an integration, we have four kinds of *catalysts*, four kinds of *capacities*, and four *categories of action*. This chapter will also cycle around to another level of distinguishing the three key verbs that are central to this book: *manage*, *lead*, and *integrate*. In our day-to-day conversations, each term is used in multiple ways, so, for the sake of clarity, we'd like you to understand the specific ways we will be using the following terms.

Catalysts for Integration

In chemistry, a catalyst is any substance that is used to start a reaction and then becomes discarded once its job is done. The catalyst is never altered itself, but it creates a transformation or it speeds up a process in that to which it is applied. For example, in organic systems, enzymes are biological catalysts for all cellular functions.

We have taken that concept and applied it to the business of organizations. We see four catalysts for organizational change integration.

1) *Educate*: Bring forth or draw out learning through inquiry. This term comes from the Latin, which means "lead forth" or "draw out." In our work with clients, we are fond of saying that everything you need to know about leading change is already within yourself; you just have to discover it and get it out there. The path of education is through observing yourself and your world, then inquiring for deeper meaning. Education involves making distinctions—"aha!" moments—that change the way we operate and interact. Education is a process that's never completed; we continue to build upon our learning.

2) *Develop*: Unfold and expand through application. This is not about one "aha" moment, but rather about gradual growth through testing new behaviors and trying out novel approaches to problems as we learn (Senge 2006). Development is practical in the context of a particular situation, and it is also expansive as we learn to transfer new behavior and approaches from one situation to another (Harris et al. 2019).

3) *Train*: Acquire skills through teaching. We perceive a big difference between developmental learning and being taught a skill. Training is limited to a one-directional path from the teacher to the student. As such, a defined amount of information—knowledge—is transferred to the recipient. Once the transfer is concluded, training is complete.

4) *Instruct—Drill*: Practice and condition through rigor. After training, a student can improve in a defined set of skills through repetitive practice.

Capacities for Integration

We see four capacities for organizational integration of change.

1) *Create*: Invent; make something up that is held to be of value.
2) *Innovate*: Find new applications for existing technology and add value.
3) *Adapt*: Learn from experience to eliminate surprise and preserve value.
4) *React*: Respond to unwanted surprises and minimize loss of value.

Figure 6.1 suggests that catalysts and capacities are correspondents; they are interdependent and each requires another for existence. Also, the

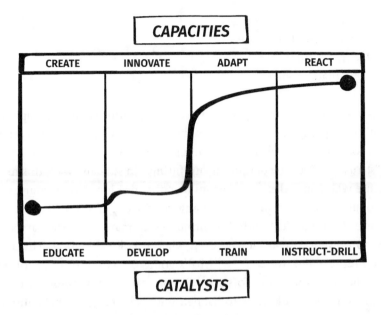

Figure 6.1 Capacities and Catalysts are Interrelated

quality of the existence of one mirrors the quality of the other. For example, the quality of creativity in a business is a direct reflection of the quality of education afforded members of the business.

Notice the middle line. It represents rising capability. To the degree that an organization applies the four catalysts, its capability to create, innovate, adapt, and react will grow.

Finally, let's look once more at the four relationships within catalysts and capacities: education and creativity, development and innovation, training and adaptation, instruction-drill and reaction. Our research and experience dealing with the integration of change strongly suggest that the effectiveness within each relationship and across relationships is governed by four types of action.

Four Types of Action for Integration

The four types of action for integration of change in organizations are each in some relationship to established norms and the status quo. In order to have breakthroughs for higher performance, there must be discontinuous change. Each action for integration will be described in more detail below. These four actions are:

1) Disintermediate Resources
2) Intermediate Possibilities
3) Mediate Differences
4) Remediate Problems.

We have all seen how initiatives that provoke systemic change call up forces intent on stopping them in their tracks. Systemic change is often treated like an organizational disease. Because such change can't help but disturb the "status quo," it is by definition "un-fitting." In so many ways this makes no sense when one takes into account that organizations have resources and are populated with bright people doing good work. Yet our organizations appear unsuited to deal with discontinuity—in many ways they are structured to prevent discontinuity—even when it is for the good. This is the natural result when we can't see what's going on except in terms of what should not be happening. To satisfy the prevailing organizational norms, systemic change would have to happen with reliability, predictability and certainty ... and that is paradoxical. Transformational change by definition is not reliable, predictable, or certain. It is a probability phenomenon and by seeing it that way, systemic change can be dealt with effectively.

Disintermediate Resources

This is the structural disassembly of established norms that may result in freeing up resources. Disintermediation is a precursor to integration. There may be other types of disintermediation, but we have identified two. The key inquiry for disintermediation is "What can we afford to stop?" For example, on an individual level, you could ask yourself: "Of all the things I do, what could I afford to stop and still get my job done?" On an organizational level, projects and processes can be analyzed for efficiency, effectiveness, and overall contribution to the organization's performance. For example, during a systems-wide change process at Honeywell's Large Computer Product Division, teams analyzed how many signatures were needed in order to get things done. Often as many as 11 or 12 signatures were needed when as few as two or three made sense.

Disintermediate by Circumstance

Circumstantial disintermediation is unplanned change characterized by increasing disorder and uncertainty with no apparent prospects for the future, thus a future of negative possibility can only be predicted. Ongoing degeneration leads to breakdowns (an outcome inconsistent with what has been intended or committed to), and these in turn lead to more degeneration. This often leads to false and misleading reports being circulated on the condition of the company, which results in negative possibility and a vicious cycle begins. These cycles often end with a collapse of the company. The collapse can be precipitous, as was the case with Digital Equipment Corporation (DEC).

DEC enjoyed 25 years of uninterrupted top- and bottom-line growth. Then in the mid-1980s, after failing to integrate changes, the corporation began to lose profits. Layoffs followed. In June 1992, Robert Palmer replaced Ken Olsen as president. Palmer was unable to stem the losses. More layoffs followed and assets were sold. DEC shrank into oblivion in six years.

- Worldwide training was spun off as Global Knowledge Network.
- The DEC database, Rdb, was sold to Oracle.
- In 1994, DEC sold its tape technology to Quantum Corporation.
- That same year Mentec bought the PDP-11 and some PDP-11 operating systems.
- The text terminal business was sold in August 1995 to Boundless Technologies.
- In March 1997, the DEC CORBA-based product, ObjectBroker, and its messaging software were sold to BEA Systems, Inc.
- In 1997, DEC sued Intel for infringing on its Alpha patents in designing the Pentium chips. As part of a settlement, Intel bought the DEC chip business and the StrongARM implementation of the ARM architecture.
- In 1997, GENICOM bought the printer business.
- At about the same time, the networking business was sold to Cabletron Systems.
- The DECtalk and DECvoice voice products were spun off and ended up at Fonix.

Finally, on January 26, 1998, what little remained of DEC was sold to Compaq.

Disintermediate Through Facilitated Intervention

This is the intentional disassembly of the organization for the purpose of generating new order and prospects for the organization. The dismembering of the company consists of action shaped by possibility. Here disintermediation is characterized by increasing order and certainty, and, in tandem, compelling prospects emerge for the future, thus the generation of new possibilities. The presence of new possibilities hastens the dismantling of preexisting norms and that clears the way for growth.

This kind of disintermediation is well exemplified in the courageous, high-risk path chosen by Ann Mulcahy in 2000 shortly after she ascended as CEO to the helm of foundering Xerox. Urged by financial advisors to declare bankruptcy in order to clear $18 billion in debt, Mulcahy responded, "Bankruptcy is never a win." She refused to shut down R&D and field sales. Despite shareholder opposition, she instead took on the arduous tasks of trimming the company's bloated infrastructure, replacing jaded manufacturing processes with cutting edge technology, and turning a traditional business model into a flexible plan to generate growth (Mulcahy 2006).

Intermediate Possibilities

Intermediation is the action of integrating discontinuity to generate possibilities and break through established norms. Change initiatives can bring new and lasting value to an organization. Intermediation is a process of "triaging possibilities" to identify and evaluate those possibilities with higher or lower probability of success. Triage is a system used to allocate a scarce commodity and direct it to where the greatest benefit can be realized. (We usually associate triage with responding to medical emergencies during disaster relief or military encounters, not with organizational change, but the concept applies.) Triage favors probability for any possibility through the use of priority order, which might include highest return on resources, time to return on resource, greatest need, and/or probability of success. Decisions are arrived at through alignment of the parties involved.

Integrating discontinuous change grows naturally from a breakthrough outcome—a new product, service, or technology—that breaches the current norms by generating possibility, creating opportunity and taking action. We arrive at intermediated decisions through alignment of parties and interests. This includes the triage of possibility, opportunity, and action. Intermediated change is about holding the space for the interplay of uncertainty and our need for understanding.

The mode is creative. Self-actualization and whole-process learning shape actions. A high tolerance for ambiguity and uncertainty exists. The intermediator sees all the elements that constitute Organization as being interwoven and interconnected. The key inquiry is: "What is the competing influence?"

Mediate Differences

This is the process of assessing different possible actions for higher or lower certainty of success. It is the process of conflict resolution during the process of organizational change. Mediation sounds "legal" and may bring to mind "settling out of court," but in a broader sense it is a neutral assessment of strengths and weaknesses between competing influences, such as tolerance for uncertainty versus the need for certainty. An organization in midst of change may identify a possibility (intermediation) and then grant authority to one or more individuals whom they deem to be qualified to act as mediators of differing choices or best paths to follow to turn that possibility into reality. A mediated decision might also be reached through consensus or agreement within parties.

We mediate to reduce deviations from the new norm with the intention of increasing predictability, reliability, certainty, and repeatability of the application of breakthrough efforts. Integrating this kind of change is in the realm of continuous improvement. Mediated change requires committed neutrality, while assessing strengths and weaknesses among competing influences. To arrive at mediated decisions, the organization might engage an authority (as simple as a check-off list or more often an expert individual) or rely upon agreement between several parties to set standards. Lean (manufacturing or production), Six Sigma, and TQM (total quality management) are examples of disciplines used for this level of integrating change. The mode is stoic, with carefully thought-out actions shaped by reason. The ideal mediation (or mediator) is committed to relinquishing passionate and political influences. Commonly, there is surrender to unavoidable necessity of considerations associated with maintaining the organization. The inquiry for mediation is "What's missing?" (not "What's wrong?").

Remediate Problems

The focus here may be on either restoring or maintaining order to reduce risks and increase certainty. The aim is to repair, refurbish, reestablish, and/or recover all or portions of pre-exiting norms before the change was implemented. There are occasions when we need to integrate throughout an organization the kind of change that returns things to normal. Remediation is about fixing what's broken. The need arises from emergency, adversity, and other unforeseen events. The focus is on removing unacceptable risk—not uncertainty. Remediated change reestablishes a preexisting norm by restoring order, confidence, and integrity. The mode is heroic, with bold and decisive action shaped by emergent needs. High determination combines with an altruistic concern for the organization's welfare.

The key inquiry for remediation of problems is "What's the breakdown?" (not "Whose fault is it?").

Malden Mills, manufacturer of Polartec, was a third-generation family business founded in 1906 by Henry Feuerstein in Lawrence, Massachusetts. In 1995, a boiler at the company's plant exploded and set fire to three main buildings at the plant, causing 40 percent damage to the whole plant. Aaron Feuerstein, grandson of the founder, was advised by his insurance company to take the insurance money, shut down the plant, and retire to Florida. His Jewish faith and his core values of caring for his workers and for the community would not allow him to do that. He paid all his employees their salaries and benefits for the next three months, a cost of over $25 million, even though most of them would not be working until the mill was rebuilt. Before the fire, Malden Mills produced 130,000 yards of material per week. Due to the commitment of his employees to save the plant, within ten days they were up and operating again in a partially burned building. Within six weeks they were producing over 200,000 yards per week.

While speaking to the Hillel Society at the University of Massachusetts Amherst, Mr. Feuerstein said: "It was unthinkable to put 3,000 people out of work. The moral imperative is critical and must be taken without regard to the consequences. Once I made the decision, my work was over. My people took over. They did it" (Neal 2006).

The "Big Three" Terms of Art

In this chapter we have thus far discussed 12 terms of art—all verbs—and now we come to the three overarching terms—also verbs—that we have been mentioning since the beginning of this book. These three are *lead*, *manage*, and *integrate*. Each is actually a holistic mix of activities comprising the *domains* of art, science, and craft, although the domain most emphasized varies with each term. Thus, in the metadiscipline of leadership, the principle domain of leading is art (creativity). In the metadiscipline of management, the principle domain of managing is science. Last, and certainly not least, in the metadiscipline of integration, the principle domain of integrating is craft.

Integrating breakthrough change also requires that three viewpoints be present.

(1) Human systems, where leadership focuses, must be perceived as the source of results.

(2) Business systems, where management focuses, must be understood in the context of Organization, not *as* the organization itself.

(3) Integration systems, where change-agents work, must be seen as distinct from, but relevant to, the success of business systems and human systems.

- Organizational Science/Management maintains stability. This metadiscipline focuses on the ability to deliver results with reliability, predictability, certainty, and repeatability. This work is grounded in authoritative hierarchies.

- Organizational Art/Leadership is creatively source-full. The focus of this metadiscipline is on the capability to increase the realization of human potential on behalf of organizational objectives, to bring about breakthrough-level, co-created change, and to hold the space for other leaders to emerge. This work is grounded in relational networks.

- Organizational Craft/Integration realizes potential. It might be called the midwife of change. Through trial and error all the basic processes that will be required to integrate change are ironed out. This may be continuous improvement, breakthrough, or remedial change due to fixing some imbalance. This work is grounded in dynamic matrices.

Specialization Is Both a Necessity of Change and an Obstacle to Change Integration

Most managers and leaders in any organization try to stay informed on a wide range of organizational subjects. At the same time, their roles often require one or more specializations. Specializations have a way of grow-ing in depth and complexity. Consider, for example, the evolution of Information Technology (IT) and the position of Chief Information Officer (CIO). CIOs were originally degreed in the computer sciences, software engineering, or information systems—each a specialization within the specialization of IT. Today many CIOs must also have either an MBA or an MS in Management degree; both degrees are based in management science. For CIOs, leadership capabilities, business acumen, and strategic perspec-tives have taken precedence over specialization. In fact, it is now quite common for CIOs to be appointed from the business side of the organiza-tion. This swing reflects the view that it is easier to learn the "IT stuff" than it is to learn the "business stuff." Nowadays, senior roles in their own right embrace many specializations that must integrate change vertically and horizontally.

How does anyone in senior leadership manage to do it all and do it all well? Should you concentrate on your specialization or on your people skills? It's a given that an organization of any size cannot operate effec-tively or efficiently without specialists (experts). Experts are amply suited to absorb and to generate new information within their own fields but, at the same time, this focused experience makes experts ill prepared to com-municate new information across specializations to others.

Specialists are vertically integrated, yet the exigencies created by the speed of change necessitate horizontal integration across the entire organi-zation. With each new wave of change, new specializations appear, which just compounds the challenge of making all the pieces fit and run smoothly. We have both a paradox and a vicious cycle. Specialization is a necessity born of change and an obstacle to change integration.

Communication and Specialization: How They Are Related

Communication is a contributing factor to the paradox and vicious cycle of specialization. As communication grows faster and more information becomes available, the rate of change increases accordingly. As change increases, specializations arise to handle the challenge, bringing with them the host of issues we described above.

Let's consider Corporate IT. It's a specialization in communication that arose because there was a need to find and share more timely informa-tion in business. As the rate of change in business increased, decisions had to be made faster, too. To make informed decisions, business managers needed facts and data sooner than was possible with person-to-person communication. IT pushed the automation introduced in the Machine Age to new heights of sophistication, while it drove a whole generation of non-specialists out of their jobs.

At first, integration of automated business was a messy affair, as so often happens with new endeavors. Executives controlled the funding, while technical folk controlled the process and access to the information. They spoke different languages and vendors served as translators, IBM being by far the most successful at this game.

Today, the game has changed again; now large-scale change is being led from inside organization. Vendor-mediated change integration is no longer sufficient; there are simply too many internal variables to control. While large-scale change led from the inside of an organization does benefit from well-informed external advice, guidance, and facilitation, it does so with the proviso that external providers work in partnership with one another and with internal integration leaders. Experience has shown that change integrations work best when internally led, but, given the gap in communication between leadership and management, a third metadiscipline is emerging that can weave the best contributions of both into a whole cloth.

Art and Science—Meet Craft

As you know, at the scale of Organization, we now approach change integration from three perspectives. First is leadership, which is more art than craft or science. Second is management, which is more science than craft or art. And there is the third perspective—integration—emerging as more craft than art or science, and the bridge or "missing link" between the two. Integration professionals would be those committed to mastering the craft of integration. Some who master integration will have a bias toward the *leadership arts* and others a bias toward the *management sciences*.

Let's pause here to reflect. Regarding integration, our experience suggests several useful points to remember:

- Most organizations need to integrate change vertically and horizontally.
- Integration is an embedded, and often unrecognized, requirement in executive roles such as CFO, CIO, COO, and right down to directors, group leaders, and team leaders.

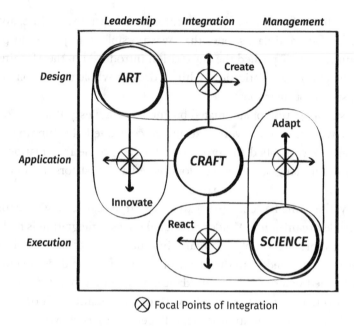

Figure 6.2 Focal Points of Integration

- Integration is an indistinct and/or undeclared organizational discipline.
- Integration is a blend of *art*, *craft* and *science*.

For the moment, imagine integration to be an undeclared universal strategic imperative, too. Use the information we outline in this book to explore ways in which your organization can benefit from a better understanding of integration. We know from our experience in helping organizations through major change initiatives that the abysmal track record for sustaining large-scale change in organizations does not have to continue. If you are willing to work toward establishing integrating change as an organizational discipline, then you can benefit from what you learn here.

Summary: Grounding the Claim

In Chapter 1 we outlined Organization's *undeclared strategic imperative*.

What's *undeclared?*
The need to develop change integration as a strategic capability; it's hidden from our view. Organization's reliance on the existing embedded change

integration capabilities found in management—react and adapt—is realizing diminishing returns. Using management capabilities for integration has reached practical limits of application. The existing approaches to change integration are best suited to maintain the status quo through continuous improvement; they are not designed for the integration of discontinuous breakthrough change.

Why is it *strategic?*

The organizations that master change integration as a strategy will thrive; those that fail to do so may not survive. Our own direct experience as business leaders, combined with data like that which the IBM Global CEO Study revealed, show us that both the rate of change and magnitude of the change that organizations must integrate are accelerating. Anything less than a strategy that underpins all planning across the organization is merely a band-aid.

What makes it *imperative?*

The acceleration of change accompanied by increases in the impact of change makes adopting integration as an organizational-scale discipline imperative. The health of organizations and human society at large depends upon the ability of enterprise systems to integrate change.

Despite overwhelming evidence that suggests that change integration should be an organizational-scale discipline, we still find a majority of organizations treating change as a "sideline," something extra we do while working on our real jobs. One root of the problem is that we have collapsed *leading change* and *integrating change* within *change management*. The understanding and the relationship between leading, integrating, and managing change is an indistinct and overlapping mass of frameworks, models, processes, and maps.

Change begins with leadership. As we've indicated before, a leader's primary job is to initiate change. Change must first be initiated, then integrated, and only then can it be managed. The successive, and usually overlapping, steps in the chain—lead, integrate, and manage—are recursive. Each round builds on the previous rounds. The portion of a change initiative that was last integrated and is now being managed forms the basis for the next round of leading, integrating, and managing change.

This chapter has described change integration as an art, and as Eric Booth (1997) points out, art is a verb. Verbs connote action, and we have offered 15 verbs that are essential to integrating change.

We described four catalysts for integration and each of these are actions organizations can take to create transformational and discontinuous change: educate, develop, train, and instruct. Each of these catalysts is in relationship to increasing the capacity for meaningful integration of change in the system: create, innovate, adapt, and react. Different situations call for different types of structured or unstructured action, and in complex change scenarios, all of these actions may be drawn upon in support of shifting away from the status quo norms to norms that allow for new possibilities: disintermediate resources, intermediate possibilities, mediate differences, and remediate problems. The 12 action verbs described here are in relationship to the "Big Three" terms of art that are central to this book: lead, manage, and integrate.

There is a strong and interdependent relationship between communication and specialization that is necessary to understand if you are taking action to create discontinuous change in your organization. This discussion of communication lays the groundwork for our deeper exploration in the next two chapters of the connections between communication, trust, and relationship and how they set the stage for breakthrough change.

References

Booth, E. (1997) *The Everyday Work of Art.* Naperville, IL: Sourcebooks Inc.

Harris, D., L. Holyfield, L. Jones, R. Ellis, and J. Neal (2019) *Spiritually and Developmentally Mature Leadership: Towards an Expanded Understanding of Leadership in the 21st Century.* New York: Springer.

Mulcahy, A. (2006) Leadership Lessons Learned on the Firing Line. MIT World Special Events and Lectures. Retrieved from https://techtv.mit.edu/videos/16167-leadership-lessons-learned-on-the-firing-line on August 29, 2020.

Neal, J. (2006) *Edgewalkers: People and Organizations that Take Risks, Build Bridges and Break New Ground.* Westport, CT: Praeger.

Senge, P. (2006) *The Fifth Discipline: The Art & Practice of the Learning Organization.* New York: Doubleday.

7

TRUST AND COMMUNICATION

Introduction

As we will see, trust in leadership does not stand by itself, it is part of a larger system of trust—a system that is manifest at many scales, such as individual, family, group, community, organizational, and governmental. While trust is a global topic, it has compelling and real local effect. Leaders deal with this local effect on a daily basis. The absence of trust has a significant cost and its presence can be a strategic advantage. This chapter addresses trust at the scale of organization, and analyzes the relationship between trust, communication, and the integration of change.

Trust, Relationship, and Communication—Setting the Stage for Breakthrough

Viewing Organization as societal provides a line of sight that is useful for core issues that need to be addressed if we are to move organizational performance to new levels. The challenge is not in addressing the issues,

DOI: 10.4324/9781003131847-7

but rather in distinguishing what issues require our attention. Once they are identified, addressing them is often quite straightforward, although it almost always takes rigorous work.

Leading breakthrough-level change is distinct from managing in almost every way and particularly with regard to the nature of our learning as leaders. Knowledge, information, and understanding as a foundation for learning are no longer sufficient. Leaders must learn to see into complexity in ways that will distinguish the basic forms (canonicals) out of which organizational complexity arises in the first place. When the quality of work performed drops, it's likely that it has something to do with trust, communication, and relationship, all of which are basic (canonical) and relevant to the quality of work performed.

- *Trust* is the medium for context, which provides meaning to the work people do.
- *Relationship* is the medium for process, which shapes the action people take.
- *Communication* is the medium for content, which establishes the value for results that people produce.

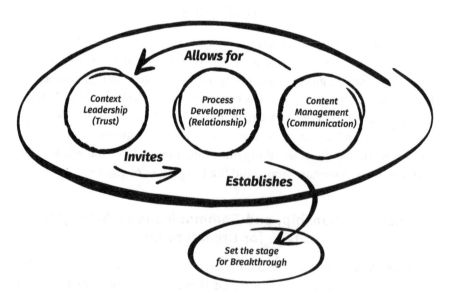

Figure 7.1 Set the Stage for Breakthrough

Trust Networks

Trust, relationship, and communication are interrelated; they form a trust network and as such are the cornerstones of societal cohesion. Why are all three so important to change integration? According to political economist Francis Fukuyama in *The End of History and the Last Man* (1992), societies grounded upon efficient trust networks will be the most successful at building sustainable, efficient economic organizations—in other words, organizations most likely to be integrated.

When trust levels are high at the business level, organizations can grow large and efficient. They enjoy lower administrative costs and higher institutional reliability. Alternatively, low trust carries with it the disadvantages of corruption, trade with influences and small, inefficient organization—all symptoms of disintegration that leads to collapse. More energy needs to be put into control systems, multiple levels of sign offs, and overall bureaucracy, thus slowing down productivity (Gibb 1978).

Peter Block and colleagues talk about the importance of trust in the virtual world we find ourselves in today.

> No matter how virtual our world becomes, having impact rests on a simple belief: relationships are decisive. If you have expertise, if you know something, and run something and you want the world to act on what you know, a trusting relationship is vital; building trusting relations is not about convenience or comfort or feeling good about working together. Your ability to engage in honest, trusting relationships is the determinant of business performance and making a difference. You need to do it because you have something to offer this world in your organization or community, so you must build that trust so that you can have impact. Tools, techniques, and methods just take us so far. But if you are focusing on relationships and their nuances, and believe that matters, your work is always engaging. It keeps you active and energized. It makes you powerful.
>
> (Block, Schimmelpfenig, and Evans 2020)

Since the 1990s, the trust system has been severely shaken by corporate financial disasters. Among these have been the Enron, WorldCom, Andersen, and Tyco accounting and reporting frauds that created a crisis in confidence in the leadership of corporate America (Reeth 2020). More recent fraud stories include that of Wirecard AG in Germany, where more than $2 billion has gone missing due to "elaborate and sophisticated fraud" (Drozdiak, Arons, and Syed 2020). And it's not just corporate fraud. In August of 2020, Steve Bannon, former political advisor to former President Trump, was arrested for fraudulently raising more than $25 million in donations to build Trump's wall but using the money for personal use instead (Lipton 2020).

Public distrust for corporate executives has threatened investor confidence and corporate productivity to the extent that Congress passed the Sarbanes-Oxley Act ("SOX," also known as the Public Company Accounting Reform and Investor Protection Act) in 2002.

The responsibility for restoring public trust has ultimately fallen to senior executives, who must model ethical leadership and spread the word to organizations themselves. Ethics are now widely acclaimed to be everybody's job.

Has Organization improved its record on trust and ethics? Has the economy expanded? The worst recession since the Great Depression recovered only to sink into deeper recession with unpredictable challenges such as trade wars, COVID-19, racial injustice, and climate crises? Major organizations continue to disintegrate; employment remains sluggish. Meanwhile, within organizations, uncertainty about the future reigns supreme, fueling fear and distrust of leadership. It's no wonder that cynicism and employee disengagement are so well entrenched.

There were strong indicators of trouble brewing dating back over a more than a decade. One example is found in this following summary of the Towers Perrin 2005 *Global Workforce Survey* (Seijits and Crim 2006) study:

- Overall, only 14 percent of employees were "fully engaged" on the job.
- The vast majority (62 percent) were "moderately engaged" at best.
- And nearly a quarter were "actively disengaged."

That same year a Gallup Research report revealed employees to be hardly more enthusiastic. While 31 percent of employees reported themselves to be "engaged" on the job, 52 percent were "not engaged" and 17 percent were "actively disengaged" (Krueger and Kilham 2006).

Earned and Granted Trust

Leadership and management require different types of trust. One type, earned trust, is familiar to us. The other, granted trust, is less familiar.

Earned trust may be increased or decreased by intentional deeds or by unforeseen circumstances. We may trust a friend who has consistently kept her promises, or we may trust a business associate who performs to high standards. We may also trust without having had a direct experience. When we go to a doctor who was recommended to us by someone we have known for a long time, we invest a degree of trust in the new doctor, even though we do not know the doctor personally, because of the recommendation and possibly because of the diplomas and certificates on his/her wall. In either case, earned trust is based in the past, whether in past deeds or on credentials.

Granted trust is distinct from earned trust. The most striking difference is that granted trust is non-contingent and non-transactional. That is, granted trust is not established or affected by deeds or by circumstances, and is granted on an all-or-none basis. Granted trust could be said, therefore, to be non-rational, or even emotional. It is neither. Granted trust is a *commitment*; it is given in one's word, and it is absolute. One grants trust based on shared commitments. When we grant trust, we are saying that the other person's deeds will be seen in the context that the person is trusted, and actions that seem to be inconsistent with their commitments or promises will be held as mistakes rather than as occasions for a withdrawal of trust. Granted trust could be said to require an act of faith; it creates a playing field of great freedom but also great responsibility.

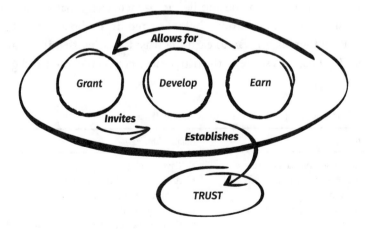

Figure 7.2 Earned and Granted Trust

When Each Kind of Trust is Useful

Both kinds of trust are important and useful. While granted trust is crucial in some circumstances, it is not helpful in all situations.

Earned trust is useful for situations requiring predictability, certainty, and reliability. For example, if you needed surgery of some kind, you would likely want to choose a surgeon who has earned your trust, whether through a recommendation or other qualifications—you wouldn't approach a stranger and offer to grant trust that they could operate on you successfully! When you board an airplane, you trust that the pilot has been properly trained and qualified by the airline. Similarly, if you have a critical project that has to meet a deadline, you will probably give it to someone who has earned your trust over a period of time by demonstrating that they could meet your expectations on timeliness and results.

The key here is to make sure that our expectations are clearly communicated in advance. We earn trust by meeting expectations, but too often, those expectations are vague or missing altogether; we assume that the other person shares our understanding of the situation, so we don't state specifically what we want to have happen. This makes it nearly impossible to meet expectations and hence to earn trust.

Granted trust is required to create futures that go beyond what is predictable. When you are creating something new, or working with a new team, it sometimes requires a large grant of trust to move the game forward. You may never have enough time to work together to earn sufficient trust with each other and still produce results on a timely basis, and consequently you will need to grant trust to one another. In particular, if what you are out to accomplish has never been done before or requires a breakthrough, then by definition there is no way to earn the trust for doing that in advance.

Table 7.1 illustrates some of the differences between earned and granted trust:

Table 7.1 Differences Between Earned and Granted Trust

Earned Trust	Granted Trust
• Entitled based on past event	• Given freely
• Shaped by one-on-one events and transactions	• A conscious choice based on shared commitments
• May be increased or decreased by deeds or circumstances	• Focused on the future
• Tends to be the automatic operating mode	• Creates the foundation for a relationship
	• Goes beyond the success or failure of the last transaction

Relationship

We are missing the mark for breakthrough change integration when we think of Organization strictly from a business-centric perspective (see Figure 7.3). Perhaps a shift in the traditional thinking about the nature of Organization will help us see what's happening within.

We believe that the business-centric view is not merely limiting to generative growth; it is in fact antithetical to the actual nature of Organization. It can be said simply as *people and organization are one*. There can be no organization without people. People are the source of everything that is created in an organization, not simply results. Yet, too often emphasis on people is underrepresented when we over-direct our focus to "the business."

When human systems—leaders—can recognize the relationships in the holographic design of Organization, we can begin to compare our thinking to thinking of others, and to see new possibilities that can lead to optimizing organization and successfully integrating change.

Communication

As our individual jurisdictions vary within our organizations, we see the purposes, goals, and responsibilities of our organizations differently. An organization that can't communicate horizontally across jurisdictions cannot coordinate activity to seize opportunities for growth.

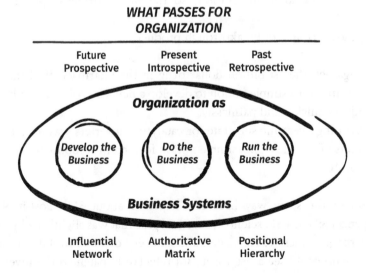

Figure 7.3 What Passes for Organization

Communication among the three systems is the "life blood" of organizational change integration. It's up to leadership to model frequent, low-amplitude communications, and to promote relational networks.

In summary, we have shown that we as leaders need to expand our awareness, lest our organizations perish in self-preservation. Treating Organization as strictly business keeps our horizons from expanding, even though we know intuitively that to compete successfully, an organization needs more creativity and courage to step into the unknown. We lapse into perceiving Organization as straightforward, repeatable acts of business that offer the seductive promise of stability.

Breakthrough by Luck?

By now you know that breakthrough is a demonstrable and positive departure in performance from what the past indicates is possible. Breakthroughs are products or services new to the company or new to the world. We've shown you that examples of breakthroughs abound and are fairly easy to recognize. You are counseled to integrate your company before you attempt to integrate change and we've done our best to help you avoid other pitfalls to success.

However, more remains to be said about the *source* of breakthrough, the *conditions* necessary for realization of breakthrough, and the *process* of breakthroughs. In organizations, these are often missed during and after breakthrough change integration, so the breakthroughs appear to be accidental.

Here are a couple of breakthrough products:

- Tagamet, the 1st billion-dollar drug in the pharmaceutical industry, began with a simple notion to develop a new class of drug for healing ulcers quickly and painlessly.
- Corning's ceramic substrate for catalytic converters was used in millions of vehicles. This simple notion formed in response to the Clean Air Act.

Remember the story way back in Chapter 1 about 3M's Post-it Notes? Dr. Spencer Silver, a 3M scientist, invented glue that was slightly tacky rather than strongly adhesive. He visited almost every division in 3M and found no one who could see a use for it. 3M reluctantly patented the invention.

Four years later, Art Fry, another 3M scientist, had a notion that Dr. Silver's reusable adhesive would solve his problem.

When Fry wrote up his idea for a reusable bookmark and presented it to management, initially they were skeptical, but soon 3M gave the invention its full support when 3M staff could not get enough of the samples Fry handed out. It took another five years to perfect machines to manufacture the product. In 1980, Post-it Notes were introduced in the U.S. Within two years, they were popular in offices, schools, labs, libraries, and homes.

It's easy to make a case for 3M Post-it Notes being the result of serendipity. The source of the breakthrough was unclear. Was it Dr. Silver or Art Fry? What conditions at 3M and in the marketplace made it possible to happen? It took years before the breakthrough finally reached the buying public. Was there any real planning or process involved?

If we look closely at this case and many other examples that have been attributed to good fortune, there are some common themes that seem to be always operating in the background. One or a few people, the source of the integrated change:

- proactively promote a simple notion;
- have a tenacious belief in a possibility they see;
- are curious;
- are willing to "stand in the face of no agreement" and to communicate their ideas.

Too often, these are the people that organizations write off. Some have strong-willed styles, while others may be soft spoken, but they are often dismissed as troublemakers. They are perceived as too radical to be team players. Their thinking is unrealistic and overly simplistic. They just don't seem to appreciate the true complexity of the situation or how many hurdles would have to be overcome. Sometimes these are the people who are nice enough and well meaning, but they always seem to be marching out of step. Know anybody who is like this?

We call these people Edgewalkers (Neal 2006) and see them as the source of integrated change in organizations. They are typically on the edge or margins of the system, with one foot in the mainstream and one foot in the external environment. They also have an ability to sense the future and are willing to take risks to follow their passion and to co-create what has never been created before. Truly innovative organizations value their

Edgewalkers and create structures and processes that allow them to be an important part of breakthroughs.

If your organization has no person who stands for the possibility of a breakthrough, then you lack source, and there is almost no hope of breakthrough occurring. If there is at least one person, then there are probably some passive enablers, too, who can help to foster breakthrough outcomes.

The conditions for breakthrough look something like this:

- The company allows individuals freedom to try their ideas without putting their careers at risk, providing they fulfill on their assigned duties. This was the case at 3M. As we will see shortly, it was not so for Sony's Honorary Chairman, Masaru Ibuka.
- The company allows individuals to explore ideas that might lead to breakthrough outcomes, even if they are not aligned with corporate strategy. The hidden truth is that this kind of work goes on whether a company sanctions it or not. Creativity is hard to suppress.
- The company fosters the expression of divergent points of view.

Breakthroughs are going to happen with or without these passive organizational enablers. When the integration of business systems and human systems is missing, breakthroughs are often attributed to good luck, for example the Post-it Note example. Case studies on breakthrough seldom reveal the *source* of breakthrough, but rather they document the circumstances in which it occurs. What if circumstances are not that relevant when it comes to breakthrough? Yes, they have effect, but they are not the deciding factor. Missing breakthrough change integration is seldom the result of a management decision and is most often a default state arising from the failure to see the benefits of integrating and the costs of not doing so.

Breaking Through on Purpose

Let's take a closer look at an organization that committed to generating breakthroughs as a strategic imperative. Engelhard is a former Fortune 500 company headquartered in Iselin, New Jersey. Engelhard developed the first production catalytic converter, which it began selling to Ford Motor Company in 1972. In 2006, BASF bought Engelhard for $5 billion.

The story begins with Orin R. Smith, Chairman and CEO of Engelhard Corporation. He joined Engelhard as a VP in 1977, became President in

1984, CEO and Chairman 1999, and retired in 2001. Smith had a vision for Engelhard and its people—what he perceived to be a strategic advantage—the ability to produce breakthroughs on purpose. His premise was simple: Engelhard would be a "net zero polluter." Engelhard products would clean up at least as much pollution as the company emitted. After two years of declaring this goal, he was dissatisfied with the low level of uptake on his vision by Engelhard leadership. He heard lots of talk but could see no meaningful action, so in the mid-1990s he hired Generative Leadership Group (GLG) to help him address the challenge of transforming his vision into a compelling new reality for Engelhard. Smith told us, the consultants, he wanted to establish a foundational educational approach for Engelhard leadership that would include breakthrough as a key component of corporate strategy.

The Generative Leadership Group's relationship with Engelhard lasted four years. Their first breakthrough using GLG's unique approach for integrating business and human systems was a transformation in the core technology behind the surface chemistry for catalytic conversion. This led to a product known today as PremAir®, the first commercial catalyst able to reduce toxic ozone in air. When air passes over an automobile radiator surface that has been coated with PremAir, up to 80 percent of the harmful ozone that PremAir touches is destroyed. Engelhard scientists found a way to lower the temperature at which the catalyst would activate the conversion from that of automobile exhaust to ambient room temperature.

This breakthrough resulted in numerous applications. Automotive radiators were among the first to be treated with PremAir. By 2005 The Sharper Image Ionic Breeze® Silent Air Purifier became the first portable air purifier to use the PremAir catalyst. The Ionic Breeze integrated PremAir into America's most popular portable indoor air purifier.

In 2001, Engelhard received the J. Dean Sensenbaugh Award from the Air and Waste Management Association (AWMA) for its development of PremAir.

Here's the story behind the story:

For six years preceding this breakthrough in surface chemistry, the VP of Sales for the catalyst division of Engelhard had been promoting a wild idea he had—the possibility of having an automobile radiator work as a catalytic converter. Such an application might even bring some autos to states of net zero pollution. No one listened to him seriously. While he was brilliant in his field, sales and marketing, other leaders at Engelhard all knew he was no scientist. Everyone understood the science: temperatures in automobile radiators were too low for catalytic conversion. Catalytic conversion requires high temperatures like those reached in the exhaust of automobiles.

GLG first worked one-on-one with Orin Smith and then with an extended executive team he formed that included 30 senior leaders, one of whom was the VP of Sales. In the first four-day off-site meeting with his team, Orin delivered a clear message: the game was in play. Engelhard was going to transform from the top down. Members of the extended executive team were each invited to play or not, as was their choice, but the game was going on, with or without them. It took most of the four days for Orin's message to sink in fully. Within the year, two of the members resigned with dignity; breakthrough was not a game they were interested in playing.

Following the first off-site, the VP of R&D invited the VP of Sales to lunch. The VP of R&D wanted to learn more about the "smog eating" radiator idea. Only a year later, this unlikely duo was featured on the front page of the Business Section of the New York Times, standing in front of a Lincoln equipped with the world's first smog eating radiator.

Orin and his extended executive leadership team worked with GLG in six three-to-four-day sessions over the next 14 months. Sessions combined leadership development work with breakthrough application on key strategic initiatives. In addition, over the next three years more than 50 key leaders throughout Engelhard attended GLG's Executive Excellence Program, to transfer the "source code" for breakthroughs. During this period, Orin Smith asked GLG to work with scores of breakthrough teams, each formed around specific breakthrough initiatives, which were sponsored by members of Orin's extended executive leadership team. The real story about the effort by Engelhard's leadership to incorporate breakthrough as a reliable element of their business strategy has never been published. Indeed, when a publication does mention something about extraordinary performance, there's likely to be an unintended misattribution of the source of breakthrough. Extraordinary performance driven by breakthrough is not well understood, even by those who play a part in it.

This is exemplified in an article titled "Why CEOs Fall: The Causes and Consequences of Turnover at the Top" (Lucier, Spiegel, and Schuyt 2002). The authors attribute Orin Smith's long tenure at Engelhard to "the idea of the long-serving CEO [which is] is deeply ingrained in the U.S. business culture." It also supports the view that "Entrepreneurial cultures also adhere to the presumption that individuals can be responsible for the success of large organizations." In simpler terms, it's all about the culture and heroes. Smith knew it wasn't the culture and it wasn't about being a hero, either. He understood that breakthrough is a discipline that can be learned. It lives in people's commitment to extraordinary results; it requires teamwork. Smith didn't think that everyone should play the game of breakthrough. He knew that breakthrough results will only come from those who choose to play the game and those who are willing to respect a diversity of views, and, in the end, agree to set aside their personal differences for the sake of playing on a winning team.

Breaking Through to Breakthrough by Standing in the Face of No Agreement

One of our favorite stories of "standing in the face of no agreement" dates back awhile. It's the tale of how the Sony Walkman came to be. Despite the age of this story, it is still relevant because nothing fundamental about Organization has changed with regard to its message. The Walkman emerged from a "failure" in Sony's Tape Recorder Division. The product would never have reached market, if it were not for the persistence of the company's Honorary Chairman, Masaru Ibuka. He succeeded in providing the leadership necessary to create a market for portable music machines despite the near impossibility of garnering agreement for his vision within Sony.

In 1978 the Sony Tape Recorder Division was working on a stereo-phonic tape recorder for journalists to replace a monaural recorder. One objective was to keep the stereo version the same size as the monaural recorder. Eventually they had stereo circuits in the device but there was no room for a recording unit. So the development team decided that it made a nice music machine, and listened to it play, while they worked on other projects.

Masaru Ibuka made it a practice to visit project teams working on new ideas. When he arrived at the Tape Recorder Division to discuss their failed attempt with the stereo recorder, he heard their "music machine" and was impressed with the quality of the sound. He recalled a project in another division to produce lightweight headphones. This inspired a vision that Nayak and Ketteringham (1986) describe in Breakthroughs:

What if you combined them? At the very least, he said, the headphones would use battery power much more efficiently than stereo speakers. Reduce power requirements and you can reduce battery consumption. But another idea began to form in his mind. If you added the headphones, wouldn't you dramatically increase the quality of what the listener hears? Could you leave out the recorder entirely and make a successful product that just plays music?

(p. 134)

To the tape recorder engineers, Ibuka's suggestions were inane. A unit with no recorder and no speaker? Who would buy such a thing?

The internal hurdles seemed endless at Sony. No matter where Ibuka turned there were people attempting to hedge their bets on his idea. Before Walkman went into manufacturing, Ibuka had to wade through endless squabbles over pricing.

An example of hedging occurred after Walkman was in manufacturing. Sony's production manager for the Tape Recorder Division, Kozo Ohsone, worried that if Walkman failed, his reputation would be tarnished. Having already spent money on the equipment to produce injection-molded cases, he did not want to risk losing on the Walkman itself. So, even though he was ordered to produce 60,000 units, Ohsone decided to produce 30,000 and lower his exposure should the product fail. He hedged his bets out of personal considerations. He did not play to win—rather he played to avoid loss. They are different games and breakthrough is not found in the second game.

Ibuka found himself standing in the face of no agreement. Yet, for him, the possibility was simple and clear, even after a miserable start for sales. During the Walkman's initial release into the marketplace in Japan in July of 1979, its sales were zero for the entire country. But by August sales suddenly exploded. By September 30,000 units had been sold and sales were accelerating. It seemed like everybody was buying a Sony Walkman. Tourists from Europe and North America packed them in their suitcases to take them home for friends and families.

Subsequently, the Sony Walkman was the model that others in the market copied and soon competitors' devices were also being called "Walkmen." The Sony Walkman became so popular that many considered it to be an indispensable product—a household word and a new category for merchandising.

The technology behind the Sony Walkman was complex, but Ibuka's vision was simple. He had a notion that if you integrated a failed recorder that only played music, with newly developed lightweight headphones this would increase battery life for the device and improve sound quality for the listener. Breakthrough and simple notions are good partners, because there is an inverse relationship between the complexity of an idea and the level of realization that is possible.

Ibuka did not attempt to solve the complex problem the development team faced; instead, he generated a possibility for a breakthrough. As Sony's Honorary Chairman, he had no authority and no budget for development, so he had to convince those with authority and budget. He had to build a network of support around his idea and find others who could tolerate uncertainty. He had no built-in way to traverse Sony's authority-based business systems (development, manufacturing, distribution). He had to rely mostly on Sony's relationship based human systems. Much of Ibuka's early work on the Walkman was accomplished using a sub-rosa network of relationships.

For every breakthrough like the Walkman there are an incalculable number of failures. Our research indicates most failures are the result of insufficient levels of integration between business systems and human systems. Business systems are about reliability, predictability, certainty, and repeatability—it's *the science of Organization*. Humans Systems are about relationships, ideas and energy—it's where the work gets done and it's *the art of Organization*.

Breaking Through to Breakthrough Can Even Happen When Leadership Is Not Getting Its Job Done

In the face of economic downturn, misguided decision-making, allegations of misconduct at the top, and questionable leadership, the employees of Ford Motor Company decided that it was in their best interest to create transformative change on their own. People from all divisions worked together to create one of the most compelling organizational-scale breakthroughs in automotive history. While many factors contributed to this breakthrough, the revolutionary design of the Taurus and the level of employee engagement were its determining factors. The Taurus design still informs the design of Ford vehicles, nearly four decades later.

The 1970s and early 1980s were not easy times at Ford. Approaching the 1980s, Ford Motor Company had lost three-quarters of its net worth and its reputation was tarnished. Sales on Pinto models introduced between 1971 and 1976, followed by Bobcats in 1975 and 1976, suffered from public disapproval over incidents of gas tank explosions in rear-end collisions. Meanwhile, foreign competition was gaining market share. Internal squabbles among senior executives did not help.

In April 1977, Henry Ford II undermined Lee Iacocca's power. Ford created an executive triumvirate, naming himself, Iacocca, and Philip Caldwell as joint leaders. A year later Ford added his brother William Clay Ford. Soon after, Ford fired Iacocca and put Caldwell in his place. Henry Ford's decisions to disempower Iacocca only exacerbated Ford's falling popularity, as he faced allegations of financial misconduct and bribery.

Henry Ford seemed destined to make one bad choice after another. He cancelled Iacocca's proposed development of a small car intended to succeed the aging Pinto just as Japanese compacts were becoming popular. In March 1980 Henry II retired as CEO and was succeeded by Caldwell.

The losses continued. The Ford Motor Company faced reduced market share and rising labor costs. Higher development expenses were required to meet new federal standards. But some important changes were coming.

Soon after Henry Ford II retired, the Escort, successor to the Pinto, reached the showrooms. A restructuring followed; several plants were closed and over 100,000 workers were dismissed. The company inaugurated a policy of employee involvement in plant operations and secured favorable labor contracts. By 1984, with overhead reduced, productivity was growing dramatically.

In 1985 Ford introduced the Taurus, a modern, full-size automobile, which had taken five years and $3 billion to develop. The Taurus was a huge hit. It won several design and safety awards. Sales and profits reached record levels. In 1986 Ford surpassed General Motors in income for the first time since 1924. The integration of the business systems (closing plants, reducing overhead) with the human systems (employee involvement, positive labor relations) was essential to this turnaround success.

Integration at the Scale of Your Breakthrough Event

In order to create integration at the scale of your breakthrough event, you need to activate the art, science, and craft of integration.

We begin this analysis with the *science* of integration, which provides the content for the breakthrough event through operationalizing the key variables of interest. Next, we look at the *craft* of integration, which provides the process for breakthrough. Finally, we discuss the *art* of integration, which provides the context for breakthrough through creating frameworks for understanding complexity.

The Science of Integration = Operationalizing Integration

Operationalizing integration consists of the work of defining a concept and related variables, so that they can be measured and expressed quantitatively or qualitatively, using scientific methods. This empirical approach *gathers information* that is observable by the senses. It is an evidence-dependent approach. For example, suppose your objective is to reduce employee turnover. This might lead to posing the question: "Does job satisfaction influence employee turnover?" To answer this question, job satisfaction and employee turnover need to be measured. The question is based upon the hypothesis that job satisfaction might reduce employee turnover.

Operationalizing this hypothesis is the *process* of moving from the idea of *job satisfaction* through defining the concept, to selecting a questionnaire to form a job satisfaction scale. This data is collected and then compared to employee turnover data. An alternative approach might be collecting qualitative data through interviews or focus groups and then comparing the results to employee exit interviews. The processes involved are scientific *research* and *analysis*.

The Craft of Integration = Internalizing Integration

The work of internalizing integration is the work of gaining acceptance for a pending shift in norms that violate established deviations to the current norm. This investigative approach discovers and communicates established norms. One effective means for accomplishing this is to conduct a cultural survey. Many existing norms are so deeply embedded and so pervasive that they go unnoticed and therefore unquestioned. Once revealed, sharing existing norms can become part of a *participative process* designed to help individuals understand why these norms have been of value and why they made sense. This can be followed by an *instructive process* that examines external shifts (shifts in market, industry structure, product, technology) that supports the rationale for the organization's break with established norms and an adoption of new norms.

The Art of Integration = Framing Integration

Framing integration is the work of creating a basic structure to organize complex issues in an easy-to-understand conceptual frame of reference.

This co-creative approach involves designing frameworks in response to situations that arise either from adversity or from opportunity. Reacting to adversity usually requires repair, recovery, and reestablishing work so it lies within acceptable boundaries of existing performance norms. It's concerned with restoring order and increasing the probability of certainty. Here the emphasis is on a *remedial process*.

Responding to (or actually creating) opportunity, on the other hand, is generative. Its focus is upon possibility and improving the odds to break with established norms in a positive way. Often perceived as breakthrough, the focus is on new and lasting value for the organization and its stakeholders. Here the emphasis is on an *intermediating process* (see Chapter 6) and the triage of possibility, nurturing the most likely options, as we have discussed before. Considerations include best use of resources, greatest need, and the probability of success. Intermediated decisions are arrived at through alignment of various viewpoints.

We can never stress too much that it's impossible to integrate change if the basic organizational framework you start with is not whole and integrated. Most organizations are not whole systems. Most organizations tend to focus primarily on the business system and very little on the human system or the development system. When organizations undertake integration, the outcomes are too often disappointing, because the platform for the integration was not whole.

Remember Francis Fukuyama's work on efficient trust networks? A weak platform for integration will also be an inefficient trust network. You can see lack of trust as one glaring indicator of poor integration.

Summary

This chapter has explored the dynamics of trust, relationship, and communication as the foundation for breakthrough. Without healthy levels of each, breakthrough cannot occur. Breakthroughs can appear to happen accidentally, such as in the case of 3M's Post-It Notes. But breakthroughs can also be the result of a commitment to breakthroughs as a strategic imperative, as in the case of Engelhard. Breakthrough is a discipline that can be learned. Breakthroughs also often occur when a champion for an innovative idea is willing to "stand in the face of no agreement," as was the case with the Sony Walkman. Finally, the case of the Ford Taurus is described as an example of breakthrough, even when leadership at the highest levels was not performing well. In each of these cases, trust, relationship, and communication were essential.

The next chapter goes more into depth on the relationship between breakthrough and breakdown in the change integration process.

References

Block, P., Schimmelpfenig, L, and Evans, J. (2020) *Building Trust in a Virtual World.* Designed Learning: Cincinnati, OH. Retrieved from https://leadershipforachangingworld.com/broadcast/?utm_source=ONTRAPORT-email-campaign&utm_medium=ONTRAPORT-email-campaign&utm_term=&utm_content=Day+8%3A+A+Blueprint+for+Change&utm_campaign=LEAD2020+LIVE+NON+Buyers+10+Day+Summit on September 22, 2020.

Drozdiak, N., S. Arons, and S. Syed. (2020) Wirecard Auditors Say "Elaborate" Fraud Led to Missing Billions. *Accounting Today.* June 26, 2020. Retrieved from www.accountingtoday.com/articles/wirecard-auditors-say-elaborate-fraud-led-to-missing-billions on September 13, 2020.

Fukuyama, F. (1992) *The End of History and the Last Man.* New York: Free Press.

Gibb, J. (1978) *Trust: A New View of Personal and Organizational Development.* Los Angeles, CA: Guild of Tutors Press.

Krueger, J. and Kilham, E. (2006) Who's Driving Innovation at Your Company? Business Journal, September 14, 2006. Retrieved from http://news.gallup.com/businessjournal/24472/whos-driving-innovation-your-company.aspx on February 13, 2018.

Lipton, E. (2020) Social Media Offered Bannon's Group a Tool to Promote Ties to Trump and Raise Millions. *The New York Times*, August 24, 2020. Retrieved from www.nytimes.com/2020/08/24/us/politics/trump-bannon-we-build-the-wall.html on September 13, 2020.

Lucier, C., Spiegel, E., and Schuyt, R. (2002) Why CEOs Fall: The Causes and Consequences of Turnover at the Top. Retrieved from www.strategy-business.com/article/20306?gko=52e87 October 10, 2010.

Nayak, P.R. and Ketteringham, J. (1986) *Breakthroughs! How the Vision and Drive of Innovators in Sixteen Companies Created Commercial Breakthroughs That Swept the World.* New York: Rawson Associates

Neal, J. (2006) *Edgewalkers: People and Organizations that Take Risks, Build Bridges and Break New Ground.* Westport, CT: Praeger.

Reeth, M. (2020) The 7 Greatest Financial Frauds in History. *U.S. News & World Report.* July 14, 2020. Retrieved from https://money.usnews.com/investing/stock-market-news/slideshows/biggest-corporate-frauds-in-history on September 13, 2020.

Seijts, G.H. and Crim, D. (2006) What Engages Employees the Most, Or the Ten C's of Employee Engagement, March/April 2006, Reprint # 9B06TB09, Iveyn Business Journal. Retrieved from https://boardoptions.com/employeeeengagement.pdf on June 4, 2021.

8

INTEGRATING BREAKTHROUGH CHANGE

Introduction

Breakthroughs are desirable outcomes that go beyond our expectation for what's predictable. A breakdown is an outcome inconsistent with that which is intended. Breakthroughs can occur through circumstance or by intention. Breakthrough outcomes are not predictable, even with clear intention. But positive outcomes are more likely with intention.

In this chapter we describe the very important relationship between breakthroughs and breakdowns. In intentional change integration processes, breakdowns have the potential for creating further breakthroughs and should not be regarded as failures. Breakthroughs and breakdowns can both be caused by circumstance or can be intentional. We offer many examples of breakthroughs of circumstantial and intentional breakthroughs and conclude by emphasizing the role of communication, building on the material in Chapter 7 on trust, relationship, and communication.

DOI: 10.4324/9781003131847-8

Where is Integration of Breakthrough Change Needed?

Better to ask where is it not needed? Throw a dart at a list of Fortune 1000 companies and you are likely to land on a company that requires a breakthrough in at least one or more of the areas listed below. This would be true in most organizations, not just those listed by Fortune. At any given moment, contemporary corporate business models lead to a requirement for one or more of the following:

- Increased revenues,
- Higher margins,
- Larger market share,
- Development of new products,
- Building new lines of business,
- Creating new categories.

These requirements stand in the face of some hard realities. Organizations need to:

- Reduce costs,
- Shorten times from the recapture of capital investment,
- Extend product life cycles,
- Shed slow-growth categories,
- Acquire and/or invest in high-growth categories.

Economic pressure from every corner of the globe on every aspect of organizational operation is dictating the ever-increasing need for companies to produce breakthrough-level outcomes. The only way to survive is to innovate and that makes organizational-scale breakthrough everybody's undeclared strategic imperative.

Breakthroughs and Breakdowns

Breakthroughs are desirable outcomes that go beyond our expectations for what's predictable. Here is our formal definition:

A breakthrough is any outcome that exceeds, by a notable margin, highest expectations that would be remotely predictable as a function of past performance.

Breakdowns, in contrast to breakthroughs, have outcomes that are significantly short of expectations. Here is our formal definition of breakdown:

> A breakdown is an outcome inconsistent with that which is intended and to which a commitment has been made.

When you're working to achieve breakthrough-level change, you can expect that some breakdowns will happen along the way. You may even need to nudge a breakdown to get past a sticking point in a change integration. In fact, breakthroughs always cause breakdowns—the change will be destabilizing, and reactions will occur—but the reverse it not true. Breakdowns provide opportunities for breakthroughs, but they do not actually cause them.

Breakthrough can occur at almost any scale, be it personal, group, team, organizational ... or all the way up to encompassing an entire society. By integrating breakthrough-level change we also gain an opportunity to generate additional breakthroughs. Thus breakthroughs are *recursive*. At any scale, both breakdowns and breakthroughs can result from *circumstance*—be coincidental—or they can result from *intention*—being purposeful.

> Circumstantial Cause: Coincidental activity with consequences unforeseeable or unforeseen.
>
> Intentional Cause: Purposeful action with consequences unforeseeable or unforeseen.

The 1965 Northeast blackout is a well-known, societal-scale example of circumstantial breakdown. It provided opportunity for an intentional breakthrough.

Breakthroughs at the Scale of Society

1965 Northeast Blackout

On November 9, 1965 a power station in Niagara Falls, New York, unexpectedly shut down because one small protective relay the size of a coffee tin failed. The relay on the transmission line was calibrated for power demands that were exceeded at 5:16:11 pm. As it tripped, the relay triggered a chain of shutdowns that affected Ontario, Canada, Connecticut, Massachusetts, New Hampshire, Rhode Island, Vermont, New York, and New Jersey. Nearly 30 million people were left without electricity for as long as 12 hours. This breakdown led to the need for collaborative R&D in the power industry.

Breakthrough in 1970s—Collaborative R&D

In the early 1970s the U.S. Senate held hearings on the lack of R&D within all sectors of the American electric utility industry. In response, the industry voluntarily pooled member funds to begin one of the most successful collaborative R&D programs in the world. Electric Power Research Institute (EPRI, a Generative Leadership Group client) was formally established in 1973 as an independent, nonprofit organization to manage this public-private research program on behalf of the electric utilities, their customers, and society at large.

Today EPRI focuses on environmental protection, power delivery, retail use, and power markets. EPRI provides solutions and services to more than 1,000 energy-related organizations in 40 countries. Some of their breakthroughs include:

- More than 900 patents,
- The groundwork for Flexible AC Transmission Systems,
- The largest electric and magnetic fields health program in the world, playing a pivotal role in resolving scientific questions concerning potential links to cancer,
- The world's largest center for nondestructive testing, used first for nuclear inspection and now for internal diagnostics of fossil power plants and industrial systems.

To better understand the integration of breakthrough change, let's visit a few events in history. Within each of the two constant and overarching influences—*circumstantial cause* and *intentional cause*—certain grouped consistencies arise. You can depend upon *religion, warfare, environment,* and *beliefs* to create the conditions for circumstantial breakthroughs. We'll see how religious practices led to a breakthrough in timekeeping, how warfare led to a breakthrough in maps, how a big freeze led to a breakthrough in building safety, and how a certain set of false beliefs led to a breakthrough in quality of life.

Within intentional cause, *context shifts* and *goals with unexpected results* open doors to important benefits beyond wildest expectations. Princeton University's PEAR (Princeton Engineering Anomalies Research) Lab, led by

Robert Jahn and Brenda Dunne (2011), created a wealth of small-scale, statistically significant results that show a direct causal relationship between subjects' intention and otherwise random results. Their experiments using Random Number Generators (RNGs) demonstrated that one person's intention is enough to create statistically significant results, that is, deviation from established norms—or breakthroughs (Radin 2018). When there are two people in a relationship, such as a couple in love, or two people with a common intention, the results are significantly greater than those expected if the two worked alone—a strong case for alignment around organizational intentions. We define intentionality as a "state-of-mind" that increases the potential for an intended reality. When you clearly express your intention, you put the game in play and that intention becomes the focal point for alignment.

Before we look at intentional cause, let's examine four stories of circumstantial cause.

Breakthrough: Four Stories of Circumstantial Cause

Whenever we talk about breakthrough integrations, pretty soon someone repeats the old saying that "necessity is the mother of invention." This certainly applies to breakthroughs with circumstantial causes. Breakthroughs like these are never cut and dried. The changes can be gradual, over numerous recursions, with many contributors over long periods of time. The motivations are as varied as the people driving the changes, as we will see in the four short stories that follow.

A Breakthrough in Timekeeping

Were it not for the need of some medieval monks to know exactly when to pray each day, we might not have a watch to wear. The religious necessities and technical skill of the medieval monks were crucial factors in the development of modern-day clocks. Medieval religious institutions required timepieces, because daily prayer and work schedules were strictly regimented, a constant reminder in the Middle Ages that God's work was to bring order out of chaos. For centuries, regulating schedules was achieved with devices like water clocks, sundials and marked candles. For obvious reasons, these weren't very reliable. Then mechanical clocks were conceived and perfected through trial and error. Improvements were shared among religious communities. Mechanical clocks could be used to broadcast important times and durations in combination with bells, rung either by hand or by a mechanical device. The Salisbury Cathedral clock, a large, iron-framed clock without a dial, sits right in the aisle of Salisbury Cathedral in England. Some claim that this is the oldest working mechanical clock in the world (Wikipedia—Salisbury Cathedral Clock 2020).

Some Breakthroughs Beget Breakthroughs

The maps our parents and grandparents looked at in grade school geography class were made possible by cannons. The invention of the cannon—most likely a Chinese breakthrough in warfare based upon the innovative use of large balls—forced towns to reconfigure their layouts for their defenses. This new specialized science of town planning created a demand for precision surveying instruments that could measure longer distances and "turn" exact angles. The new equipment was another breakthrough that was later used to produce still another breakthrough in the accuracy of maps.

Environment and Chimneys

The fireplace you enjoy during winter months descends from a hot new idea that was all the rage when a cold snap in Europe lasted several hundred years. In the 12th century, fireplaces with chimneys appeared in northern Europe in response to a bitterly cold period. Chimneys provided a safer method to direct sparks and smoke up from rooms indoors and away from rooftops outside. Safer living spaces allowed for the luxury of several fires to heat a single building, creating more warmth and light. People could move their activities inside, work and play longer hours more comfortably. Chimneys radically changed how people lived in buildings and the ways that they used their buildings.

False Beliefs and Air Conditioning: A Cool Combination!

The air conditioning we take for granted is possible because someone held a hair-brained notion about disease. Dr. John Gorrie, a 19th-century Apalachicola, Florida, physician is considered to be the father of refrigeration and air conditioning, because he believed in the miasma theory that heat and "bad air" from swamps caused malaria. He was wrong (and others with him!). However, his belief inspired him to experiment with new compressor technology to try to cool the air for patients in his small hospital. In time, his experiments paid off and he was able to freeze enough water into ice to create air conditioning. Dr. Gorrie had a vision that one day his invention would be used to cool large buildings and even cities. He never lived to see that day, but as we know from personal experience, it did come (Wikipedia—John Gorrie 2020).

Breakthrough: Three Stories of Intentional Cause

Upon deeper consideration of the idea that necessity is the mother of invention, we'd like to distinguish that most inventions are actually the brainchildren of intent. An invention starts with some specific purpose. The inventor is searching for a one-time, exclusive solution to a problem. The search is not so much out of necessity as it is based upon perceived benefit. There's often a motive of profit driving the invention. But then something unexpected happens and the breakthrough takes the inventor in a new direction that could never have been anticipated.

From Organs to Looms: When Existing Technology Goes Visiting

Aunt Agnes could afford those fancy paisley cushions in her living room because in 1801 French weavers transferred an existing technology into a new context. They saw it might be possible to apply principles behind an invention used for controlling automatic organs to build looms capable of weaving complex, repeatable patterns. The breakthrough result was the Jacquard Mechanical Loom. It was controlled by punch cards. This innovation allowed Joseph Marie Jacquard to use his loom to manufacture elegant textiles at affordable prices. If Jacquard were advised by a modern-day business consultant, the accomplishment would be characterized as "having monetized hole-punch technology by successfully scaling its application to looms."

Surprise! A New Product Category Arises When Intention and Chance Combine

This one will make you wonder just how many possibilities in your company are lost because the outcome doesn't match the goal. William

Perkins, in London in the mid-19th century, was attempting to make artificial quinine. The white powder he produced was not quinine. Whether in frustration or from curiosity, he threw it in some water; the liquid suddenly turned a beautiful mauve. Perkins had invented the first artificial dye entirely by chance.

Communication Drives the Velocity of Change

What's making change happen faster? Increases in the ease and speed of communication are primarily responsible. Here are two macro examples:

1. Following the Dark Ages, there was a surge of invention in Europe once safe communication between cities was established.

   In the 1450s one such invention was the printing press. By the 16th century this breakthrough led to the ability to print affordable books in large numbers, which gave scientists the means to share their discoveries with multiple others.

2. About a hundred years ago we marked the emergence of telecommunications. Here we have, perhaps, the best modern-day example of a correlation between ease of communication and rate of change.

Using book publishing and telecommunication as our starting point, let's examine how the rate of change increases with the ease and speed of communication.

Publishing

The ability to publish knowledge in machine-printed books marked the beginning of the rapid growth of *specialization*. It allowed those who specialized, like scientists, to coin and publish terms that only others in their fields could understand—professional jargon. It's interesting to watch the ripple effect (and paradox!) that developed with the printing press. One breakthrough change—the printing press—allowed for faster and easier and more communication. Improved communication led to specialization, a breakthrough for building knowledge but also a breakdown, because specialization is the most challenging barrier to the integration of change in organization. Specialization both helps and hinders communication.

When any big change is underway, it is not uncommon to find that the specialists and executive leaders who are introducing the change don't speak in terms meaningful to those at other levels within their organizations who must cope with the integration. Precious little of the information imparted helps us to see how we will be impacted or how we can support the change beyond doing what we're told to do or how the organization will register the difference we and others make. Is this new arcane language a power play on the part of the change initiators? Hardly. This stressful situation happens because in many ways *change* and *integration* are also developing their own specialized vocabulary as the process unfolds. Even the change sponsors are asking one another, "So what is it we're doing here? Can you repeat that, please?"

Telecommunication

A later familiar breakthrough in the speed and ease of communication, telecommunication significantly increased expansion opportunities for trade and commerce. Businesses grew in number and size. The complexity of doing business increased accordingly, and integrating changes in the ways in which business was conducted grew increasingly difficult. As commerce grew, out of necessity organizations of all types began to subdivide work into specialized activities. Each specialization created its own lexicon. Over time these specialized activities broadened into specialized fields of learning, each with its own language. Today, we take many specializations for granted and can find many types represented in the management sciences.

Breakdowns and Breakthroughs—The Practices
Principles for Change Integration

Does our knowing that these and other breakthroughs have all happened, help us to cause new breakthroughs or increase our ability to integrate change? In other words, if we somehow recognize patterns and influences, can we plan in advance to leverage and manipulate change? Not likely! There are too many variables and permutations. That is Newtonian thinking, and breakthroughs are built on quantum thinking—being open to unpredictable possibilities.

There is *no* way to know enough before engaging with change, but important learning happens in your engagement with change itself. There is *no* way to know if something you are creating will eventually be useful or where it will lead. It is virtually impossible to forecast change with one exception—the *rate* at which change will occur. It's going to occur faster than it did before. Abundant historical evidence suggests that this is a predictable constant (Aburdene 2005). At best, you can be prepared to follow wherever the path of breakthrough may lead. We conclude this section with two guiding principles of change integration.

1. If you're not prepared to be wrong, you can't lead a change initiative.
2. If you're not prepared to be surprised, you can't integrate change.

Working Through Breakdowns

Leaders are distinguished by their ability to quickly adapt and re-group their efforts to restore momentum to their initiative. When momentum is lost, we call this a "breakdown." This can occur when the project is stalled, when you encounter unanticipated results or there is conflict between people. In this section, we will examine the nature of breakdowns and discover how to turn breakdowns around quickly.

Any time you take on a big commitment or commit to a big result, you will inevitably have breakdowns. It is almost impossible to foresee every element of a project plan (and probably not a good use of the team's time to even try!). Once a project is in action, unforeseen circumstances and interim results will undoubtedly surprise or thwart the original intentions of a team.

Breakdowns are good indicators of what is missing in a project or in teamwork, and so are useful to understand. It is also important to know how to get projects back on track quickly. Breakdowns can also be opportunities for breakthroughs!

Using these tools, you will be better able to:

*   "Mine" or analyze breakdowns for learnings.
*   Turn breakdowns around with power and velocity to get projects back on track.

- Treat setbacks as an opportunity to catalyze team communication, innovation and refocused action.

Process for Resolving Breakdowns

It is helpful to follow along by looking at Figure 8.1 as you read.

1. Declare the breakdown. Remember, it can only be a breakdown because there is a commitment in the background.
2. What is the commitment in the background that has this be a breakdown? It is important here to have the commitment at the same scale as the breakdown, i.e., at the systems level, team level, or interpersonal level.
3. State "what happened." Distinguish the facts and interpretations. List the facts only, no interpretations.
4. Ask: "Are we committed to the original vision, project, result?" If not, then there is no longer a breakdown.
5. If you are still committed, do a quick analysis. Regarding fulfilling on your commitment, ask:

   - What is working and making a difference?
   - What is not working, that if it were would make a difference?
   - What is missing, that if it were provided would make a difference?
   - What is working but making no difference?

6. Go through the conversations:

   - Relationship: Is relationship missing? On the team? Between the team and the project?
   - Possibility: Brainstorm all the possible ideas and actions. Look to leverage what is working, fix what is not working, and provide what is missing. This is where the opportunity for a breakthrough may occur.
   - Opportunity: Create the pathways that make the possibilities real.
   - Action: Who's going to do what by when?
   - Completion: Who needs to be told? Acknowledged?

7. You're back in business!

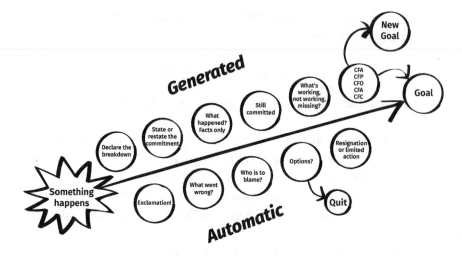

Figure 8.1 Process for Working Through Breakdowns

Breakthrough Process

When we say "breakthrough," we mean a result that is created under a very specific set of conditions, as we shared in the overview of this book:

1. Not predictable from past performance, even highly successful past performance; a quantum leap in results; one that is discontinuous with the past.
2. Produces significant value in terms of forwarding the organization's vision and/or goals.
3. Creates a new reality for the organization about what is possible.
4. Is committed to in advance, without knowing how.

Some notes about these conditions:

- You can't have condition #1 without clear measures in place, including measures for the results that would be produced under "business as usual" conditions.
- You can't have condition #2 without a clear view of the organization's vision, mission and goals.
- Condition #3 is the difference between a breakthrough and a breakthrough outcome. It is possible that a result can be produced that is beyond what is predictable, but has no lasting effect on the organization's view of what is possible; it is, therefore, the organizational

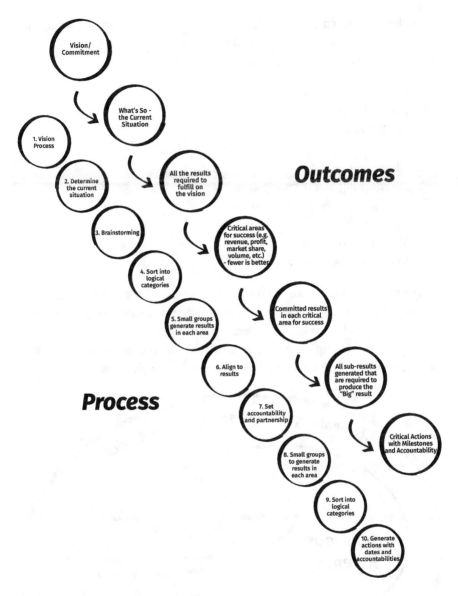

Figure 8.2 Breakthrough Framework

equivalent of what would be a "peak experience" for an individual. A breakthrough, on the other hand, includes one or more breakthrough outcomes and leaves the organization at a new level of possibility in performance.

- Regarding condition #4: If it's not committed to in advance, it's a happy accident, not a breakthrough.

To design and achieve breakthroughs, you will need to know, be able to use, and learn to think from a number of "foundational concepts" which have been discussed throughout this book:

1. Generous listening
2. Point of view
3. Earned and granted trust
4. Scale
5. Alignment
6. All speaking and listening create reality
7. Context, process and content
8. Source of action
9. What is obvious, isn't
10. Co-creation and ownership.

The Concept Map indicates the relationship of these ideas. For example, by looking at the map you can see that co-creation is related to generous listening, trust, and point of view. Here is a useful exercise: Look at the map, see if you can determine why and how each distinction is related to the others, and how they are related to your Breakthrough Initiative.

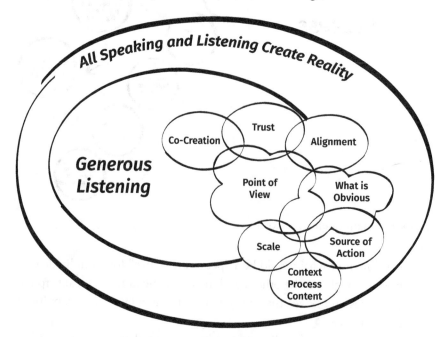

Figure 8.3 Breakthrough Concept Map

More About Intention

Throughout this and the previous chapter we have talked about the importance of intention in creating breakthroughs. The impact of intention varies significantly based on your view of organizations.

In the traditional view of organizations, the structures are rigid and hierarchical, and the person at the top of the hierarchy is expected to have the answers and tell everyone else what to do and how to do it.

In the view of organizations and leadership we present in this book, organizations are seen as complex, living systems, continually changing and adapting. Leadership is distinguished from management, and the role of the leader is one of guiding, influencing, and co-creating an environment in which people can flourish and contribute to their fullest. Leaders create fresh and novel possibilities that draw the organization toward a new future. To do this, we as leaders must be clear about what we are creating around us. Our organizations will be a reflection of our leadership.

Consider this example from the physical world: imagine you have a bottle of baby oil with iron filings in it. If you hold a magnet up to the side of the bottle, you can see the magnetic field that is created, as the iron filings dance through the oil, forming patterns within the magnetic field.

This is one way to think about leadership—like a magnetic field forming patterns of action consistent with our intention. Leaders set up conditions that create a "field" around them, similar to a magnetic field. This field attracts some behaviors and outcomes and not others, just like the magnet attracts iron filings and not plastic pellets.

So how do we do this? How do we create a field that attracts the outcomes we desire? One way is by being very clear about our intentions. By creating clear intentions and communicating them broadly, we can affect our relationship with behaviors and outcomes, like the magnet attracts iron filings into clearly formed patterns.

A business vision and mission statement is also an intention. These types of documents, when they are brought to life in an organization like the J&J Credo, create a field that helps guide people's action in many different situations.

Creating intentions matters. Having a clearly defined and articulated intention helps to guide our actions and influence outcomes in surprising and powerful ways.

The Power of Intention

There is a great deal of both scientific and philosophic evidence for the power of intention to affect the world around us. We discussed the PEAR findings at the beginning of this chapter. Quantum physics is discovering many kinds of new relationships between particles, one of the most stunning being the "entanglement" of particles at a distance—the concept of "non-locality" (Radin 2006). According to Chris Laszlo:

> [W]hen two quantum entities are paired, they become intermingled in such a way as to remain forever linked together. Once connected, their wave functions become phase entangled with each other, such that there are no longer two independent wave functions but one which encompasses both quantum entities evermore. Even when separated over large distances, and diverted along different axes, the paired bonding remains instantaneous.
>
> All the results are, to a very good approximation, what quantum mechanics predicts. One striking fact emerges: that entanglement is non-local. i.e. it is not due to local hidden variables as Einstein/ Podolsky/ Rosen had postulated in their "EPR paradox" first advanced in 1935.
>
> (Laszlo 2021)

In Meg Wheatley's book *Leadership and the New Science*, she discusses the idea from quantum mechanics, in which relationship is the key determiner of everything. Werner Heisenberg, a prominent physicist, characterized the world as "a complicated tissue of events, in which connections of different kinds alternate or overlap or combine and thereby determine the texture of the whole." Wheatley continues, "These unseen connections between what were previously thought to be separate entities are the fundamental ingredient of all creation" (Wheatley 1994: 11). We would say that intention is one of these unseen connections. In organizational application, creating clear, shared intentions for breakthrough (without having to know how it may occur) is a form of human "quantum entanglement" that keeps the team aligned, even when separated over large distances.

Prayer, or sending healing energy or white light, is another example of intention. Scientific experiments have validated the effectiveness of this form of intention as well. Holt (2001) reported a Columbia University study found that women at a fertility clinic were almost twice as likely to get pregnant when, unknown to them, total strangers were praying for their success. The clinic was in Korea, and the praying strangers were members of various Christian denominations in the United States, Canada, and Australia. Women in the prayed-for group had a pregnancy rate of about 50 percent, versus 26 percent for women in the control group. The Columbia researchers expressed surprise at the magnitude of this difference, saying that they did not expect to find any benefit to prayer at all.

Business vision and mission statements are also intentions. These documents, when they are brought to life in an organization like the J&J Credo, create a field that helps guide people's action in many different situations.

Creating intentions matters. Having a clearly defined and articulated intention helps to guide our actions and influence outcomes in surprising and powerful ways. The following exercise has been used by GLG clients and our students to use the Attractor Model to create intentions.

Process for Creating an Intention

Using the Intention Attractor Model in Figure 8.4 with your team, answer the following four questions:

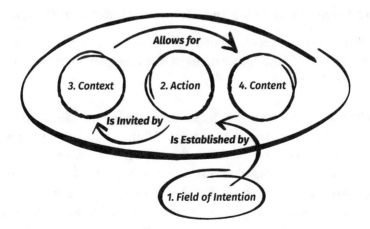

Figure 8.4 Intention Attractor Model

1. What is the *field of intention* that you want to create? What do you want the coming year to be like? What do you want to establish for yourself, your team, or function? (Write your response on a post-it and put it in the bottom oval.)
2. What *actions* will most allow that field to be established? What actions will give rise to that field of intention? (Write your response on a post-it and put it in the middle circle.)
3. What *context* do we need to create that will invite those actions? What meaning, future, or culture will most invite the desired actions? (Write your response on a post-it and put it in the left-hand circle.)
4. What *content* most allows for that context? What do we need to have in order to create that future, vision, culture, meaning? (Write your response on a post-it and put it in the right-hand circle.)

Now, check for resonance, for internal validity. Read through your statement, starting from the field of intention and following the steps in the order in which you placed them. Read through it again, this time starting from the content—which allows for the context—which invites the action—which establishes the intention.

Do both ways make sense to you? Do they validate your experience? Does it create your desired outcomes? If not, but you like the ideas on the post-its, try moving them around. Or ... start fresh! Trust your instincts. Listen for fit and resonance (does it "ring true" or go "cha-ching"?).

Some Examples of Using the Attractor Model as a Design Tool

Our clients and students have used the model as a design tool at many scales (individual, team, organizational, for example) and for many purposes, including:

*   *Designing culture change:* Use the model to distinguish the elements that comprise the inherited or current culture, and then use it again to create the desired elements of your intended, newly created culture.
*   *Creating successful teamwork:* What do we have to do? What do we have to have, in order to do that? Who do we have to be, to produce the intended outcomes? You can also use the model to determine whether or not leadership, management, and development are all present on the team, by putting people's names in the circles based on their preferred mode of operation, and seeing if the team is properly composed

to produce the desired outcomes. You can also match the required attributes of the project to the team composition. For example, when you are creating something new, you will probably need more leadership and development than management. As the project progresses, management may become more important. Does your team composition match what is required for the project at that point in time?

- *Planning a meeting*: What do we want people to know as a result of this meeting? To feel? To do? What is the intention we want to create for this meeting? By being clear about your intentions, you can give yourself some flexibility in the actions you take. You can then use your intention to determine the appropriate actions to take, rather than sticking to a predetermined series of steps, especially if you sense they are not producing the desired outcomes.

- *Creating a purpose and intention for the year – or for a day*: Use the model to create a vision statement for the organization, your team, your self. Create your intention for the day, or the week, or a project. What is the field I/ we want to create? What actions will establish that field? What context will invite those actions? What content will allow for those actions?

Notes for More Advanced Use of the Attractor Model

The Attractor Model is very flexible, and can be used starting at any point in the diagram.

The "traditional" way to use it is to start with the content. Once that is clear, look to see what context that allows for. When the context is clear, decide what actions the context will invite. Then look to see the field that is established by those actions.

If you are clear about the vision (the future or context), work forward to the actions that the context invites … and then work back to see what content will most allow for the desired context.

The model can be used to distinguish the existing state, as well as to create a new or desired state. Remember that the model can be used at any scale, from a short phone call or meeting, to a year-long vision, to determining your life purpose.

In addition to designing projects and intentions, you can also use the model to establish your relationships—with your spouse, kids, parents, boss, and/or direct reports. Think about what you want life to be like with them and create the field, and so on. See what shows up! The best way to see what it's good for is to try it out, and practice with it in lots of different situations!

Summary

It's hard to imagine an organization that does not need some form of breakthrough change, given the rapidly changing and unpredictable environment. As a reminder, we define breakthrough as "any outcome that exceeds, by a notable margin, the highest expectations that would be remotely predictable as a function of past performance." A breakdown is "an outcome inconsistent with that which is intended and to which a commitment has been made." Breakthroughs always provide breakdowns, but the opposite is not necessarily true. Breakdowns can be an opportunity for additional breakthroughs.

Either breakdowns or breakthroughs can be either circumstantial, which calls for a reaction. Both have the potential for positive results. And breakdowns and breakthroughs can both be intentional, most likely leading to results far beyond expectations, and to establishing a recursive pattern of breakthrough results that can become embedded in the culture as "the way we do things here."

In this chapter we provided several cases of circumstantial and intentional breakthrough change, as well as process steps to guide your Breakthrough Initiative. The Intention Attractor Model is a very specific "machine tool" that can guide you and your team in creating your intention for your Breakthrough Initiative, and we encourage you to utilize this in a way that works for your team and your unique situation, challenges, and opportunities.

In the next chapter we offer Toomey's Three Laws for Integrating Change, along with more cases to help reveal the underlying patterns of these processes for breakthrough change and organizational transformation.

References

Aburdene, P. (2005) *Megatrends 2010: The Rise of Conscious Capitalism.* Newburyport, MA: Hampton Roads Publishing.

Holt, J. (2001) The Year in Ideas: A to Z: Prayer Works. *New York Times Magazine.* Retrieved from www.nytimes.com/2001/12/09/magazine/the-year-in-ideas-a-to-z-prayer-works.html on January 4, 2021.

Jahn, R. and B. Dunne (2011) *Consciousness and the Source of Reality: The PEAR Odyssey.* Princeton, NJ: ICRL Publishers.

Laszlo, C. (2021) *Quantum Physics and its Ontological Implications: A Primer for Management Scholars and Practitioners.* Unpublished document.

Radin, D. (2006) *Entangled Minds: Extrasensory Experiences in Quantum Reality.* New York: Paraview Pocket Books.

Radin, D. (2018) *Real Magic: Ancient Wisdom, Modern Science, and a Guide to the Secret Power of the Universe.* New York: Harmony Books,

Shaw, G. B. (1903) *Maxims for Revolutionists.* Scotts Valley, CA: CreateSpace Publishing.

Wikipedia (2020) John Gorrie. Retrieved from http://en.wikipedia.org/wiki/John_Gorrie on November 8, 2020.

Wikipedia (2020) Salisbury Cathedral Clock. Retrieved from https://en.wikipedia.org/wiki/Salisbury_Cathedral_clock on November 8, 2020.

9

TOOMEY'S LAWS OF INTEGRATING CHANGE

There is nothing more difficult to carry out nor more doubtful of success, nor more dangerous to handle, than to initiate a new order of things. For the reformer has enemies in all who profit by the old order, and only lukewarm defenders in all those who would profit by the new order. The lukewarmness arises partly from the fear of their adversaries who have law in their favor; and partly from the incredulity of mankind, who do not truly believe in anything new until they have had actual experience of it.

Machiavelli

Introduction: With a Big Nod to Newton

As we said earlier, the rulebook for change integration has not been written, and it is unlikely there will be a rulebook anytime soon. However, there may be *laws* for integrating change that can provide some guidance. We propose three universal laws as a starting point. But first an acknowledgment is in order.

It is said that plagiarism is a high form of praise. In this sense our "three laws for change integration" are high praise for Sir Isaac Newton, because we have unabashedly borrowed upon his "three laws of motion"

DOI: 10.4324/9781003131847-9

in modified form for our purposes. Newton did the heavy lifting and basic thinking. We have taken his breakthrough work in physics for use in a different context. This is a good example of *innovation*. Innovation is a form of change that is the product of intention. We innovate by taking something that has been established and applying it in a new way, for different purposes with the intention of producing a useful outcome. The Jacquard Mechanical Loom mentioned earlier was another innovation.

Here's the quick refresher on Newton's three laws of motion. His laws are used to explain *cause and effect* phenomena observable in the physical world. In their most simplified form, they are:

1. A body persists in its state of rest or of uniform motion unless acted upon by an external force.
2. The net force on an object is equal to the mass of the object multiplied by its acceleration.
3. To every action there is an equal and opposite reaction.

Editing each of Newton's laws of motion, while maintaining the integrity of his thinking, brings new meaning to the nature of integrating change in organization.

Building on Newton's three laws of motion, we offer these three laws of change integration:

Toomey's Laws for Integrating Change

Toomey's First Law for Change Integration

Survival and change amenability are inversely related.

The longer a system survives, the less amenable it is to change. For example, an organization persists in its current state in the absence of an energetic intervention. It is a natural tendency of an organization to keep on doing what it's doing, like Newton's body in motion. All organizations resist

Table 9.1 Toomey's Laws for Integrating Change

First Law	Survival and change amenability are inversely related.
Second Law	The work needed to change is equal to the complexity of the system multiplied by the needed rate of the change.
Third Law	To every act of change integration there is an equal and opposite reaction directed at disintegrating the change.

changes to whatever state they are in. In the absence of an intervention, an organization will maintain its state—homeostasis. From the organizational perspective, interventions are a form of "unbalanced energy." This kind of energy is the ally of leadership and the bane of management. Leadership generates interventions to create discontinuous change—to shake things up, move forward, and keep ahead of the curve. Remember the *disintermediation through facilitated intervention* conversation in Chapter 6? Management is charged to maintain states of reliability, predictability, and certainty, so it strives to neutralize unbalanced energies. It's little wonder that there can be so much tension around integrating change.

Toomey's Second Law for Change Integration:

The work needed to change is equal to the complexity of the system multiplied by the needed rate of the change.

Three corollaries to the Second Law for Change Integration are:

- A system's complexity is a function of the number of specializations and their interrelatedness.
- The capacity to absorb change increases with each successful change.
- The capability to cause change may exist at levels that exceed the organization's capacity to absorb change.

Change is initiated when work is directed at the organization to be changed, the target system. The greater the complexity of the system, the more energy (work) is needed to initiate change. If you are wanting to create a stronger culture of customer service, it will take a lot more work to initiate change in a large pharmaceutical company than in a small family clinic.

When integrating change, a balance between capacity and change can be achieved by modulating the expected rate of change against the capacity of the system to absorb change. Here we are using "capacity" to refer to the amount of tolerance available to receive or accommodate destabilizing energy, as opposed to the four capacities for integration—create, innovate, adapt and react—identified in Chapter 6. Carefully stretching an organization's capacity to absorb change by modulating the frequency and amplitude of the change being integrated reduces uncertainty, minimizes collateral damage, and grows more capacity (Conner 2006). Apple is an organization that shines in this area.

Sometimes an organization has the capability—technology and "brain power"—to effect change, and does so, without being able to absorb the destabilizing energy that it releases. Several such events come to mind; the deployment of the atom bomb to end World War II and the BP oil spill in the Gulf of Mexico are just two.

Toomey's Third Law for Change Integration

To every act of change integration there is an equal and opposite reaction directed at disintegrating the change.

Experienced leaders know it best—estimate the amount of work needed for integration and then double the estimate. (And now the budget will only be exceeded by half the amount it would have been otherwise!) This means that the system naturally works to counter attempts to change it. Skillfully designed change integrations absorb and neutralize this "reactive energy." It also follows that every large-scale change requires a certain amount of work to integrate change and additional work to neutralize and convert opposing forces (Lewin 1943, Kegan and Lahey 2009). Typically, in organizations the planning for change integration fails to account for the additional work required to stabilize and sustain changes that constitute discontinuities for the system.

Disintegration: When Organizational-Scale Communication is Missing

Ever wonder why, when a business emergency occurs or when there is a material decline in performance, there often appears a positive response from employees? People rally. There is an organic response to emergency circumstances. Ad hoc groups and teams form to deal with the issues. Differences and disputes are set aside, and adversaries work together. Situations that appear to be dangerous and emergencies are circumstances that provide clear consequences for a failure to take corrective action. The amplitude of the breakdown overrides most barriers and people are motivated to figure out how to communicate and work together.

On the other hand, have you ever wondered why compelling new opportunities fail, particularly those with apparent potential to break with existing norms? Let's use British Petroleum (BP) and their campaign to go "Beyond Petroleum" as an example. Despite a well-publicized, well-financed foray into new sources for energy, the alternative energy business offices for BP closed, investment was cut, and its chief executive took early retirement according to a *Financial Times* article (Crooks 2009). A dramatic but not uncommon example, BP belongs to an industry faced with extinction if the company does not transform and it chooses to hunker down around its core business. But somehow the core became sloppy and BP was criticized for taking its eye off the ball. How did BP loosen its grip on the core business in the first place? What did BP sacrifice in declaring its position as an industry leader in alternative energy?

Crooks (2009) wrote:

> Rarely have two words proved as powerful, or as troublesome, for a company's reputation as "beyond petroleum." Launched in July 2000, the slogan—with a new logo and a lavish advertising budget—sent BP's brand awareness soaring in the U.S. and helped it craft an image as the world's best-run oil company. <u>Critics argued that it also sent a message to the majority of the company's workforce that theirs was an outdated part of the business.</u> It also set BP up for attacks from green campaigners, who could never be persuaded that the company had done enough to live up to its promise …
>
> … [E]ven the biggest enthusiasts failed to predict the slogan's impact. While the detail of BP's advertising made it clear the company was setting out in a new direction rather than changing overnight, the impression was created that it was no longer in the dirty—and sometimes hazardous—old oil and gas business.
>
> There was substance behind the slogan: BP committed more strongly to renewables than other oil companies. <u>Its downfall was that it failed to maintain the highest standards in its core business</u>. When problems emerged, they were seized on vigorously by BP's critics.

We have underlined two seemingly unrelated statements from the *Financial Times* article, because we think these explain why BP lost its grip on the core business.

The first statement:

<u>Critics argued that it also sent a message to the majority of the company's workforce that theirs was an outdated part of the business.</u>

The critics' observations were ignored. BP treated the warnings as mere speculation in the swirl of commentary on the new corporate direction.

Surely stakeholders and the public could see the bigger picture. The message that BP sent in 2000 announcing the new slogan "Beyond Petroleum" was right on the money for the world's needs, where the industry needed to focus, and promised a bright new future for BP and its workforce.

The CEO's declaration was no empty statement. Capital was allocated; a new logo was adopted, and an aggressive ad campaign followed. The message raised brand awareness and polished up the BP image, both very desirable outcomes. By promising to take leadership in finding alternative energy sources the CEO took a courageous stand on BP's behalf. Certainly, all would come to see the wisdom of this momentous course of action.

Given that BP is an energy company built on petroleum-based products, this new direction with its clear and compelling intentions would require fulfilling upon many breakthroughs. BP has a long history of engaging in breakthrough work and in developing leaders who can lead breakthroughs. So there was no reason to believe that this company-wide initiative would not succeed. What was missed?

Executive leadership at BP failed to recognize how business systems and human systems interrelate at the scale of organization. The announcement might have made explicit that the new endeavor was possible only because the excellent work accomplished by people in the core business would be the company's rock-solid foundation for transition into the future. Instead, BP put a macro game into play: The core business was pitted against "the new thing." The deadly game of "us against them" is never conducive to the integration of change. Put on the defensive, people are marginalized. They cannot see how their day-to-day jobs will contribute to making a difference. Nor can they see ahead to how their "obsolete" team or division will fit into a changed organization.

This leads us to the second statement:

> Its downfall was that it failed to maintain the highest standards in its core business.

Obviously, BP didn't do "downfall"; companies don't do anything. It is people who do things. One thing they do is to contribute excellence, but another thing they can do is to withdraw their contribution. When people contribute excellent work, they communicate that they believe in what they are doing. They can see how their work makes a difference and their work occurs for them as relevant. A company cannot buy excellence from its employees. Time, work, and reasonable quality can be purchased, but excellence is a gift given by employees. This gift maintains the high standards that every company needs in order to thrive. But the workforce at BP withdrew their gift. Over time, their pain in being marginalized was communicated in terms of sinking performance. The second underlined statement, "it failed to maintain the highest standards," reflects how employees at BP sent a message back to leadership.

It's this simple: People, business, and organization are one. There is no business or organization without people and these people are listening very carefully to what their leaders have to say. This seems obvious on its face. Why don't we design and integrate companies like this is true? Human performance in all its forms depends upon trust, communication, and relationship (Chapter 7).

As if the first insult in 2000 were not enough, the new president of BP, Tony Hayward, issued another slap in 2007. He remarked that BP had "too many people that were working to save the world." How many times does the same lesson need to be delivered before leaders see that people—not just some people, but all—in an organization are an interrelated whole? It's this simple: People, business, and organization are one. There is no business or organization without people and these people are listening very carefully to what their leaders have to say.

The quality of any business, its products and services, is mainly dependent upon employees and their relationship with the business end of the organization. Yet leadership too often takes that relationship for granted and behaves as if signing on for the job makes it reasonable to expect high performance. This is valid only up to a point. The limits to application are reached when a compelling reason to rise above a prevailing norm surfaces within the organization. Human performance in all its forms depends upon trust, communication, and relationship. Employees in an empowered relationship with their organization are a source of energy, flexibility, and creativity. That priceless equity is lost when human systems and business systems are not integrated. BP missed integration and this oversight was ultimately the source of its downfall.

Breakthrough—Art, Craft, and Science

At this moment, before we proceed further, let's briefly review what we've been discussing.

Breakthroughs at inception take form through art, the work of leadership; they are creations. Therefore, conceiving a breakthrough is an art form.

Breakthroughs have the quality and impart the feeling of being unique. Each is very much one of a kind, beginning existence as somebody's inspiration, which is the case with all art.

Once in demonstrable form, breakthroughs move from the conceptual level of *art* toward functional reality via *craft, the work of integration*. A good example of the role of craft is the Sony Walkman. Its first expression, while functional and working in Sony laboratories, was crude in comparison to the portable little marvel that started the "small" revolution in consumer electronics. During *craft*, the path that the rough prototype followed from the lab to a finished product was, in part, a function of *dialectics*. (Should it look like this or like that? Should it work like this or like that?)

In *craft* the focus moves from "Can we make it work?" to "Can it be made to be effective?" Now more refined examples of the possibility demonstrated in the lab are crafted and tested. Can a prototype work smoother or faster … be bigger or smaller … cost less to produce … or look more attractive? Only once the *craft* phase has demonstrated reasonable feasibility and efficacy, is the last phase, *science*, undertaken.

With science, the work of management, the game takes a turn to *method* and *methodologies*. It's all about efficiency, cost reduction, and quality control. In this phase multiple disciplinary areas must coordinate: manufacturing, packaging, branding, distribution, marketing, sales, and service.

These three phases—*art, craft,* and *science*—are all forms of integration, each with unique effects and unique challenges. For the successful integration of breakthrough change, the "artful" leaders, the "crafty" integrators, and the "methodical" managers will keep communication flowing vertically and horizontally through all the levels of organization, until a new organizational paradigm is safely in place and all the stakeholders are satisfied winners in the new game. We can think of no better example of the relevant phases that art, craft, and science play in breakthrough than this story of change that took 800 years to integrate, as breakthroughs begot others.

Double-Entry Bookkeeping: 800 Years of Integrating Breakthrough

Art in 1211

Eight hundred years ago a breakthrough occurred that planted the seeds of modern bookkeeping. We can see the earliest known evidence of what we now know as the double-entry-system in paper fragments found in Florence, Italy, and dated 1211. The fragments were once part of an account book that belonged to a Florentine banker. Why would we consider this newly conceived idea from the science of mathematics to be an art form? Because it was born in the realm of creativity. From 1211 forward we can watch bookkeeping evolve and integrate.

Craft in 1458

As the practice of double-entry grew in the fertile soil of commerce in Renaissance Italy it began to shift from art form to craft. This phase took over 250 years. The "rules" were developed and codified through trial and error. Benedetto Cotrugli is believed to have written the first book to mention double-entry bookkeeping in 1458. It was titled *Libro de l'Arte de la Mercatura* (*Book on the Art of Trade*) (Cotrugli 1458). His and other similar hand-written manuscripts circulated throughout Italian city-states during the 15th century. We next see that in Venice in 1494 the Italian monk Luca Pacioli published a book on mathematics. *Summa de Arithmetica, Geometria, Proportioni et Proportionalita* (*Everything About Arithmetic, Geometry and Proportion*) was a digest and guide to mathematical knowledge, a kind of "Everyday Math for Dummies." Double-entry bookkeeping was one of five topics covered in 36 brief chapters. *The Rules of Double-Entry Bookkeeping: Paticularis de computis et scripturis*, excerpted from *Summa de Arithmetica*, is still available on Amazon. com (Pacioli 2010). He made no claim to the invention of the double-entry system. He is, however, generally recognized as the author of the first published double-entry bookkeeping text.

Science in 1890

In the craft phase of bookkeeping, work was done by hand. Some rules were developed that allowed for shortcuts in record keeping, but it was still all work by hand. Then in 1880 a clear and compelling need for speed with accuracy presented itself. The U.S. Constitution mandates a census every ten years to apportion taxation between the states and to determine Congressional representation. Thanks to the rapid growth of the U.S. population, the 1880 U.S. Census took seven years to complete, which made the data already obsolete by the time it was tabulated. Between 1880 and 1890, immigration continued to drive the population explosion. The Department of Commerce feared that if the snail's pace 1880 processes were used, the 1890 census could take over 13 years to complete.

They found a faster way—remember punch cards used to manufacture the intricate patterns of Jacquard weaving discussed in Chapter 8? The German-American statistician Herman Hollerith invented a mechanical tabulator. Once again based upon punch cards, it could rapidly tabulate statistics from data. The advantages of his technology were obvious for accounting and tracking inventory. Hollerith founded the Tabulating Machine Company in 1896. In 1911, four corporations, including Hollerith's firm, merged to form the Computing Tabulating Recording Corporation (CTR). Under President Thomas J. Watson, it was renamed International Business Machines (IBM) in 1924. Tabulators were used widely until 1940 when the first electronic computers began to appear. Here's a bird's eye view of the progression of the science of automated bookkeeping:

From the first tabulators to the early accounting machines (also called bookkeeping machines), to today's super computers, a myriad of applications have developed for recording data and reporting information. Today companies of all sizes have ready access to bookkeeping, accounting, and finance applications.

The capability in computer technology from 1990 forward allows for huge and complex applications. Today's *Enterprise Resource Planning* (ERP) systems such as SAP and Oracle, exemplify just two of many. While obvious, it's worth noting that advances in any technology lead to corresponding advances in application and compounded complexity. These combined factors necessitate the integration of change on a company-wide scale and the concurrent integration of breakthroughs at multiple levels.

Table 9.2 Progression of the Science of Automated Bookkeeping

Year	Technology
1880	Hollerith Census Tabulator
1940	Computers based on vacuum tubes
1960	Computers based on discrete transistors
1964	Computers based on Solid Logic Technology (SLT)
1981	Computers based on microprocessor central processing units (CPUs)
1990	Computers based on discrete integrated circuits (IC) CPUs

As growing complexity drives the need for breakthrough at multiple levels, so the rate at which breakthroughs are required is increasing just so we can cope. Viewed from our current perspective, some might say that this 800-year historical outline is a continuous integration of breakthrough change all in the name of saving time. It began slowly and inconspicuously with one initial notion of double-entry bookkeeping and has gained momentum right through to automated ERP, accounting, and financial systems. Are we there yet? When do our heads stop spinning?

From this page forward, each story you read in the book will demonstrate successful change integrations. We have already shared with you a number of breakthroughs at the scale of society, beginning with the 1965 blackout and ending with double-entry bookkeeping. Let's turn now to look at breakthrough at the scale of organization and two companies that amply demonstrate that concept. We invite you to consider, too, that both companies were led by individuals who were deeply committed to improving communication.

Breakthrough at the Scale of Organization

In the context of business, breakthrough is commonly held to be an outcome that goes beyond what past performance indicates is likely to happen. To elaborate further, a breakthrough is a *positive discontinuity*—an outcome that exceeds what the most optimistic extrapolation of past performance might indicate is possible. If we use this as a reasonable working definition, then we might add that breakthroughs have been going on in business forever. Any core business, and sometimes even the formation of companies, is based upon somebody's breakthrough. You can probably think of others, but here are two well-known stories rewritten from the context of "the American dream" into the context of breakthrough and change integration.

Samuel Morse Invents the Telegraph

Breakdown in 1825

In 1825, in the midst of working on a portrait commission in Washington, D.C., Samuel Morse (1791–1872), an accomplished portrait artist, received a letter from his father. Morse read a single line: "Your dear wife is convalescent." He immediately left Washington for his home at New Haven,

Connecticut. But by the time he arrived his wife had already been buried. Heartbroken and guilt-stricken about being unaware of his wife's decline and her lonely death, he shifted his life work from painting to achieving a technology for rapid long-distance communication.

Breakthrough in 1832-

In 1832, Morse took ideas from Charles Thomas Jackson's experiments with electromagnets and developed a working model of a single-wire telegraph. But Morse's telegraphic signal would fade beyond a few hundred yards of wire.

Integration

Morse elicited the expertise of Leonard Gale, a chemistry professor at New York University. With Gale's insights and experimentation, Morse was soon able to send a message through ten miles of wire. This was the level of integration Morse needed to commercialize the telegraph. Alfred Vail, who had excellent skills and money to invest, soon joined Morse and Gale. Morse could now begin to develop his telegraph very rapidly.

Recursive Integrations

In 1845, Morse hired former postmaster general, Amos Kendall. Kendall extolled the value of the device and had little trouble convincing others of its potential. He assembled a small group of investors who put up $15,000 and formed the Magnetic Telegraph Company. Many new telegraph companies were formed as Morse sold licenses across the United States and eventually across the globe. When he died, he was a wealthy and honored man.

In 1851, industrialist and entrepreneur Hiram Sibley organized the New York & Mississippi Valley Printing Telegraph Company in Rochester. Sibley envisioned uniting a number of small telegraph companies into one great, efficient system. Meanwhile, Ezra Cornell (who would cofound Cornell University in 1865) bought back one of his own bankrupt telegraph companies and renamed it the New York & Western Union Telegraph Company. Initially fierce competitors, by 1855 both men agreed that consolidation was in their best interests and Western Union was born. In 1861 Western Union strung the first transcontinental telegraph wire, finally linking the East and West coasts.

Xerox—A Core Business Based in Breakthrough

Breakthrough in 1959

Founded in 1906 in Rochester, New York as The Haloid Company, Xerox came to prominence in 1959 when it introduced the Haloid Xerox 914. This first Xerox was a plain paper copier that used a breakthrough technology developed by Chester Carlson with backing from the Battelle Memorial Institute. Xerography, which means *dry writing*, formed the core business of Xerox. By 1961 Xerox reached almost $60 million in revenue. In 1963 it was already on the *Fortune* 1000 list ranked number 423 with just over $100 million in revenue. By 1967 it was ranked at number 145 with $525 million in revenue.

Expertise is Antithetical to Breakthrough

In 1959 Haloid Xerox hired the management consulting firm Arthur D. Little (ADL) to conduct market research to ascertain the potential market for the 914. ADL asked secretaries how many copies they usually made each day using then-current technologies (carbon paper, dittography, and so forth). Based on the data, ADL concluded that the market opportunity was 5,000 machines, far too few to justify the investment required to manufacture the 914. ADL's report concluded: "Although it may be admirably suited for a few specialized copying applications, the Model 914 has no future in the office-copying-equipment market."

Xerox moved ahead anyway, betting the company on their risky plan. They developed a new business model, leasing the machines for only $95 per month, which included 2,000 free copies. Each additional copy cost 5 cents. Soon, companies were averaging 2,000 copies per day, and Xerox was well on its way to being a billion-dollar company. Xerox eventually manufactured over 200,000 Model 914s and estimated that total placements was over 600,000. (Some machines were placed in multiple companies during their lifespans.)

Recursive Breakthroughs and Integration

We've already seen with Morse's telegraph that under the right conditions breakthrough begets breakthrough, in recursions. Oftentimes, too, with each recursion the rate of breakthrough outcomes accelerates. This is what happened

Table 9.3 Breakthroughs at Xerox

- Carlson filed his first preliminary patent application on October 18, 1937.
- Just one year later, Carlson's backroom laboratory produced the first near-perfect copy several times, thus establishing the efficacy and reliability of the process.
- After several failed attempts to find financial backing (breakdowns!), in 1942 Carlson met with senior members of Battelle Memorial Institute in Columbus, Ohio. That led to significant investments in the development of the process.
- By 1946 Battelle successfully established the feasibility of the process on larger scale.
- Between 1946 and 1953 Battelle negotiated a series of licensing agreements with Haloid (Xerox) that would lead to significant wealth for Battelle and Carlson.
- On October 22, 1948, Haloid made the first public announcement of xerography.
- In 1950 the first Haloid Xerox Copier was sold.
- By 1953 Haloid demonstrated that the process was commercially viable.
- By 1959 the concept was refined to the point where the Haloid Xerox 914 was produced, the first truly simple, push-button, plain-paper copier.
- The first six months of sales volume for the 914 equaled projections for the entire life cycle of the product. So much for planning!
- The physics behind xerography led to other breakthroughs like the laser printer.

(Owen 2004)

at Xerox; it's obvious in revenue growth after the introduction of the Xerox 914, but look also at the breakthroughs that were behind its introduction.

Summary

Based on our experience of working with organizations and our understanding of the literature on organizational change and transformation, this chapter has presented Toomey's Laws of Integrating Change. We presented case studies of change integration breakthrough at the scale of society and the scale of change that are clear demonstrations of these three laws.

1. Survival and change amenability are inversely related.
2. The work needed to change is equal to the complexity of the system multiplied by the needed rate of the system.
3. To every act of change integration there is an equal and opposite reaction directed at disintegrating the change.

Here are other key points to remember as you undertake your own breakthrough projects.

- *Art, craft,* and *science* are discrete phases of change integration.

- Breakthrough change can emerge in response to need or because someone sees a new possibility for something that could be and would bring about positive change.
- Breakthroughs fall into two temporal categories:

  1) Some breakthroughs emerge across generations. Some take hundreds of years to fully integrate because the initial breakthrough leads to other breakthroughs, setting off a chain of breakthrough.

  2) Some breakthroughs must integrate within a single generation of management. This challenge is made more complex by a new phenomenon. For the first time in history there are now five generations in the workforce (Gourani 2019), each with distinct world views, and therefore likely to approach integration in diverse ways.

- There is always at least one committed individual who stands for a possibility. It's someone committed to change who takes action and demonstrates results.
- People are at the source of integrating breakthroughs and where breakthroughs occur; it is people who cause them. Societies, communities, and companies do not cause breakthroughs, but they are the social systems where breakthroughs register—become visible to the rest of the world.
- Employees in an empowered relationship with their organization are a source of energy, flexibility, and creativity, and this is lost when human systems and business systems are not integrated.
- Breakthrough begets breakthrough. Each breakthrough that is sustained leads to other breakthroughs.
- With each new technological breakthrough, we become increasingly dependent upon things we understand little about. This leads to specialization, which involves knowing a great deal about a small part of a larger whole.
- Sophisticated systems such as business organizations are technologically advanced entities that depend upon a wide variety of experts having disparate knowledge. Experts understand important, although small, parts of the whole. They provide little insight into the elements that hold the interdependent whole of organization together. They are

likely to miss the forces that shape organization and provide cohesion for those who do the work that produces results.

In Chapter 10, we offer more specific guidance in implementing your own breakthrough efforts.

References

Conner, D. (2006) *Managing at the Speed of Change: How Resilient Managers Succeed and Prosper Where Others Fail.* New York: Random House.

Cotrugli, B. (1458) *Della mercatura e del mercante perfetto.* Facsimile Publishers, Delhi, India. Translated by Carraro C. and G. Favero (2017) *The Book of the Art of Trade.* New York: Palgrave Macmillan.

Crooks, Ed. (2009) Back to petroleum, *Financial Times.* Retrieved from https://www.ft.com/content/b8626bf4-6b20-11de-861d-00144feabdc0 on January 10, 2010.

Gourani, S. (2019) Leading multiple generations in today's workforce, *Forbes,* April 25, 2019. Retrieved from www.forbes.com/sites/soulaimagourani/2019/04/25/leading-multiple-generations-in-todays-workforce/?sh=6c4c0e4b4636 on November 14, 2020.

Kegan, R. and Lahey, L. (2009) *Immunity to Change: How to Overcome it and Unlock the Potential in Yourself and Your Organization.* Cambridge, MA: Harvard Business School Publishing Corporation.

Lewin, K. (1943) Defining the Field at a Given Time. *Psychological Review* 50(3): 292–310.

Owen, D. (2004) *Copies in Seconds: How a Lone Inventor and an Unknown Company Created the Biggest Communication Breakthrough Since Gutenberg—Chester Carlson and the Birth of the Xerox.* New York: Simon and Schuster.

Pacioli, L. (2010) *The Rules of Double-entry Bookkeeping de computis et scripturis.* Scotts Valley, CA: CreateSpace Independent Publishing Platform . (Originally published in 1494.)

10

CREATING YOUR OWN BREAKTHROUGH

Introduction

Breakthroughs can happen at any scale. You can have breakthroughs at the team level, business unit level, or corporate level. You can have breakthroughs in manufacturing, marketing, or accounting processes. Breakthroughs can occur in research settings, educational institutions, non-profit organizations, and healthcare organizations. We contend that regardless of the scale or setting, there are some underlying patterns and conditions that are more likely to create breakthrough results.

Our experience in breakthroughs contrasts with some of the standard thinking and research in the field. We offer new ways to think about breakthrough that are more empowering and purposeful than the research would have you believe is possible. This chapter offers a case of "interrupted breakthrough" that taught us some important lessons, so you don't have to learn them the hard way.

We revisit the relationship between risk and uncertainty in the context of breakthrough change and continue our exploration of how the imbalance between business systems and human systems in Organization gets

DOI: 10.4324/9781003131847-10

in the way of potential breakthrough. This chapter concludes with several basic guidelines for attempting your own breakthrough. One of the most important principles to remember throughout this chapter is that while breakthrough change cannot be managed and controlled in the traditional business-centric way of approaching change, you can create the conditions in Organization so that you are designing for breakthroughs.

Designing for Breakthrough

If you are a seasoned manager, most likely you have witnessed at least one breakthrough in your career, though it may have occurred under a misnomer of *incremental results* or *stretch goals*. Companies know how to plan for *incremental results* and *stretch goals*. The challenge lies in finding ways to achieve breakthrough with similar levels of certainty. On its face, the notion that we can plan for breakthrough seems to be an oxymoron. This view is heavily supported by a number of research initiatives that looked at the source of breakthrough results in companies of all types.

Breakthroughs, by Nayak and Ketteringham (1986), is one of the most quoted bodies of research on this subject. We have examined some of the results presented in *Breakthroughs*, but we've come to considerably different conclusions on the sources of breakthrough from those offered in that book and other business literature.

Nayak and Ketteringham drew two notable conclusions:

1. Adversity drives breakthroughs.
2. Breakthroughs can also be the fortuitous results of serendipity.

While both conclusions may be valid, they also can be misleading, because they present an incomplete and less-than-empowered picture. Since the publication of their book, we have learned:

1. The view that "adversity drives breakthrough" can destroy the possibility of creating breakthroughs if audacious mandates are used to create the appearance of adversity. In short order, employees see through this for the inauthentic manipulation that it is, and breakthrough gets a bad name.
2. The view that "breakthroughs can also be the fortuitous results of serendipity" suggests that we can do no better than wait and prepare

to take advantage of good luck. This view disempowers those who are invited to work on breakthrough, because others see them as the merely lucky recipients of good fortune (or worse, the chosen few).

3. Breakthroughs can be *generated on purpose* and as part of an *organizational scale strategy*. To generate the opportunity takes tolerance for ambiguity and a willingness to engage in what might be seen as "fuzzy thinking."

Some of the questions corporate leaders often ask when considering breakthrough results include:

- Can corporate mandated outcomes be reliably fulfilled if they require breakthroughs?
- Can leaders deliver on a promise of breakthrough if it's not possible to plan for breakthrough in the way we plan for other strategic imperatives?
- Can our people really create useful notions for breakthrough products and services—ones that no one else has thought of?
- Do our people have the means—talent, skills, time, finances, dedication—to transform notions into rich and compelling ideas?
- Is there a way to express our vision so that it communicates the possibility and enroll others?

Each question is in service to the answers being a qualified "yes," which makes each somewhat rhetorical, but each also (1) frames the body of concerns that arise when leaders consider the scope of the challenge to deliver on breakthrough outcomes, and (2) frames an argument for breakthrough requiring a distinct approach from that needed for planning for non-breakthrough strategic imperatives.

Our field-based research spanning the last five decades tells us that management style planning methodologies do not work well for initiating breakthroughs. Certain planning methods may be useful around checking for feasibility, efficacy, and reproducibility, the domain of management. But even within these management tools that attempt to measure the success of initial breakthrough, additional breakthroughs are often needed. Tactical planning doesn't work well for breakthrough because the very process presupposes that you know what to do or that you can find it out. Since breakthrough is about doing something that has never been done before, then how could you know what to do and plan from there?

It is possible; however, to *design* for breakthrough—to create the conditions in your organization that are conducive to breakthrough. Over the years, we have identified and refined these four "design sets" that prove to be highly effective in creating favorable conditions.

Four Design Sets

1. Create initial breakthrough notions.
2. Demonstrate early:

    a. Workability
    b. Feasibility
    c. Efficacy

3. Scale up to pilot and from there to full production.
4. Reset and create another breakthrough.

We've told you a lot of stories about how other people did it. Now let's take a look at a case study from Generative Leadership Group (GLG) records.

Stumbling Blocks to Change Integration: A Case of Interrupted Breakthrough

Back in the mid-1990s, a large high-tech product company hired GLG to work with a team of scientists and engineers. Their mandated objective was to come up with a new product breakthrough. After weeks of brainstorming the team thought they could create a machine that would use a dry photograph development process to replace the existing industry-standard wet process. Such a product would revolutionize film developing and make them an instant market leader.

Now they had to demonstrate that a dry process could actually work for the intended industry application. Within a few months the team presented a working model, and, after some fine-tuning, they also demonstrated efficacy; the model made reproductions that exceeded the quality of the current industry-standard for wet process. But up to this point they were unable to demonstrate feasibility. The light source for the working model burned out too fast, and the expense to replace it raised cost per copy so high that the product could not compete. So the team needed another breakthrough—a better light source.

To make the product economically viable, the team would have to refine the process to work with 50 percent less light intensity. They scrutinized all the related science available, but their research indicated that at best a 35 percent reduction could be achieved and that looked like a long shot. Frustrated and empty-handed, they turned to GLG. We helped them to design their own framework for producing breakthroughs. By adhering to the framework parameters, in only four months the team built a new device with a light source that reduced light intensity by 90 percent. With feasibility demonstrated, they realized that they had invented a core technology that could be applied to many other uses and products as well. Next the team collaborated with manufacturing to calibrate tolerances and to optimize the use of existing manufacturing equipment to build the new product. Their level of cooperation substantially reduced the investment cost for new manufacturing equipment.

So, returning to our earlier design sets, we all agreed that design sets 1, 2, and 3 were accomplished. It was time to look at design set 4, "Reset and create another breakthrough." The team was riding high. They felt good about their accomplishment and their contribution to their company's future. The team leader—"Bob" for the sake of anonymity—and his core team asked the VP in charge to keep their group in place. They also presented some new ideas for recursive breakthroughs, achievable by applying all that they had learned. The VP promised them a response in a week and, true to his word, a memo arrived seven days later. It expressed the company's appreciation for the team's accomplishment, and it outlined sizable bonuses for the team members. The last paragraph said that senior management would be disbanding the team; each member would be receiving a new assignment in a few days.

As part of a completion process for our consulting engagement, we asked the VP to share the reasons behind senior management's decision to disband the team. His answer was troubling. Bob had peers—not on the team—who perceived him to be a loose cannon. Bob did not fit senior management's profile for a good manager. His project reports had often been late. He exceeded his budget for the project. Everyone agreed: "It is best to discontinue." The VP concluded that, while the outcome was outstanding, no one had really expected the team to succeed. And no one believed a long shot like that could happen again.

GLG had worked with this team for nearly a year. Bob was smart, inspiring, tenacious, and fully supportive of each member of his team. He was deeply committed to creating a breakthrough product, even though he felt out of place in this large company. Bob's own small company had been acquired by this organization a few months before the team was formed. Some of the people on the team had come with him, acquired for their skills and their reputation for creating new technology. Bob was convinced that he was assigned this team and project because the acquiring company did not know what else to do with him.

Lessons Learned

At that time, GLG had no idea that the ongoing generation of breakthroughs is related to what we now call "integrated organization." In light of the team's contributions, we were sure that its continuance was a given. Our client's decision to disband came as both a shock and a big wake-up call for us. This outcome was a line of demarcation in our learning. Since then we've discovered that it is possible to design for breakthrough *at scale*. In other words, an entire company does not have to be integrated to have sustainable breakthroughs at lower levels.

Over time we've also learned that *producing a breakthrough and then disbanding is* not an uncommon outcome for breakthrough teams. Reasons for stopping vary, but the end result is the same—*the source of breakthrough is lost*. The culprit? Preconceived notions about how things should be done. Preconceived notions are useful for running a business, but they are harmful to creative and innovative breakthrough pursuits.

Unwittingly, Bob also played a part in the demise of his team. Further conversations with Bob, his team, and senior management revealed to us that the team's data had made sense within the team but lacked credence with their superiors and their peers. Bob might have been more successful if he had been able to present information in a context that was relevant to the concerns of his new sponsors. Failure to communicate is more often a byproduct of failure to create relevance for your listener.

To summarize:

1. Never take for granted that the design for breakthrough results will be obvious to others in the company. Always connect the dots for others.

2. Team leaders must communicate project status often and widely, and not just to their sponsor(s). The communications, at a minimum will include:

    a.   Breakthroughs ("We have a working model!")
    b.   Breakdowns ("The working model has efficacy but does not yet appear feasible. We're working on it.")

3. Running a business is more about science than art.
4. Creating and innovating are more about art than science.
5. Breakthroughs are precursors to strategic business products and services.
6. Disciplines for running a business are distinct from those for creating and innovating.
7. These disciplines often appear as opposites—seemingly antithetical.
8. Confusing these discipline leads to misplaced expectations.

To Integrate Breakthrough, Keep Risk and Uncertainty Distinct

Uncertainty arises naturally as a bedfellow of the creativity and innovation required for breakthrough (see "Change, Risk and Uncertainty" in Chapter 1). As the story about Bob and his team demonstrates, most organizations, to their detriment, operate under the preconceived notion that they should tolerate uncertainty only when existing products are commoditizing but not at other times. Yet there could be no more risky time to seek a breakthrough in product development than in the last moments of the product cycle, when the odds of failure are highest.

When presented with the opportunity to continue breakthrough product development with a team of people who had demonstrated they could do it, management in Bob's company instead elected to disband the team because it was nonconforming. It was too much on the edge of the norms associated with management and predictability (Neal 2006).

Such decisions are direct reflections of Toomey's Third Law for Change Integration:

> To every act of change integration there is an equal and opposite reaction directed at disintegrating the change.
>
> (Mel Toomey, Chapter 9 in this book)

More specifically, they are based in a failure to distinguish risk from uncertainty. This constraint operates against organizational integration and breakthrough growth. The failure is exemplified in the statement: "The increased competition we anticipate next year puts the margins in our core business at risk."

Uncertainty, you may recall, is not about protecting something we have; it's about daring to reach for something we don't have. Uncertainty is messy business. It requires a tolerance for "not knowing." It makes us live without the comfort of answers to the questions: What will it look like? How does it work? When is it going to happen? Economist Frank Knight (1921) first identified the "radically distinct" difference between uncertainty and risk.

When Knight studied the "radically distinct" difference between uncertainty and the more familiar notion of risk, he discovered profound differences in outcome depending upon which of the two is actually present and operating. What Knight called "risk proper" is measurable, unlike "uncertainty," which is not measurable. He noted that uncertainty, when it is misidentified as risk, hamstrings decision-making by leaders at all levels of organization. This phenomenon was evident in our client's decision to disband Bob's high performing R&D team. Leadership was snagged because "the fear of the unknown—approaching uncertainty as if it is risk—will hobble attempts to put creative initiatives into play" (Knight 1921).

Risk can be measured quantitatively in numbers or in dollars and cents. As such, it is properly the jurisdiction of business systems—the day-to-day operations for efficiencies, reliability, and repeatable results. Uncertainty lies in the realm of human systems that are capable of new beginnings, generating breakthroughs and morphing to meet needs.

Breakthrough change integration is not the place for a conservative stance. This is where we must acknowledge that "pit in our stomach" sensation. At the same time, we must not freeze into inaction or abandon the game. Before you start, make certain that sponsors and everyone who will be affected by change understand that the uncertainty of breakthrough change integration cannot be measured quantitatively. Begin your breakthrough by setting agreed-upon qualitative terms dealing with effectiveness, efficacy and to some degree, feasibility, then throughout the process, communicate frequently to keep everyone in the loop (Conner 2006).

We now examine four barriers to breakthrough, (1) Business-centric integration, (2) Specialization, (3) Myth and superstition, and (4) Linear thinking.

Barriers to Breakthrough

Business-centric Integration

At the time of our story, we did not understand how an undertaking that had so much potential and was of such obvious value could be discarded because of "rules." We searched for clues and began to recognize that Bob's case was similar to other cases. They all worked in organizations based upon *business-centric integrations*. Those leaders who decided to disband the team were very smart people. They had a committed and compelling understanding of the value of conformity from the perspective of managing business; that is, *developing business, doing business,* and *running the business.*

Developing business is the work done today so that at some time in the future we can increase the business the company does: opening new locations, entering new markets, increasing product lines. *Doing business* is the day-to-day transactional work of selling goods and services. *Running the business* is all about fulfilling on the business the company is already doing. Each of these three aspects of business requires a high degree of discipline and conformity. Weakness or absence of any one is a real threat to efficiency, effectiveness, and even a danger to the business itself. Members of the senior management team in Bob's organization headed the business, operations, and finance units. In retrospect, it's easy to understand their decision, given the context in which they worked.

Most companies "integrate" their organization by putting business at the epicenter of concern. This practice fosters a dichotomy—on one hand there is business and, on the other, everything else. Everything else is seen as satellite. From the perspective of business, the value of other parts of an organization lies only in their abilities to serve the needs of business. There's nothing wrong with seeking the comfort of a well-oiled and stable operation, as long as we recognize that seeking stability necessarily puts limits to growth. At some point "business-centric" designs reach barriers to growth that cannot be breached at the scale at which they manifest.

Table 10.1 Business-Centric Integration

	Develop the Business	Do the Business	Run the Business
System Main Activity	Influential Network Expansion	Authoritative Matrix Sales/Order Taking	Positional Hierarchy Operations
Orientation	Prospective	Introspective	Retrospective
What Shapes Action	Future Needs	Present Conditions	Past Experience

Specialization – The Saboteur of Change

Beyond business-centric design, what ultimately sources the opposing forces to change in organization? What's being protected besides the status quo? Our experience in systemic and integrated change initiatives indicates that what's being protected is all the *specialized work* that it took to create the status quo. No small matter when you consider the diversity of specializations in organizations, the delicate interrelationship of the specializations, and the effort it took to sculpt that amorphous mass of human inventions, ideas, opinions, and emotions into "how things are done" today.

When change is seen as a threat to stability, there will be pushback, in large part due to the threat of work that is anticipated as needed to reestablish post-change stability. The increasing ease and speed of communication within organization, and between organizations and their stockholders, customers, suppliers, and the general public, is driving the need for more change at an ever faster pace. To keep up with change, specializations are on the increase, in turn increasing the work needed to integrate cross-disciplinary change in large, complex systems like your organization.

Myth and Superstition – The Party Crashers of Integration

Advances in communication and computers led to the formation of Information Technology (IT) departments. Soon there emerged Chief Information Officers (CIOs). More recently, we find companies with both a CIO and a CTO (Chief Technology Officer). Can you begin to imagine how much leaders and managers today must learn about specializations other than their own just to carry on a conversation and to communicate basic needs? Frustration leads to so much dissatisfaction and alienation among employees. Most of this registers in employee engagement surveys such as the ones reported in earlier chapters.

Never before have so many people at work understood so little about so much. This sorry condition is the product of the complicated interdependencies among increasing levels of specialization, combined with the rate of change that is making organization ever more complex. In this environment it is not uncommon to find weaknesses:

* Integration is not treated as an organizational discipline.
* Decision makers drive change without considering the interrelatedness of specializations.

- Communications from the top down are directives.
- Communications from the bottom up are status reports.
- Those who do the work of integration lack input and access to related decisions.
- The goodwill of those needed to integrate change is missing because they feel powerless.
- Myth and superstition substitute for reality.

It's a given that most of organization's attention falls on "doing business" and directly related matters. Integrating change is usually not approached as a directly related matter, unless an emergency arises. It's also a given that we understand a great deal more about business but comparatively less about integrating breakthrough change at the scale of organization. Any time we are confronted by something that goes beyond our current understanding, myth and superstition appear to serve as stunt doubles for fact. These two compadres become the means of explaining "the truth" about whatever is foggy. Myth and superstition thrive around integrating breakthrough change. They're always ready to crash the party.

To counter threatening weaknesses when your organization is in a state of change, try mapping out the lines of communication through which necessary knowledge and information are spread. Mapping can empower change integration. The map is likely to look different from the layout needed to operate the business. The communication map during change should go beyond spreading directives from decision makers downward to the workforce. It should also empower anyone who is developing the change to provide knowledge and understanding to decision makers above. Keeping the channels of communication open both ways while integrating discontinuous change goes far beyond what little we can understand or anticipate in advance. Much understanding is derived in the moment and has implications that differ across specializations as well as within the hierarchy.

Our experience suggests that, when businesses attempt to integrate change wrapped in myths and superstitions, widespread misapplications of the change ensue. Integrating change requires a holistic kind of communication—*communication at the scale of organization*. It is no longer sufficient for individuals to understand their parts, to do what the job calls for, and to cooperate in contributing their piece only. New, higher levels of coordinated action between players are needed and this mutuality can happen only through communication at the scale of organization (Kotter 2012).

Linear Thinking Inhibits Breakthrough Change

When we lapse into perceiving organization as straightforward and repeatable acts of business, our seeming lack of will actually reflects our habitual reliance on *linear thinking*, a left-brain activity that we can trace back over five millennia to the introduction of the alphabet. Let's consider a brief history of how business evolved to where we are today, to add some context to this discussion.

According to neurosurgeon Leonard Schlain, author of *The Alphabet Versus the Goddess—The Conflict Between Word and Image* (1998), reliance on linear thinking is probably programmed by our predominant left brains. Schlain argues that wherever alphabets were adopted, a destabilizing imbalance in human relationships ensued. This imbalance reflected a radical physical change in the structure of the human brain to accommodate literacy. In order to interpret strings of letters arranged in lines as abstract symbols for words, the left side of the brain—our "male" side—enlarged to favor focused, linear, sequential thinking. Along with these attributes, other left-brain functions became exaggerated too; concepts of time, numeracy, aggression, strength of will, and "if this, then not that" reductionist logic. Our thinking became lopsided, at the disadvantage of the right side—our creative "female" side—which governs images, pattern recognition, and holistic, simultaneous, synthetic, and intuitive thinking.

Our propensity for linear thinking places constraint—in the broadest terms—upon the ability of people in Organization to imagine new possibilities for organizational growth. Consider that if we associate linear thinking with business systems, which are the domain of management, we can likewise associate creative thinking with human systems, the domain of leadership. The good news, as Schlain points out, is that with awareness and some practice, we can generate balanced use of both sides of our brains. We can be focused and think holistically, too—both advantages for different purposes—particularly when applied to breakthrough change integration!

Breakthrough Initiative

Now that you have learned the four design sets for designing for breakthrough and have a better understanding of the barriers to breakthrough change, it's time to put these concepts into practice in your own Breakthrough Initiative. Integrating change begins with leadership, as we said earlier, and we'd like to offer these basic principles for leading breakthrough change. These are valuable principles to explore with your team, since everyone on the team will take on leadership in the service of breakthrough. We provide some guiding questions following this list.

Principles for Leading Breakthrough Change

- You must be absolutely clear on what you're up to.
- You must be willing to stand in the face of no agreement.
- Many will say you and your people can't get it done.
- You can't get it done by yourself.
- The initiative can only be carried out through influence, which means you need to build it through leadership.
- You need to build a story around a Breakthrough Initiative.
- Some people will come in early.
- Some people will come in in the middle, when there some inkling of proof.
- There will be some late adopters.
- The design is one where there will no penalty for arriving late.
- The deal is to keep the game in play. Don't let a non-player stop the play. Listen to them.
- Walk into that future we are envisioning and coming back to tell the story of what we saw. And creating a likely story that's believable (not true because the future is not certain and has not yet taken place).
- One doesn't have to be in a state of adversity to depict and drive towards a compelling future.
- Leading. It's lonely.
- Expectations will foster belief in the value of the intentions.
- Expectations identify outcomes.
- Design objectives identify performance characteristics.
- Performance characteristics begin to shape the expectation.
- Leadership is an act of existential courage.

Summary

The leader who takes on integrating breakthrough change is seldom given a "pat hand." There is an art, craft, and science to any successful change integration, and it has much to do with striking the right balance among these three domains. Before you even attempt breakthrough, doing what it takes to integrate human and business systems at the scale of organization ensures that this earthmoving change has a reasonable opportunity to succeed.

Breakthrough outcomes are not new to companies. Breakthrough occurs with some degree of frequency in most organizations. These extraordinary levels of performance have been studied, documented, and reported for decades. As mentioned at the beginning of this chapter, a strong case can be made—and indeed has often been made—for the notion that break-throughs often happen when a company is faced with adversity ... or sometimes they happen just because of "good luck." Not very encouraging news, if true! Management works to avoid states of adversity and we have yet to meet the leader who has successfully proposed a strategy that was based upon good luck.

Literature on breakthrough suggests all manner of causes. Yet none that we have found gives much insight on how to go about *generating* break-through. Here is brief list of some things we have learned that deserve consideration, should you attempt your own breakthrough outcome:

1. You *can* design for breakthrough.
2. Breakthroughs can be a useful and grounded part of strategy.
3. Reaching more than one breakthrough requires

    a.   A generous allowance for strikeouts and multiple times at bat
    b.   Understanding that players do not hit the ball every time
    c.   Knowing that most hits will not be home runs.

4. Breakthrough is not the common symptom of adversity; failure is.
5. Good luck is not a determining factor in breakthrough.
6. The notion that good luck is causal masks the actual source of breakthrough—people are the actual source of breakthrough.
7. Mandates are antithetical to breakthrough.
8. Sustaining breakthrough change requires co-designed, scaled integration.
9. While a breakthrough may be a positive break with established norms, it does not insure a positive response from the employee population. (Remember Toomey's Third Law of Integrating Change.)
10. The integration of breakthrough change is possible to the degree that an organization is integrated. The more integrated an organization, the greater the likelihood that the benefits of breakthrough change will be realized at whatever scale the breakthrough is attempted. Most

organizations are sufficiently integrated to handle most mediation (Six Sigma, reengineering, and lean manufacturing, for example) and remediation. This is not the case for the intermediation and integration of breakthrough change.

This chapter has discussed several challenges to keep in mind when you are attempting your own breakthrough change. They include the challenge of keeping risk and uncertainty distinct, and understanding (1) the challenges of business-centric integration; (2) the resistance that comes from specialization; and (3) the ways in which linear thinking inhibits our attempts at breakthrough change.

Chapter 11 takes an organizational systems approach to integrating change, which helps to overcome the challenges of attempting your own breakthrough change.

References

Conner, D. (2006) *Managing at the Speed of Change: How Resilient Managers Succeed and Prosper Where Others Fail.* New York: Random House.

Knight, F. (1921) *Risk, Uncertainty and Profit.* Boston, MA: Houghton Mifflin Co.

Kotter, J. (2012) *Leading Change.* Cambridge, MA: Harvard Business Review Press.

Nayak, P.R. and Ketteringham, J. (1986) *Breakthroughs! How the Vision and Drive of Innovators in Sixteen Companies Created Commercial Breakthroughs That Swept the World.* New York: Rawson Associates.

Neal, J. (2006) *Edgewalkers: People and Organizations That Take Risks, Build Bridges and Break New Ground.* Westport, CT: Praeger.

Schlain, L. (1998) *The Alphabet Versus the Goddess—The Conflict Between Word and Image.* New York: Viking Press.

11

CONSTRAINT AND CREATIVITY

Introduction

Reflecting on our work with organizations and with the executives and managers who lead and run them, there are some thoughts and observations that we want to share with you. They center on performance indicators and their effect in Organization as well as the challenges Management and Leadership face in designing and establishing performance indicators.

As we have said many times, Management and Leadership are distinct organizational disciplines and at times their objectives appear to be at odds. Our intention is to provide some resolution and clarity on how Management and Leadership can coexist as complements in Organization. Their functioning as complements depends in large part on Development, an often under-appreciated and poorly understood organizational discipline.

This chapter focuses on a systems view of Organization, continuing our dive into the details of the subsystems and their interrelatedness. How we think about Organization has significant implications for the systems optimization of any kind of change or breakthrough we wish to integrate. We begin with an outline of the basic functional attributes for Management,

DOI: 10.4324/9781003131847-11

Leadership, and Development as they relate to performance in Organization. This is followed by an assertion that shifts in perception lead to shifts in action, and that the thoughtful design of Key Performance Indicators (KPIs) is one of the highest leverage points for creating systemic shifts.

Organization as a System

Integrating Human Systems and Business Systems

The experience we have with perceptions and jurisdictions, linear thinking, our relationship with risk versus uncertainty, and applying rules we use for working with tools to working with people all illustrate a fundamental concept; *how we think* about organization puts constraints—limits—on how far the system can grow (Meadows et al. 1972, 1991). Any crisis has its roots in organizational thinking that has reached its limits of usefulness. When we apply a holistic view to Organization, integrating Human Systems with Business Systems, Organization will prosper.

Human systems integration is a phrase seldom used in business. However, many familiar methodologies depend on the integration of Human Systems for their success. Some examples: Project Management, Governance, Risk Mitigation, Total Quality Management, Reengineering, Six Sigma, Lean, Human Factors Engineering, Safety, Training, and Simulations. When applied to business, these methodologies can produce valuable results but there are limits to their application.

There are two basic assumptions underlying the application of traditional disciplines within Business Systems (the processes for acquiring, developing, and fulfilling on business objectives). The first assumption is that as Business Systems are changed, people will fall in line. The second assumption is that an explanation regarding what is being done, why it is being done, combined with information and training, will ensure that people fall in line. While there are compelling examples of these traditional approaches providing real value, research indicates that it only happens in 20 percent to 30 percent of the cases (Hammer and Champy 2006). Our experience indicates that this traditional approach to change works at certain scales and not others. The larger the change that is undertaken, the less likely it is that the traditional approach will meet expectations. Examples of large-scale systems change include mergers and acquisitions, total quality management, reengineering, and the implementation of enterprise-wide software systems.

To be successful in flipping the odds from 20/80 to 80/20 in large-scale change, when what is possible takes on new meaning, we need to shift contexts by placing Human Systems Integration in the context of Organization rather than in the context of Business Systems. An approach in which Human Systems are dealt with in the context of Organizational Systems is distinct from the traditional one. In this new approach, Human Systems are addressed concurrently with Business Systems and both are now integrated into the larger context of Organization. One of the earliest mentions of the idea that Human Systems are essential in change processes was a Harvard Business Review article in the 1980s regarding the implementation of new technology (Leonard-Barton and Kraus 1985). However, even now there does not appear to be large-scale adoption of this concept.

Such a shift raises an expanded set of implications, including significantly improved adoption rates and considerably increased leverage, particularly when dealing with what seem to be recurring, unsolvable, or insurmountable business problems.

State Shift in Thinking—The Inflection Point

To address Human Systems in the context of Organization requires a state shift in our thinking. The first step in shifting our thinking is to begin to see and understand "Organization" as a whole system. The second step is to see and understand that Business Systems are one part of the whole, and that these two terms (Business Systems and Organizational Systems) are not alternate ways to say the same thing. The third step is to recognize that a state shift in thinking from the scale of Business Systems to Organizational Systems is the same kind of shift needed when one moves from a Newtonian "cause-and-effect" view (how we tend to think of Business Systems) to a quantum view. The quantum view is how we are beginning to think of Organization (Tsao and Laszlo 2019). Besides a state shift in our thinking, we also need to understand that state shifts can occur in organizations (Barrett 2017).

Think of an inflection point as that point in a system where there is a state shift. When there is a state shift, the content remains constant and the form and shape shifts, that is, there is a shift in state. The phrase "Inflection Point" is used here as a term of art because it provides the basis for a useful metaphor, the metaphor of state shifts in water. The metaphor will help us to see why Human Systems Integration is such a powerful place from

Table 11.1 A Systemic View of People in Organization

A Systemic View of People in Organization

The Systems	Systems' Concerns	Systems' Primary Functions	Systems' Inflection Points	States of Existence
Organization	Optimization of Resources	Balancing Trade-Offs Potential, Efficiency, Effectiveness and Results	Outer-World Relationships	Chaotic Field
Business	Delivery of Business Results	Providing Assurance Stability and Organic Growth	Relationships with Human & Developmental Systems	Authoritative Hierarchy
Human	Realization of Potential	Creating Beyond Norms Grounding Possibilities as Potential Realities	Relationships with Business & Developmental Systems	Relational Network
Development	Transfer of Realized Potential to Operational Reality	Demonstrating Feasibility Establishing Efficacy and Resolving Effectiveness	Relationships with Business and Human Systems	Dynamic Matrix

which to leverage large-scale organizational change. It is also a powerful place to address the knotty problems that arise in the organization's three subsystems.

There are two temperatures at which water goes through a state shift. At 212° F water ceases to be liquid and becomes gas. At 32° F water ceases to be liquid and becomes solid. Gas, liquid, and solid are the states in which water is the constant and 212° F and 32° F are the inflection points for state shifts occur.

With this example in place and the idea that people are the constant in the existence of organization in all its states, consider this: Human Systems Integration is about managing the state shifts within an organization and between the organization and the world in which it exists. It is about working at the inflection points (the liminal, in-between, threshold places) where state shifts occur. Organizational, Business, Human and Developmental Systems exist distinctly much the same as steam, ice, and liquid water (the common element being H_2O). The common element for Organization and its three subsystems is people. In the same way that H_2O has particular properties and unique behaviors in the various states of Organization. Working with gas, liquid, and solids requires differing methods of interaction. This is also the case when working with organization and its three subsystems. How we work to change Business Systems is not the way we must work to change Human or Developmental Systems. Each requires a significantly unique approach.

Groups of people in each of the states are both the source of results (positive leverage) and the most likely place for breakdowns (negative leverage). When people are, on one hand, integrated with the whole system, and, on the other, dealt with in terms of the concerns that arise when they are working within a particular subsystem (the state), a synergy occurs that cannot be explained in terms of the sum of the parts. This is what integrating change is about.

Viewing the organization in quantum terms, as we do, means that we must examine Organization from this question: "What is the smallest discrete indivisible physical property that Organization possesses?" People are the smallest discrete indivisible physical property that constitutes organization; and while the answer is obvious, its implications are far-reaching. One implication is that people working in groups give rise to effects that are based in *probability*, not the kind of effects based in *predictability*. There are exceptions such as is found on an assembly line, but this Newtonian view does not apply in most parts of the organization. The final step is to see and understand that the kind of thinking that works well at the scale of Business Systems is largely invalid at the Organizational Systems scale.

The value of Human System Integration at the scale of Organization is the optimization of the total systems equation. Think of "total systems equation" as an equivalent for Organizational Systems. The evolving design of organization has been dominated by the concerns of business, the business-centric approach to integration. We are not suggesting that this should be different. Business concerns are foundational for any organization. It's obvious that if business concerns aren't managed effectively, there is nothing else to talk about. We *do* suggest, however, that not all business concerns can be addressed successfully within the context of Business Systems. Some business concerns, such as those that are recurrent and/or seem unsolvable, are better addressed once removed (one-scale-up) from where they occurred; that is to say, at the scale of Organization. In addition, we suggest that business concerns are, at the scale of Organization, an incomplete set of concerns; that by themselves, these concerns do not and cannot address the needs of the whole system.

Organizational Systems are the "whole" in which Business Systems reside. What Business Systems are about is obvious to most of us. Said simply, they are about providing reliability, predictability, and certainty in the conduct of business. We are not as confident that we have a similarly cogent and concise answer to the question, "What are Organizational Systems about?" We propose that Organizational Systems are about optimizing resources by balancing tradeoffs between results that could be and aren't yet there (potential), reducing the cost of producing results (efficiency), and the efficacy and quality of results (effectiveness).

If Business Systems are one part of the whole, that is, Organizational Systems, what are the other parts? Consider thinking about this question in the following way. Suppose that Organizational Systems are the field within which Business Systems (about reliability, predictability, and certainty) exist, and that there are two additional systems within this field, Human Systems (about possibility and unrealized potential) and Developmental Systems (about efficacy and effectiveness). Now add in this thought. All three systems in the field of Organization are both self-serving and in the service of the purposes and concerns of the organization as a whole.

Think of Organization as "a resource-dependent optimization system"— a system that works to produce the most valuable results possible with the least number of resources. "Optimization" includes increases in effectiveness (bringing new things into existence) and efficiency (making more with less). Organization is "resource-dependent" because without resources it cannot exist. However, resources alone are insufficient to constitute an organization. Organization's constitution also depends on the presence of three subsystems: Business Systems for operating the business, Human Systems for conducting the business, and Development Systems for evolving the business.

Organization as a system works to optimize results and resources through Development's skillful integration of Business and Human Systems. Business Systems are optimized by improved efficiency (i.e., processing sales). Human Systems are optimized by improved creativity and innovation (i.e., making sales). Many would say that "making sales" is a Business System—there are rules, processes to follow, and measures for success. However, sales organizations that are not creative and innovative underperform. At the point of sale, one usually finds a creative action in some form.

System Optimization

In Organization, "optimization" is the process of modifying the system to improve something. There are three different areas of focus, depending on which subsystem of the organization you are looking at. In Business Systems a key area of improvement is efficiency, and it is the concern of Management. In Human Systems a key area of improvement is effectiveness and it is the concern of Leadership. In Development Systems a key area of improvement is efficacy, and it is the concern of Integration.

"Optimization" shares the same root as "optimal," but rarely will optimization produce an optimal system. A system optimized for efficiency will work under very limited conditions and is virtually useless outside a narrow range of conditions. A system optimized for effectiveness on the other hand will have broad application but will tradeoff efficiency for its flexibility. There are always tradeoffs when optimizing a system and the basic tradeoffs are between efficiency (rigidity) and effectiveness (flexibility).

Optimization of a system must be approached with caution. Premature optimization embeds flaws, which can be hard to find after a system is normalized. So, it is important to first have a sound and workable prototype. Prototyping is one of the main jobs for Development Systems.

Optimization of a system does not mean the system will retain the same functionality. There are limits to optimization as much as there are limits to growth. Significant performance improvements are sometimes achieved by optimizing a small set of functions or by removing extraneous functions. For example: A small parts warehouse currently has 10,000 different parts and uses 100 differing sized boxes for shipping. It is determined that per capita labor cost will rise, and the number of parts will double in the next five years. One way to optimize the system is to reduce 100 box sizes to say ten. This reduces labor cost by reducing headcount, storage-cost by reducing inventory, and increases buying leverage through larger orders of each size box. It also increases the use of bubble-wrap and shipping costs, however the increased costs are less than the savings.

This example demonstrates tradeoffs. Efficiency with shipping cost was better at 100 box sizes but the overall system efficiency was best at ten box sizes. To work, optimization must focus on one or two things: time to results, workspace, storage space, capacity, or some other resources. This will usually require a tradeoff in which one or two are optimized at the expense of others.

One opportunity to optimize is when there is a need to relieve a bottleneck. Look for the fewest functions that account for the most results (Goldratt and Cox 2014). Applying the 80/20 rule of thumb and you are likely to land in the right "zip code." A note of caution: Optimization codifies process into a reduced number of steps. This can often create a situation where understanding of underlying processes is reduced and the need for specialization is increased. This may complicate hiring practices and training programs.

For those familiar with software systems optimization, it may be easy to see some correlations for Organization. Software systems can be optimized by automated compilers or by programmers. Gains are usually smaller for local optimization, and larger for global optimizations. Perhaps the most powerful optimization for software systems is to find a superior algorithm. Business System optimization requires human intervention, but many of the principles of automated software systems optimization will apply.

System Interrelatedness and its Effect

Business and Human Systems are deeply interrelated, and because of this we tend to think of them as one system—Organization. When this happens, we miss seeing how they are distinct, and thus the effect each has on the other is masked. A small change in the Business System can bring about many changes, sometimes quite large changes in the Human System. The reverse also holds true. Therefore, it is important to look deeper than *cause and effect*; we must also examine the more subtle *influences* of *potential*. A failure to discern these subtle influences leads to unmet expectations as well as unintended and sometimes undesirable outcomes. When making changes, additions, or deletions, even small ones, to Business or Human Systems it is important to recognize that Business Systems are deterministic and Human Systems are probabilistic. The nature of each is therefore subject to quite different rules-of-engagement, which suggests the expectations for each should also be distinct. For example: Generally speaking, the elimination of variables in Business Systems is beneficial. This is not the case with Human Systems—having people think the same way is not best for most work environments.

Systems and Perception

Systems, in the broadest of terms, can be seen as being in a certain state, and having certain content that is subject to inflows (content coming into the system) and outflows (content going out of the system). Examples of content for organizations are money, people, products, ideas, methods, processes, practices, and so on, each flowing in and out.

The state of an Organizational System is dependent on many factors. Perhaps the most influential of those factors are KPIs, for they determine a great deal about how we perceive the system's state. This point is important because perception shapes action. Action, in turn, produces results. Some actions produce results directly, but most actions produce results indirectly through systems. Something seemingly as simple and ordinary as making a phone call requires a complex system of communication. Actions within Business Systems produce results that are more a function of *cause and effect*, as is the case with the phone system example. Dialing a number on our phone (the cause) leads to a phone ringing elsewhere (the effect) with several *cause* and *effect* events along the way.

Actions within Human Systems produce results that are more a function of *influence* on *potential*. Making a presentation (influence) to a CIO or CTO who has a budget and need (potential) for the type of software your company provides is an example of *influence* and *potential* within Human Systems. Human Systems are *pattern-based*, not *process-based* (as is the case with a phone system) and therefore they must be measured in terms of probability, not predictability. Weather is an example of a system of patterns (Spring, Summer, Fall, Winter) that arise in chaos. When speaking of weather, one can generally be correct about a season but much less likely to be correct about a particular day within a season.

Sustained Shifts in Perception Lead to Systemic Shifts in Action

In Organization, sustained shifts in perception can bring about systemic shifts in people's actions. Shifts in perception can change the actions we are likely to take. Think of perception as an intermediary for action. People think they act in response to the facts, not in response to their perception of the facts. Two people, making the exact same money, get the exact same raise. Are they both equally satisfied? Maybe, maybe not. It depends on lots of things, like their perception of their salary before the raise (was it enough to start with?) and their perception of the size of the raise (was it commensurate with their perception of their value to the organization, their effort?).

Perception can change through *cause* or it can change through *influence*.

An example of change through *cause* is the election of a new method of depreciation for capital assets. The *effects* of the election are to either increase or decrease expenses and in turn to increase or decrease taxable earnings, depending on the method selected. This effect can lead to changes in decision-making about capital spending. This could be a means of changing capital spending in an organization.

A change through *influence* can be seen in this example that deals with a possible way of evaluating the performance of managers. Imagine all operating managers' performance reviews included a "promotion index" for their direct reports. The index shows the percentage of directors in the manager's group that are found by the Executive Committee to be candidates for promotion within the next 24 months. The Executive Committee's evaluation is based on a consistent set of KPIs for directors. This can lead to managers becoming more rigorous in hiring, investing more in their director's development, and becoming better mentors and coaches. This could also lead to building a deeper bench of directors who qualify as future managers.

The first example is a direct way of bringing about change in a Business System. The second example is an indirect way of bringing about change in a Human System. Both examples can drive sustainable shifts in perception, which in turn will encourage systemic change in action and, in turn, results. While one might find isolated examples to the contrary: Business Systems are most responsive to *cause* and Human Systems to *influence*. Another way to say this is that this example of indirect influence through changing key performance indicators is one way to create a state shift in thinking that becomes sustainable in the system.

Table 11.2 Organizational Sub-Systems: Characteristics Recap

Human Systems	Business Systems	Development Systems
Diagnostic Evaluation	Analytic Assessment	Feasible Efficacy
Leadership	Management	Development
Influence	Cause	Buffer
Probability	Predictability	Feasibility
Discontinuity	Continuity	Transfer
Creativity/Innovation	Reliability/Certainty	Efficacy/Velocity
Characterize	Define	Interface

Designing Key Performance Indicators That Shape Perception

Shaping perception is not just a matter of the presence of key performance indicators. It is also important to attend to their design. Let's look how we might apply mathematics in the design of performance indicators. In mathematics, three ways of finding the value of a list of numbers are mean, median, and mode.

Arithmetic mean – finding an average.

Median – finding the middle value

Mode – finding the most frequently occurring value within set ranges. /

Taking a closer look at *mean* and the design of performance indicators helps us see why careful attention to KPI design can prove beneficial.

The arithmetic mean is one type of mean—another type is a geometric mean. The geometric mean is typically used in cases of *exponential* growth or decline. There is a third mean used in statistics; the mean of a random variable is its expected value—that is, the theoretical long-run arithmetic mean of the outcomes of repeated trials, such as a large number of tosses of a die.

This suggests that geometric mean is useful in designing performance indicators that detect discontinuities (i.e., breakdowns and breakthroughs), while an arithmetic mean would be useful in designing performance indicators that detect continuities. When we need to buffer decisions, then the statistical mean is useful in designing performance indicators for guessing. In the early and intermediate stages of the development of something new, something that has never been done before, there is a need for guessing about *how long* or *how much*.

Using the arithmetic mean to find "data-points" may have the most value for Business Systems where efficiency, control, and continuity are important. On the other hand, the geometric mean is likely to have the most value for Human Systems where creating, innovating, and discontinuity (exponential growth) are important. The integration of Business and Human Systems at the scale of Organization suggests that Development Systems may find value from using the statistical mean for prediction around the socialization of breakthroughs. Think of "socializing a breakthrough" as the integration of results that are outside of the established norms. Remember Bob's story?

There are other areas of design for KPIs to explore but for now the examples above are sufficient to show why the *application* and *design* of performance indicators deserve considerable thought and attention.

When fundamental changes in *behavior* (the actions people take) are needed in organization, then we must be careful when deciding not only *what* is to be measured but also *how* it will be measured. Measuring a system alters the perceived state of that system and in turn the system itself. Organizations are complex (cause at a distance), chaotic (starting condition sensitive) systems. A small change in the design and presence of performance indicators can lead to significant and unintended changes in the whole system.

Articulation of Organizational States

Most organizations have an expressed goal to be in a certain state. KPIs are a means for articulating that state. The difference between the current perceived state and the goal state represents a discrepancy in state. The challenge is one of determining what will alter the perceived state in favor of the goal-state. It is this challenge that has occupied Mel for the last 30 years. We are not suggesting that the design and presence of key performance indicators are the only thing needed to change perception, behavior (action), results, and the perceived organizational state. But we are suggesting they are causal and influential, and they are therefore critical to the sustainability of perception, behavior, and results in organization.

Business, Human, and Development Systems each provide different aspects of optimization, the overarching object of the Organizational System.

Business Systems *govern* the conduct of business (software applications, accounting conventions, processes, procedures, etc.). The goal for Business Systems is to increase *throughput efficiency, reduce resource utilization* and to provide continuity through *reliability, predictability,* and *certainty.* Business Systems can be changed through the application of *causal performance indicators* and they can be measured quantitatively. Management is responsible for the quality of Business Systems in Organization.

Human Systems *influence* the nature and quality of interactions between individuals, groups, and teams. Human Systems do not lend themselves to definition the way Business Systems do. However, they can be characterized as those systems that increase the probability of certain types of results—the ones that are not predictable. Human Systems are further characterized by the observable behavior of individuals, groups, and teams through evaluations. The objective for Human Systems is increased *effectiveness*—that is the ability to bring something new into existence. The more effective the system, the more *discontinuity* it will generate. Human Systems can be changed by the application of *influential performance indicators* and they can be measured qualitatively in terms of increased *creativity,* and *innovation.* Leadership is responsible for the quality of Human Systems in Organization.

Summary

The responsibility for the overall integration of Business Systems and Human Systems within an Organizational System rests with Development. Development is the *interface* between the Management of Business Systems and the Leadership of Human Systems. Development can be measured in terms of the levels of buffering it provides plus the velocity with which it moves new possibilities along the spectrum of feasibility. If Organization is also a system of constraints—that is, a system of limits to what can be included and a limitation of possibilities—then the disciplines needed for calibration of the organization (deciding on the tradeoffs and designing KPIs) are Management, Leadership, and Development. So, calibration refers to a combination of tradeoffs between effectiveness and efficiency and designing KPIs. A discussion of calibration, constraints, and leverage follows in Chapter 12.

References

Barrett, R. (2017) *The Values-Driven Organization,* 2nd ed. New York: Routledge.

Goldratt, E. and Cox, J. (2014) *The Goal: A Process of Ongoing Improvement.* Great Barrington, MA: North River Press.

Hammer, M. and Champy, J. (2006) *Reengineering the Corporation: A Manifesto for Business Revolution.* New York: Harper Business.

Leonard-Barton, D. and Kraus, W. (1985) Implementing New Technology, *Harvard Business Review,* November 1985. Retrieved from https://hbr.org/1985/11/implementing-new-technology on November 21, 2020.

Meadows, D.H., Meadows, D.L., Randers, J., and Behrens III, W. (1972). *Limits to Growth: A Report for the Club of Rome's Project on the Predicament of Mankind.* New York: Universe Books.

Meadows, D. (1991) *Global Citizen.* Washington, DC: Island Press.

Tsao, F. and Laszlo, C. (2019) *Quantum Leadership: New Consciousness in Business.* Stanford, CA: Stanford Business Books.

12

CALIBRATION, CONSTRAINT AND LEVERAGE

Introduction

In the last chapter, we explored ways of optimizing Organization through integrating Human Systems and Business Systems. State shifts in thinking and perception, or inflection points, become powerful ways to integrate meaningful change. Key performance indicators are not the only way to bring about state shifts in thinking and perception, but they are among the most powerful tools we have.

Throughout this book we have talked about the constraints inherent in any system, and in this chapter our intent is to expand your understanding of how to calibrate constraints and to distinguish the points of leverage available to optimize organizational transformation. We pose questions that may seem simply philosophical, but they are meant to provoke real dialogue among those who are committed to the success of the organization. We encourage you and your team to wrestle with these questions and to find real answers. In the process, you will perceive your system in expanded ways, and new possibilities will emerge.

DOI: 10.4324/9781003131847-12

Calibrating Constraint at the Scale of Organization

Organization has three primary constraints. They are the three organizational disciplines: Management, Leadership, and Development. Also, there are three secondary transcendent constraints: Design, Application, and Execution that transcend Management, Leadership, and Development. That is to say, each secondary constraint has, within it, one element of each primary constraint.

Constraints and Real-World Systems

Goldratt (1999) observes that applied real-world systems have at least one constraint otherwise they would be capable of infinite throughput, which is not possible.

In the application of linear programming models, which are capable of solving optimization problems for systems with hundreds of constraints, researchers have found that all but a few such solutions with more than three constraints were so unstable that they are completely impractical amid the noise of a real-world system. The stability of optimization systems has a strong correlation to the number of constraints—the more constraints, the less stability.

The application of our approach to organizational integration has provided compelling evidence that optimization of Human Systems results from initiating "self-organizing processes" that are low in constraint and high in relationship. On the other hand, it is the imposition of "prescribed processes" high in constraint and low in relationship that optimize Business Systems. Both have critical limits in application and these limits are generally poorly understood, which can result in some very undesirable outcomes.

When Mel first came across the Goldratt's (1999) work regarding constraints he thought: "This whole approach is counterintuitive." It was obvious to him that complex systems such as organizations have many more than three constraints. He remembers thinking that perhaps Organization is one of the exceptions to the rule. This proposition of only three constraints called into question everything he had thought through regarding Organization. On reflection, he began to see that perhaps what Goldratt and others working on the Theory of Constraints found actually did apply to Organization.

Theory of Constraint practitioners claim that in practice three constraints is the realistic maximum for stability. In adopting their thinking and findings we can see that at any given scale of Organization it is possible to have only three constraints. One implication of this: impacting a complex system can be made both simpler and more effective, by providing methodologies for *scaling points-of-view* (perception) and for *calibrating constraints* (controls and influences) in sets of three. This is the basis for our assertion that at the scale of Organization there are three primary constraints: Management, Leadership, and Development, plus three secondary, transcendent constraints: Design, Application, and Execution.

Now that all of this background is in place, how do we find the leverage points to effectively bring about changes in such complex and chaotic systems such as an organization? The next section will address this more directly.

Leverage in Organization

Donella Meadows' (et al. 1972, 1991, 1999) work in systems analysis revealed the possibility of leverage points for system interventions. She proposed that the success of an intervention is scale dependent. Our work indicates that successful integrations are the result of major interventions that require finding points of leverage quickly. Meadows goes on to say that to the degree that the observer is part of the system, awareness and calibration of these leverage points is an aspect of self-organization (we would also add self-generation). She suggested that when this is done collaboratively, intervention reveals a collective intelligence, which is greater than the sum of parts. Her observations on this point are often cited in energy economics, green economics, and human development theory. We figure this is good company to be in, so we are citing Meadows' observations and building upon them for our purposes.

Meadows started with the observation that there are levers, or places within a complex system where a small shift in one thing can produce big changes in everything. Meadows tells us that we not only need to realize the existence of these leverage points, but also to know where they are and how to use them. According to Meadows, most people know instinctively where these points of leverage are, but tend to calibrate them in the wrong direction. What this typically looks like *on the ground* is applying more resources and realizing diminishing returns. This is like doing more of what will never be enough.

Trimtabs—A Simple Application

Buckminster Fuller said this kind of leverage is about finding the "trimtabs." Val Jon Farris was Fuller's event producer where thousands of people would fill auditoriums around the country to hear him address the question: "How can an individual make a difference in the world?" She describes the origin of the "trimtab" concept:

> At those events, Bucky told a story of when the Navy commissioned him to solve a critical engineering problem at the height of World War II. As the war raged on the high seas ever-larger battle ships were needed to seize the advantage. As these "great ships of state" as Bucky called them grew in size, their steering mechanisms required more power to turn their rudders than their engines could produce. His revolutionary invention not only solved this crucial military problem it created a new paradigm for human greatness.
>
> Bucky's invention was called a "Trimtab," a small six-inch wide strip of metal attached by hinges to the trailing edge of a ship's rudder. As an engine's hydraulics force the Trimtab into the path of oncoming water, the pressure generated against it assists the rudder in making its turn. Next, Bucky posed that like this tiny sliver of metal can alter the course of a great ship of state, you and I as little individuals can change the course of humanity.
>
> (Farris 2014)

Turning a ship's wheel at the helm applies force to the trimtab, not to the rudder. The trimtab is turned opposite to the direction the rudder needs to go in. Turning the trimtab on a ship's rudder takes a small fraction of the energy needed to turn a rudder itself. In fact, it's impractical to build a system that can withstand the kind of force generated by the energy it takes to turn a rudder large enough to turn a battle ship or an ocean liner. If energy is applied directly to the rudder, rather than leveraging force through trimtabs, diminishing returns will have the steering system fail long before enough force is applied to turn the rudder of the ship.

Turning a trimtab has the effect of amplifying energy (an exponential return) and therefore produces leverage. The speed with which the ship moves through water determines the amount of potential energy available. This potential energy is transformed into kinetic energy by turning the trimtab. When a trimtab is turned toward port, the resistance of the water flowing against the trimtab turns the rudder in the opposite direction toward starboard. When the rudder turns into the resistance of the water, it transforms potential energy into kinetic energy. This provides the energy needed to help the ship change direction. Notice there are three constraints: the ship, the rudder, the trimtab—each one moving through water and overcoming resistance in distinct but related ways. Their relationship is a function of strategic-design; their effectiveness is a function of objective-application, and turning the ship is a function of the tactical-execution.

This trimtab example makes some useful points. Once we think a mechanism through, like the steering system for a ship, we can build the systems for reliable, predictable, and repeatable results. These are the kind of systems that Management is most concerned with—ones that produce repeatable results in a reliable way. Because they are systems based on *cause* and *effect* their design makes it relatively easy to figure out what is needed to correct or calibrate them. The construction of this kind of system tends to be resource-intensive. This makes changing them after construction costly and difficult. Therefore much attention must be paid to getting it right the first time. This is the part of organization that is "build to last." Frequent swap-outs of most management systems are not practical. Management systems' flexibility is achieved through increased articulation within the systems (increased points of leverage and control) and increased articulation increases complexity, which in turn increases the cost of maintaining the system after it is built.

Leadership on the other hand is challenged with creating trimtabs that are simple in their design and that can morph as they are applied. These trimtabs are often designed on the fly and always with insufficient data to validate their effectiveness in the design phase. Validation occurs in application and it is in application that they morph. Leadership's trimtabs are not based in *cause* and *effect* but rather they are more a product of *notions* and *probabilities*—ones that appear on their face to be valid and to hold potential.

Because Leadership systems are based on probability and possibility they are almost never just right in their early application. Their flexibility is, in large part, a product of the simple concepts from which they flow. Their elements are high on relationship and low on constraint, so they allow extraordinary flexibility. Leadership's trimtabs certainly don't meet

Management's standards for stability and continuity but they can bring new possibility into early-stage reality with considerable velocity.

It is Development's job to foster the morphing of Leadership's trimtabs— building new forms of control that take early-stage reality into a state of increased stability. When there is enough stability to reach the outer margins of what is acceptable to Management, then Management takes over to integrate the new "emerging reality" into existing established Business Systems. Management's challenge is to take what Leadership created and Development has piloted, and then bring it to stability through optimization of efficiency and control by applying continuous improvement models.

Performance Indicators as Trimtabs

All examples have limitations, but they can be useful for distinguishing and teasing out new ideas. What the example of trimtabs for rudders on battle ships and ocean liners suggests is that KPIs can be used like trimtabs for organization. It further suggests that performance indicators are more than measures; they are also influencers and, as such, are potential points of leverage for intervention and large-scale change. It also suggests that the design and nature of performance indicators for Management, Leadership, and Development need to be thought through in different contexts. At the risk of overburdening the use of examples, let's extend what we learned here by using one additional example.

Aircraft flight controls allow a pilot to safely guide a plane to the desired destination. The example used here describes controls for a single engine monoplane of conventional design. Other fixed-wing aircraft configurations may use different control surfaces, but the basic principles remain. The controls for rotary wing aircraft (helicopter or auto gyro) are completely different and might be an appropriate example for extending this thinking even further at some future time.

Axes of Motion

What if we were to think of an organization like an aircraft in motion? It is free to rotate around three axes (There's that three thing again!). The axes are perpendicular to each other and intersect at the center of gravity. In order to control position and direction we must be able to control rotation about axes. Not too bad a way to think about organization and ... it opens up the possibility of designing an organization's instrument panel, controls, and influencers in new ways. The idea of "designing instrument panels" is not a new idea, but the approach we are suggesting does go beyond what has been previously put forward and has major new dimensions for application.

Some organizations can be likened to a single aircraft, flying in one direction with a clear destination or target. Other organizations look more like a squadron, sometimes flying in tight formation and at other times flying in a loose formation. A squadron can have many destinations or targets. Think of squadron members as operating groups and divisions of an organization. Certainly, having an overall view of the statistical results for the squadron helps establish its level of its effectiveness but one cannot control a squadron in the strict sense of the term. You can only orchestrate it by setting clear objectives for its members. Members, however, can direct the planes by using instrument panels in combination with controls, and guided by clear objectives. This opens up the idea that the nature of performance indicators for a squadron (the organization) are quite different from those of its members (operating groups and divisions) and raises these two questions:

1. What is the right center of gravity for the organization?
2. What are the three performance indicators that intersect the center of gravity?

Vertical Axis

Suppose an organization has a vertical axis that passes through it from top to bottom. In aviation the rotation about this axis is called yaw. Yaw changes the direction from left or right. The primary control of yaw is with the rudder. Ailerons also have a secondary effect on yaw.

This suggests four vertical axis design questions:

1. What forms the top and bottom of organization?
2. What three performance indicators effect direction for organization?
3. What three performance indicators have secondary effect on direction?
4. What is the right relationship for these performance indicators?

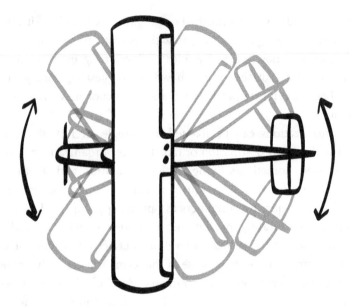

Figure 12.1 Vertical Axis

Figure 12.2 Longitudinal Axis

Longitudinal Axis

Extending this example, organization also has a longitudinal axis passing from front to back. In aviation, rotation about this axis is called bank or roll. Bank changes the orientation of the aircraft's wings with respect to the downward force of gravity. Bank angle changes by increasing the lift on one wing and decreasing it on the other. This differential lift causes bank rotation around the longitudinal axis. The ailerons are the primary control of bank. The rudder also has a secondary effect on bank.

This suggests four longitudinal axis design questions:

1. What forms the front and back of organization?
2. What three performance indicators effect lift for organization?
3. What three performance indicators have secondary effect on lift?
4. What is the right relationship for these performance indicators?

Lateral Axis

Next, think of organization as having a lateral axis that passes through it from left to right. In aviation, rotation about this axis is called pitch. Pitch changes the vertical direction the aircraft's nose is pointing. The elevators are the primary control of pitch (up or down). The elevator also has a secondary effect on pitch (how far up or how far down).

This suggests four lateral axis design questions:

1. What forms the left and the right of your organization?
2. What three performance indicators determine pitch (or the vertical direction) in your organization?
3. What three performance indicators have secondary effect on pitch, in other words what affects how far up or down your organization is headed?
4. What is the right relationship in your organization for the performance indicators that affect your lateral axis? For example, which performance indicators are most important?

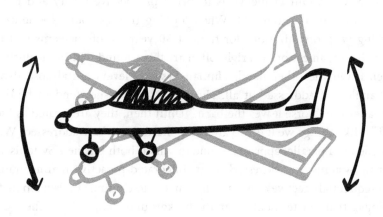

Figure 12.3 Lateral Axis

There is far more complexity regarding aircraft control than represented so far. The distinctions we could draw from expanding on this example would be overkill. However, the design questions for each of these axes can lead to whole new ways of perceiving Organization, which in turn can lead to new actions, leading to breakthrough results. These are discussions worth having!

As previously stated, Meadows found that most people instinctively know where the points of leverage (trimtabs) are, but tend to calibrate them in the wrong direction. Our experience suggests that most large-scale systems changes (M&As, enterprise system implementations, TQM, reengineering, downsizing, etc.) fail to meet expectations for the very reason Meadows states—points of leverage are calibrated in ways that produce the exact opposite of the intended effect. One case that exemplifies Meadows' point:

A large Canadian telco was "downsizing" in the mid-1990s. They designed a severance package intended to encourage people to leave the company. They overlooked one important item. Those with the best track records were the ones most able to land new, and often better jobs than the one they had with the company. Guess who left and who stayed. Because the downsizing was not put into proper context, the company lost many of its best people because those people could not see their future in the organization in light of the downsizing. The downsizing happened, expenses were reduced to acceptable levels, and the company survived, but it did so at an unnecessarily high and unplanned cost in human capital and to the Human Systems.

There are numerous cases that make this point and in retrospect their flaws are clear. Our challenge is to bring prospective clarity and not to wallow in "20-20" hindsight. When looking through our experience of working with organizations for the last 50 years, it often seems that the levers that organizations get right often are those found within the Business Systems. On the other hand, Human Systems levers are almost always mishandled, if addressed at all. Human Systems issues tend to be dealt with after the "horse leaves the barn." Until then, they are treated as "soft stuff"—like things we'll get to after the "hard issues" are addressed. What is needed is a parallel approach—one in which both Business Systems and Human Systems are addressed in an integrated-proactive manner rather than sequential-reactive one. Our challenge is to continue to develop methodologies that isolate clients from the background complexity of these concepts and bring them to direct, immediate, and useful applications.

A Hierarchy of Leverage for Organizations

Meadows' (1999) work on leverage in systems has a strong correlation to leverage in organizations. What follows is an adaptation that draws heavily on her thinking.

Leverage and Key Performance Indicators are like the front and back our hand. One requires the other, and they arise together. Trying to run an organization without performance indicators and understanding where the leverage points are, is like running the organization using a Ouija Board. Sometimes we have to make what you might call "Ouija Board decisions"—there just is not enough data, information, or knowledge available at the time the decision must be made. So we do the best we can with what we have, throwing in as much intuition and instinct as we can muster. But this approach represents a necessary exception, and it is not the way to run an organization.

So, how can we increase the amount of data, information, and knowledge available to us, and how can we refine our intuition and instinct? There isn't just one answer to this question but if we are willing think through the right performance indicators and locate key points of leverage for our organizations then we will have made a major dent in the questions.

Twelve Points of Intervention

The following 12 points of intervention in performance indicators will help you to think through the integration of points of leverage. We have adapted Meadows (2014) Twelve Points of Leverage to our model of integrating change in Organization. The least powerful interventions are listed first, followed by the most powerful interventions at the bottom. It's important to keep in mind that sometimes you will want to use a less powerful intervention if that will accomplish the outcome you are looking for. At other times you want to be sure that you are not using too weak an intervention when a more powerful one may be needed. After each description of the 12 interventions, we provide questions that can be used by you and your team to help you apply each intervention to your organizational situation.

12. Parameters

Examples of parameters for organization are the size of permissible variances, credit card charge limits, size of a single capital purchase that requires prior approval, and so on. Parameters have the lowest leverage for intervention of all performance indicators; even though they are the most clearly perceived. Parameters have little impact long term, and they are not likely to change behaviors in any meaningful way.

A widely changing organization will not be made stable by a change of parameter, nor will a stagnant one suddenly "come to life" through the use of parameters. Parameters can help regulate—they can be like a "canary in the mine"—an early warning system for danger.

Awhile back, Mel and three of his colleagues were dinner guests of a large client. There were six executives from the client organization. Dinner was good. The meals were moderately priced. Everyone had a couple of glasses of wine. When the check came the most senior executive (let's call him Frank) collected his colleague's American Express cards. Frank added his card to the pile and then gave them to the waiter to pay the bill.

The next day at a morning meeting with Frank, Mel thanked him again for dinner and asked him why he used six credit cards to pay for the meals. Frank responding by saying that beginning this week his company put a limit on what they would reimburse one person for business meals without prior authorization. He laughed and said, "I just don't have time for this kind of nonsense."

If you have the authority, you might do your organization and its people a big favor by getting rid of "parameters that make no difference." Clearly some do make a difference and they should be supported. But parameters are often used to try to control things and that does not work. Take Frank for example. An executive with 25 years of service, working as a division head for a very large organization being required to get prior approval for meal charges over $100.

1. What three parameters make a positive difference in the function of your organization?
2. Name three parameters that interfere with the function of your organization.

11. Buffers and Calibrating Expectation

Buffers can have significant influence over organization improvements, particularly if they are not physical buffers where size is critical and can't be changed easily. Non-physical buffers can stabilize an organization when applied to things such as communication, data flow, and the minimization of external effects.

Calibration of expectations is a very effective means for buffering. However, for many organizations, expectation is a one-way street where it is good to raise them and bad to lower them. Appropriate performance indicators can help us understand how to calibrate expectation, learning where to "raise the bar" because that part of the organization has the "capacity and stock" to take it on and where to "lower the bar" to create some breathing room.

1. What are the three central expectations for your organization?
2. What are the three KPIs to measure each of those expectations?

10. Organizational Structure

Organizational Structure has a major effect on the function of Business and Human Systems, and it is therefore a potential point of leverage. No news here! This is obvious. However, refitting a structure can be risky. The costs and delays of restructuring may be prohibitive if externalities (uncalculated indirect effects) are not recognized. If costs make it impractical to change structure then some leverage points might be to: (1) Understand and work on correcting system limitations, (2) Relieve bottlenecks, and (3) Reduce fluctuations.

1. What are the three externalities critical to restructuring your organization?

9. Length of Delays and System Change Rate

The premise for this point of leverage is that information and action are related by cause (information) and effect (action). The validity of this premise depends on the context. Information delivered outside of its intended context is likely to result in one of two things; no action or inappropriate action. A leverage point change is the length of delay around information. Information received too quickly can lead to an overreaction. Information received too late can cause an underreaction.

Improperly calibrated delays cause oscillations when trying to adjust a system. Meadows provides a simple example of this:

The city council is considering building the wastewater treatment plant. However, the plant will take 5 years to be built, and will last about 30 years. The first delay will prevent the water being cleaned up within the first 5 years, while the second delay will make it impossible to build a plant with exactly the right capacity.

(Meadows 1972)

1. Provide three examples in your organization where information has arrived too quickly.
2. Provide three examples in your organization where information has arrived too late?

8. Negative Feedback Loops

Negative feedback loops work to slow down change processes. We invent them as controls to keep important system states within safe boundaries. In a system experiencing discontinuities, a negative loop will tend to promote stability in the early and intermediate stages of its application. When negative feedback loops are over applied, as is the case when stability is the dominant measure of success, their application leads to stagnation. Negative loops help keep outcomes near the target goal. These loops are useful when exceeding objective is as undesirable as falling short. Negative loops tend to provide regular, frequent feedback, high accuracy, and tightly calibrated variances.

1. What three negative feedback loops promote desirable stability in your organization?
2. What three negative feedback loops promote instability in your organization?

7. Positive Feedback Loops

A positive feedback loop is a self-reinforcing loop that tends to speed up change. Positive feedback loops spur growth and exploration. Examples: The more money you have in the bank, the more interest you earn, so the more money you have in the bank. The more babies that are born, the more people grow up to have babies. Or a recent example—the more people who have Covid-19, the more people infect others, causing the disease to grow exponentially.

The loops are useful when exceeding objective is desirable. They also lead to collapse when control of gain is lost. Positive loops tend to provide less frequent, irregular feedback, and are less concerned with accuracy and more concerned with timing. Meadows and colleagues' (1972) work indicates that in most cases, it is preferable to dampen the gain in a positive loop (slow it down), rather than increase gain in a negative loop (speed it up).

1. What three positive feedback loops are spurring growth and exploration in your organization?
2. What three positive feedback loops demonstrate potential for spinning out of control in your organization?

6. Structure of Information Flow

Who has and does not have access to information, and how information flows in Organization is a very powerful point of leverage. It is neither a parameter, nor a positive (re-enforcing) or a negative (slowing) loop, but a new loop for information delivery—the kind of information that goes beyond what is delivered normally, therefore causing people to behave differently. This powerful point of leverage is much less costly than changing infrastructure and it is also easier.

Meadows tells the story of a subdivision where all the houses were identical except for the placement of the electric meters. In some homes the meters were in the basement, and in other homes they were installed in the front hall, where residents could easily see how much electricity they were using. All other things being equal, electricity consumption was 30 percent lower in the houses where the meter was in the front hall (Meadows 1999: 12).

1. Where are the three highest leverage places in your organization to improve the structure of information flow?

5. Rules of the System

"The rules of the system define its scope, its boundaries, its degrees of freedom" (Meadows 1999: 13). Three places where it is easy to see rules in Organization are around incentive, punishment, and conduct-constraints. Rules can be a very high leverage point for change. However, rules cut two ways. They can provide positive or negative leverage depending on rule-cost relative to benefit. Rules are never natural in their effect and they always have a cost—mostly hidden. Rules in Organization have what we call a "rule-tax." Rules are taxed because they are implemented in the name of the common good and they are paid for by all—the same way a community is taxed for education, even those members who have no children in school.

There are many reasons for rules. Some rules are driven by outside regulation and they must be followed because they are needed for compliance—Rules for Compliance. Some rules are needed to maintain order in the system—Rules for Order. In this last category Rules for Order, the operative word is *maintain*. Rules can maintain order ... they are not likely to cause order. There are also Rules for Prevention—and these can be the mischief makes. This category is one where rules are often justified by isolated events. The rule that follows the event is set to make an example so that, whatever it was, does not happen again. This is a costly misapplication of rules and creates unmanageable bureaucracy.

1. What are three rules in your organization that keep it the way it is?
2. What are three for your organization that promote needed change?

4. The Power to Add, Change, Evolve, or Self-Organize System Structure

Self-organization refers to the capacity of a system to change itself by creating new structures, adding new negative and positive feedback loops, promoting new information flows, and making new rules. Meadows writes:

> Further investigation of self-organizing systems reveals that the divine creator, if there is one, did not have to produce evolutionary miracles. He, she, or it just had to write marvelously clever *rules for self-organization*. These rules basically govern how, where, and what the system can add onto or subtract from itself under what conditions.
>
> (Meadows 1999: 15)

A very strong case can be made that in Organization, self-organization systems are Human Systems dependent. As the business environment changes, Human Systems not only change to fit, but they also undergo an evolution that makes them able to break down and accumulate the changed content within their new environment. It is this capacity that has systems self-organize.

One example of a rule of self-organizing systems comes from our work with leaders. We are committed to working with leaders so that they are developing other leaders in the system. This is built into their key performance indicators as a way of creating a catalyst for integration between the Human Systems and the Business Systems.

Judi worked with the Honeywell Defense Systems Division to enhance their approach to Socio-Technical Systems (Pasmore et al. 2019). The Socio-Technical Systems approach puts all members of the organization into self-organizing teams. The leader's role transformed from supervising and controlling to advising, facilitating, and developing.

1. Where are three opportunities to enhance self-organizing systems in your organization?

3. The System Goal

A goal change has impact on every point of intervention listed above including parameters, feedback loops, information flow, and self-organization. There is not much to say about this one. What is important is to keep in mind is that when a system goal is changed, "business as usual" is subject to change. Everything within the system is subject to a reset to zero—that is, back to the beginning—starting over again from scratch. This reset does not happen with every part of the system, but every part should be called into question regarding its suitability in its current form.

> Whole system goals are not what we think of as goals in the human-motivational sense. They are not so much deducible from what anyone *says* as from what the system *does*. Survival, resilience, differentiation, evolution are system-level goals.
>
> (Meadows 1999: 16)

People within the system don't usually recognize the whole-system goal that guides the organization. The typical response to questions about the goal of a corporate organization is "we are here to make a profit," or "our purpose is to increase stockholder wealth." However, very few employees get out of bed in the morning excited about increasing stockholder wealth for their employer. In the mid-1980s, Ian Mitroff and Ed Freeman each detailed a new way to think about the systems goal of Organization called Stakeholder Theory, arguing that the firm should create value for all stakeholders, not just shareholders (Mitroff 1983; Freeman 1983). While some companies have given lip-service to a stakeholder approach, most still focus on goals such as profit, stockholder wealth, and market share.

This focus on bottom-line measures is despite evidence from several studies that demonstrate that an organizational focus on positive societal goals actually has a more powerful impact on organizational performance (cf. Sisodia, Sheth, and Wolfe 2014; Collins 2001).

1.   What whole-systems goals are currently based on what the system does, not on what people say?
2.   What whole-systems goals are currently based on what the system is designed to create for breakthrough at the scale of Organization?

2. Organizational Mindset (A Paradigm)

It is from the organizational mindset that Organization organizes. Think of organizational mindset as a societal paradigm made up of ideas and unstated assumptions that all established members share, not to be confused with culture. It is the thoughts and states-of-thought which arise in this paradigmatic framework that generate most organizational systems. Any commonly held set of assumptions forms a paradigm at the scale of Organization. Most sets of assumptions go unexamined and therefore re-examining these fundamental assumptions often leads to the formation of new paradigms. An organization unexamined is no organization. This iconoclastic approach has advantage in that it is a quick way to bring about certain kinds of change. Its disadvantage rests with its limits in application. Relating to this approach as a "silver bullet" for change leads to failures that ultimately invalidate what does work about paradigmatic change.

> Paradigms are the sources of systems. From them, from shared social agreements about the nature of reality, come system goals and information flows, feedbacks, stocks, flows and everything else about systems … The ancient Egyptians built pyramids because they believed in an afterlife. We build skyscrapers because we believe that space in downtown cities is enormously valuable.
>
> (Meadows 1999: 20)

Some suggest that paradigms are very hard to change, and others suggest there are no limits to paradigm change. Our experience indicates that there are limits and changing paradigms is not all that hard. It is relatively easy for a paradigm to shift at the scale of the individual. It can happen almost instantaneously in what Neal, Lichtenstein, and Banner (1999) call moments of "grace, magic and miracles." It can be more challenging at the systems level. Where the evidence for "hard to change" comes from is working on paradigmatic changes when something else is needed. Changing paradigms requires another way of seeing things and begins with those with open minds. Meadows provides this guidance:

> So how do you change paradigms? ... In a nutshell, you keep pointing at the anomalies and failures in the old paradigm, you keep speaking louder and with assurance from the new one, you insert people with the new paradigm in places of public visibility and power. You don't waste time with reactionaries; rather you work with active change agents and with the vast middle ground of people who are open-minded.
>
> (Meadows 1999: 18)

1. What are three assumptions in your organization that are unexamined?
2. Who are the active change agents who support the new paradigm?

1. Transcendent Organization

Organizations that demonstrate transcendence go beyond changing paradigms or challenging fundamental assumptions. These are organizations that demonstrate the ability to change the values and priorities that are the background to the assumptions. They are able to establish value sets and choose among them. This point of intervention is Human Systems and Business Systems dependent. It holds the most potential for fundamental change in Organization, and calls the Development Systems into play—the home of "Integrating Change." Transcendent organization is the highest leverage point of all.

> There is yet one leverage point that is even higher than changing a paradigm. That is to keep oneself unattached in the arena of paradigms, to stay flexible, to realize that no paradigm is "true," that everyone, including the one that sweetly shapes your own worldview is a tremendously limited understanding of an immense and amazing universe that is far beyond human comprehension. It is to "get" at a gut level the paradigm that there are paradigms, and to see that that itself is a paradigm, and to regard that whole realization as devastatingly

funny. It is to let go into Not Knowing, into what the Buddhists call enlightenment.

(Meadows 1999: 19)

Some human development models can be very helpful in guiding us to discern our own particular worldview or paradigm and to see the range of other possible paradigms. Examples include the Enneagram (Appel 2011), Spiral Dynamics (Beck and Cowan 2005), or Edgewalker Organizational Orientations (Neal 2011). If you delve deeply into any of these models of paradigms, you begin to see that none of them are "true," even if there is value in their perspective. According to Meadows (1999: 19), "If no paradigm is right, you can choose whatever one will help to achieve your purpose." Perhaps this is the most freeing thing of all.

1. What paradigm could your organization transcend that would be the most freeing and empowering?

This chapter concludes with "Six Rules for Engagement" that can guide you in calibrating the three primary constraints in Organization—Management, Leadership, and Development. There are two rules for each of the primary constraints. You might think of these as mathematical rules that define the relationship between variables, or alternatively, as dials that calibrate the balance between variables. As a reminder, continuity is related to the stability of the system and discontinuity is related to potential breakdowns and breakthroughs in the system. A stable system that never has any discontinuities will not be able to adapt to its environment over time. Conversely, a system that is constantly changing with discontinuities will not have enough resilience to hold itself together over time. Management and Leadership must learn to calibrate these different forces in order to find the right balance.

Six Rules for Engagement

First Primary Constraint—Management

Calibrating Constraint on Behalf of Continuity

*   Rule 1

    ○   Efficiency and control are directly correlated to constraint and continuity.

- o   Increasing constraint can improve efficiency and control.
- o   Improved efficiency and control increase continuity.
- o   Increased application of constraint produces diminishing returns.
- o   Optimizing diminishing returns is a function of calibrating constraint levels upward or downward and:

Estimating the resource needed to maintain constraint relative to the estimated value produced through a focus on efficiency and control.

- Rule 2
  - o   Increasing constraint will ultimately lead to a loss of efficiency and control and a collapse of the system.

Second Primary Constraint—Leadership

Calibrating Constraint on Behalf of Discontinuity

- Rule 3
  - o   The potential for creativity and innovation is inversely correlated to constraint and discontinuity.
  - o   Decreasing constraint can improve creativity and innovation.
  - o   Improved creativity and innovation increase discontinuity.
  - o   Decreased application of constraint produces exponential returns.
  - o   Optimizing exponential returns is a function of calibrating constraint levels downward or upward and:
    Estimating the capacity to buffer and socialize breakthrough and discontinuity relative to ...
    Risks to the stability of established systems.
- Rule 4
  - o   Decreasing constraint will ultimately lead to a loss of creativity and innovation and a collapse of the system.

Third Primary Constraint—Development

Calibrating Constraint on Behalf of the Socialization of Discontinuities

- Rule 5

- ○ Discontinuous growth is influenced by the socialization of breakthrough.
- ○ Capacity for socialization is proportional to tolerance for uncertainty.
- ○ Increased tolerance for uncertainty is a function of buffering.
- ○ Optimizing socialization of breakthrough is a function of calibrating tolerance levels for uncertainty through:

  Management's willingness to temporarily reduce constraint and accept less efficiency and control during the socialization of a breakthrough.

  Leadership's willingness to temporarily increase constraint and accept less creativity and innovation during the socialization of a breakthrough.

- • Rule 6
  - ○ Socialization of breakthrough depends on temporary states of compromise.

Summary

Leverage and key performance indicators are like the front and the back of the hand. They mutually arise. This chapter has presented new ways to think about leverage and key performance indicators in new ways, drawing on the work of Donella Meadows (1999; Meadows and Wright 2014) and Buckminster Fuller (Farris 2014).

Throughout this chapter there are questions that can guide you in Design, Application, and Strategy. We encourage you to seriously delve into these questions and arrive at concrete answers about your organization. You will find your thinking changed, leading to new opportunities for breakthrough and action.

The next chapter will build on the Model for Organization and will reveal the source code for an integrated organization.

References

Appel, W. (2011) *Inside Out Enneagram: The Game-Changing Guide for Leaders.* San Rafael, CA: Palma Publishing.

Beck, D. and Cowan, C. (2005) *Spiral Dynamics: Mastering Values, Leadership and Change.* New York: Wiley-Blackwell.

Collins, J. (2001) *Good to Great: Why Some Companies Make the Leap and Others Don't.* New York: HarperBusiness.

Farris, V.J. (2014) The Power of "Trimtabs": What Bucky Fuller Taught Me about Human Greatness. *Huffington Post.* Retrieved from www. huffpost.com/entry/the-power-of-trimtabs-wha_b_5863520?utm_hp_ref=impact&ir=Impact on November 24, 2020.

Freeman, R. and Reed, D. (1983) Stockholders and Stakeholders: A New Perspective on Corporate Governance. *California Management Review,* 25(3), 88–106.

Goldratt, E. (1999) *Theory of Constraints.* Great Barrington, MA: North River Press.

Goldratt, E. and Cox, J. (2014) *The Goal: A Process of Ongoing Improvement.* Great Barrington, MA: North River Press.

Meadows, D. (1991) *Global Citizen.* Washington, DC: Island Press.

Meadows, D.H., Meadows, D.L., Randers, J., and Behrens III, W (1972). *Limits to Growth: A Report for the Club of Rome's Project on the Predicament of Mankind.* New York: Universe Books.

Meadows, D. (1999) *Leverage Points: Places to Intervene in a System.* Hartland, VT: The Sustainability Institute.

Meadows, D. and Wright, D. (2014) *Thinking in Systems: A Primer.* White River Junction, VT: Chelsea Green Publishing.

Mitroff, I. (1983) Archetypal Social Systems Analysis: On the Deeper Structure of Human Systems. *Academy of Management Review* 8(3), 387–397.

Neal, J., Lichtenstein, B., and Banner, D. (1999) Economic and Spiritual Arguments for Individual, Organizational and Societal Transformation. *Journal of Organizational Change Management,* Special issue on spirituality and work, 12(3), 175–185.

Neal, J. (2011) Edgewalker Organizations, in L. Bouckaert and L. Zsolnai (eds.), *Handbook of Spirituality and Business.* New York: Palgrave.

Pasmore, W., Winby, S., Mohrman, S., and Vanasse, R. (2019) Reflections: Sociotechnical Systems Design and Organization Change, *Journal of Change Management,* 19(2), 67–85, DOI: 10.1080/14697017.2018.1553761

Sisodia, R., Sheth, J. and Wolfe, D. (2014) *Firms of Endearment: How World-class Companies Profit from Passion and Purpose, 2nd edition.* Upper Saddle River, NJ: Pearson FT Press.

13

SOURCE CODE FOR AN INTEGRATED ORGANIZATION

Introduction

Is it possible to understand organizational change the same way we understand changing how computers work? What would be possible if we were to understand organizational change at the level of its source code? This is what is needed to reliably integrate organizational change. In this chapter we will explore this possibility.

This chapter takes a taxonomical approach to understanding organization. Taxonomy is the branch of science concerned with classification, particularly of organisms, based on shared characteristics. The source code presented here is a taxonomy of systems and subsystems in Organization and their relationship to one another. One of the useful outcomes of this model is a classification of the nine archetypal roles in organizations. By the end of this chapter, you will have a much better sense of when and how to activate each role in your change integration efforts.

DOI: 10.4324/9781003131847-13

Source Code

Source code for computers is all about control. If you have the source code and you understand the computer's programming language, then you have control. You can make changes and additions to how the computer functions. In a similar way, this is also true for Organization. If you have the source code for Organization and you understand the language in which the code is written, then you can bring about change and integrate change into the system.

There are differences between computer source code and organizational source code that are worth noting. The main difference is that computer source code is built on instruction-sets and organizational source code is built on patterns-sets. To understand the language of patterns and pattern-sets, the source code for Organization, we must trust our "sight" at least as much as we trust our "analytic-cognitive" ability. Much of what we see happening in Organization does not lend itself to analysis, but this does not mean we can't see it, haven't seen it or that we will not recognize it when we see it again.

Very little of what we are asked to do in bringing about change in our organizations trains us to recognize pattern-sets, so we use "instruction sets" (encoded process steps) for most every form of change and integrating change within our organization. This approach works some of the time and not others. It works well for things that repeat. It does not work well for unique events.

When the imposition of process does not work, we seldom think that the use of process is invalid, rather we look for a new, better or different process. It just does not occur for most to question process as a means for change. This in part is because we don't readily have a means of distinguishing repeatable events, like manufacturing a battery, from unique events like coming up with a new kind of battery. It does not dawn on us that unique events cannot be addressed in reductionist terms and therefore the act of causing unique events, what is often called innovating, is not amenable to repeatable processes. We suggest that process is not a high-leverage means by which to innovate. To deal successfully with unique events we need to understand the function of patterns and "pattern-sets" in Organization. This means we need to learn to think differently. This does not mean that we should rid ourselves of the way we now think! How we think now is good ... and we need to expand our modes of thinking.

With computers, instruction-sets are identical every time they are used. The context for use, that is, the computer, is also unchanging and therefore every execution produces a consistent result. Not so with unique events and the application of pattern-sets, where the context (in this case the organization) changes from day-to-day. This means the use of pattern-sets is always starting-condition-sensitive. In chaos theory this is called "sensitive dependence on initial conditions," also known as the "Butterfly effect," based on Lorenz's (1972) paper titled, "Predictability: Does the Flap of a Butterfly's Wings in Brazil Set Off a Tornado in Texas?" Minute changes in the system's initial state will lead over time to large-scale consequences (Capra 1996)

Pattern-sets are never identical—they may be similar, that is, recognizable as belonging a group, but they are never identical. Classic physical world examples include snowflakes, evergreen trees, and ocean waves.

To recognize patterns we must be willing to "look" just to see what there is to see. This is like looking without expectation. Take a moment and reflect. See if you can remember a time at work when you were looking, and aware that you were looking, and were looking without expectation. Looking without expectation is foundational to the process of discovery. The greater the expectation we bring to seeing, the less likely we are to discover anything other than what we expect. However, looking without expectation does not mean we are looking without intention. When we are engaged in intentional looking, pattern recognition is the precursor to seeing pattern-sets. Unlike so many of the other things we deal with, analysis is not a point of leverage when it comes to patterns—however, seeing patterns and pattern-sets can provide significant leverage.

Analysis allows us to differentiate and separate things, while seeing allows us to distinguish and relate things. Differentiation is about taking things apart, separating, looking at pieces, recording differences and mapping fixed relationships onto "fault-intolerant" processes that are not change-amenable. Distinguishing is about seeing things in dynamic relationship, looking at the whole, recording similarities, and mapping the patterns in dynamic relationships into "fault-tolerant" approaches that are highly change-amenable.

A basic challenge in all organizations is integrating the dynamic relationships of individuals, teams, groups, departments, divisions, customers, suppliers, and regulators—relationships that are constantly changing and evolving. This means we must develop as much ability within our organizations to see, to distinguish, and to relate, as we have developed to analyze, find differences, and to separate. We can impose small degrees of order on dynamic relationships but imposed order is almost never sufficient, even in the military. We need a way to work outside of "control"—a way to approach the ever-changing needs that arise day-to-day and at the same time maintain purpose, objective, and reliability in our businesses. Join us in exploring what this might take. We will not find all the answers, but we will take new ground—ground that is important.

Patterns and Organization

To lead and integrate organizational change successfully, we need to update how we think about Organization. To begin this update, it helps if we are willing to consider the possibility that organizations can be seen as a system of patterns arranged in pattern-sets. In addition, consider that all organizations produce recurring, fractal-like patterns (the same pattern of wholeness is found at every scale) and pattern-sets that are recognizable if we learn how to look for them. A large majority of these patterns are not unique to any one organization or industry. The patterns arise from entanglements between three organizational subsystems. They are:

> Human systems: the source of possibility,
> Development systems: the source of efficacy,
> Business systems: the source of stewardship.

Entanglement is an idea borrowed from quantum mechanics in which the states of objects must be dealt with in relationship to each other, even though they are distinct (Radin 2006). In the case of Organization, the objects are the three subsystems above, human, development, and business. The states for objects are possibility, efficacy, and stewardship.

When organizational subsystems are seen in relationship to each other, it is possible to draw correlations between their observable properties. "Observable properties" is a fancy way to say "the stuff that can be seen and measured." Suppose that we could go beyond measuring transactions and inventorying facts. What if our current understanding of observable properties is only a small subset of what is there? What if we could begin to measure dimensions of states like possibility, efficacy, and stewardship—and even things we call the "soft stuff?" When we begin to see and measure what is called the soft stuff, we will discover the soft stuff has as much leverage as the hard stuff.

Peter Drucker, the father of management, was incorrectly quoted as saying: "What gets measured gets managed," an idea that has primacy in the field of Management. We know how to measure the hard stuff, but to begin to measure the soft stuff we must think of "measurement" in new terms—the kind of terms needed to take a quantum view of Organization. For example, it may be that we measure too much in some places and not enough in others. Over-measuring produces a lot of static and noise (un-contextualized information) and after a while we no longer notice it. It becomes like the sound of the HVAC in our offices. It's there, but seldom noticed. On the other hand, where we measure too little, we end up being blindsided by seemingly unpredictable events. Buerkli (2019), summarizing scholarly critiques of the measurement mantra, stated: "Not everything that matters can be measured. Not everything that we can measure matters."

Measuring what we don't need to know "just in case" is as dangerous as failing to measure certain things that don't fit the conventional wisdom of what can or should be observed and measured in Organization. Imagine that any time we measure something in one area of our organization it has an immediate impact on, what appear to be, other unrelated areas. Now suppose this is the case every time we measure something, not just some of the time. This means that measurement performed on one subsystem instantaneously influences other subsystems entangled with it.

The view that the very act of observing and measuring something in an organization has unpredictable and hard-to-trace consequences, is consistent with the correlations predicted by quantum mechanics, and observed in experiment. These observations necessarily lead to a rejection of the idea of local realism—the idea that any part of the organization is a "private reality" (reality in isolation) and exists without material effect elsewhere. Therefore, the idea that any part of an organization could, in any way, operate like a "private reality" (reality in isolation) would be hard to imagine. Yet we see parts of organizations acting with impunity, taking no responsibility for negative effect on other parts or the whole.

One implication of the quantum view means that we can no longer support the notion that information about the state of a subsystem can be successfully mediated by interactions within the immediate surroundings of the subsystem itself. Said differently, we must surrender the notion that there is "my area" and there are "other areas." Then, there is the "organiza-tion" and that while my area is part of the whole we are separated in ways where many of the things we do can be isolated and have no effect on other parts or the whole. This is an unsupportable and dangerous notion. We must be responsible for designing our relationships with the whole and its parts while focusing on our very real local accountabilities. Finding the lev-erage needed to be more effective individually, and to build more effective organizations, requires seeing the organization's systems in relationship.

Looking back over the last five decades makes one thing clear; a lot has been added to the mix for Organization without much being taken out. It seems there is a creeping accretion of mass and complexity leading to a dramatic increase in work where the only work product is internal and/or external compliance. This is work that lacks economic value as opposed to the kind of value we find when providing products and services in a free market system. So most of what was there 50 years ago is still here today—largely unchanged—continuing as if it were robotic and indestructible. Most of what has been added in organizations looks like compensatory processes, internal policies and external regulations. While all three have their value, they are too often applied without the realization that organi-zations, and the larger systems they reside in (an industry, the economy), do not respond predictably to controls.

In the next section we will move deeper into exploring how we might change our thinking about Organization.

Organizational Subsystems

We will revisit Organization's three subsystems in more detail than before, but first we need to revise the dictionary definition of Organization in Chapter 2 to more closely represent what we mean when we say *Organization*. However, no matter how accurate it might be, the definition will, at its best, be a shallow representation of what is meant when we say Organization.

Organization is a complex system of mutually dependent structures that form into subsystems. The subsystems manifest fractal-like patterns at all scales: individual, team, group and organization. The actions and interactions of subsystems, within scale, and across scales and perspec-tives, produce incalculable permutations of overlapping interests that serve complementary and conflicting purposes.

So! How useful is that? If anything, the definition demonstrates the futility of any attempt at defining Organization. No matter how "right" the definition, there is little about it that makes a difference. Even if we yielded an encyclopedic definition for Organization, such a definition would be of no more value to us in understanding how organizations function around change than would be provided by a mediocre paragraph.

If defining Organization does not lead to the kind of understanding that will make the difference needed, maybe we can find a way to see into Organization—a kind of organizational X-ray vision. This seeing would yield something practical—something that we can apply and work with—something that provides power and leverage in an ever-changing reality. Be forewarned. Such an approach will take a different order of thinking and concentration than that required by more traditional approaches based on analysis and accurate definitions.

Where we go next has many parts and we need to understand each part at face value, but we don't have to remember a great deal about them. What is far more important is to see how the parts come together in patterns—in relationships. It is in the patterns of relationship that we must do our thinking. It is in the patterns that we find the leverage and rewards for our thinking.

To begin to wrap our minds around Organization, its parts, its patterns, and its singularly unique nature, we will use taxonomy as a tool to organize the complexity, relate the parts, and see the patterns. This approach allows us to check for internal consistency in our thinking, to categorize and, at the same time, see the dimensionality of the whole.

A Taxonomical Approach to Organization

We have talked about Organization as a field phenomenon and now we will look at what shapes the field. There are four attributes that establish an Organization's perimeters—its outer edges—what it is bounded by. They are: *framework*, *discipline*, *intention*, and *articulation*. These terms will be used in artful ways and the definitions below will guide our thinking about them in the context of Organization.

Framework

A framework is a support structure in which other support structures can be developed and organized. Frameworks facilitate organizational development and running the day-to-day business. They are useful in understanding the complexity of Organization. Distinct frameworks are necessary for successful integration of change.

Discipline

There are many meanings for this term. In Organization, discipline is not a means of changing behavior of individuals or groups. Nor is it a coercive mechanism. Rather, organizational discipline forms the basic branches of organizational learning and it is therefore elemental to integrating change. Organizational scale discipline provides primarily methodological approaches that have direct and indirect bearing on secondary disciplines such as business administration, engineering, and finance.

Intention

Intention is another term with many meanings in common usage. As we use the term here, it means an "organizational state-of-mind"—one that increases the potential for particular results—as can be seen in the collective intention of an organization. In Organization, well-formulated and clearly expressed intentions (often called "strategic intents") put the game in play and set the direction that has the organization reach its objectives.

Articulation

By far the most complex organizational field attribute, articulation, is a balancing factor for the other three and is the inter-mediator of organizational socio-economic structures. Because Organization is an amalgam of sociological and economic factors, these factors create the superstructures of the industry to which an organization belongs. In Organization, articulation is the creation, identification, and naming of processes and practices of participation. Articulation takes into account cultural form and ideologies—derived mostly from the organization's industry (the context), an organization's societal norms—(the content), and level-of-practice such as is found in Six Sigma—(the process).

Let's go back for a moment to review the four types of action for integration from Chapter 6 because they will help us understand how to work with conflict at the scale of Organization. The four actions are (1) Disintermediate resources, (2) Intermediate possibilities, (3) Mediate differences, and (4) Remediate problems.

Disintermediating resources is the action of structurally disassembling established norms to free up resources for change. Intermediation is the action of integrating discontinuity such as breakdowns and breakthroughs to generate new possibilities for the organization and to break through established norms. Mediating differences is the process of assessing different possible actions and assessing the strengths and weaknesses between competing influences. Mediation is done with the intention of increasing predictability, certainty, and repeatability of the application of breakthrough efforts. Remediation is about repairing, refurbishing, reestablishing, and/or recovering all or portions of preexisting norms before the change was implemented. It's about fixing what's broken.

Within and between an organization's socio-economic structures, patterns of conflict arise. Conflict normally calls for mediation. However, when there are struggles within and/or between an organization's economic structure (hierarchy—business systems) and within its social structure (relational networks—human systems), *intermediation* produces outcomes consistent with principles, values, and mutual interests. It can generate new possibilities. This is in contrast with *mediation*, which produces outcomes that are consistent with what those with authority want. Conflict that arises when integrating change is best served by intermediation, which is more likely to provide for the interests of all parties with far less compromise than that which is required in mediation.

The interrelationships of cultural forms, societal norms, and practice cannot be predetermined, mechanically or even paradigmatically, during the period of integration. Rather they are the product of negotiation, imposition, resistance, and transformation. Thus the integration of change cannot be attached to Organization mechanically or even paradigmatically. Nor can particular interpretations, valuations, and uses of form or practice. Change and its integration must evolve in play, with a commitment to playing an infinite game (Carse 2011). Attempts to prescribe the play will kill the game. This does not mean that setting objectives can be overlooked, however, the more the players can call the plays, the greater the chances for reaching objectives and successfully integrating change.

In spite of compelling evidence for its flaws in bringing about change, some in organizations embrace the view that bosses set the game rules and prescribe the play, and everyone else does as they are told. This is more in line with Carse's (2011) finite game; there are winners and losers, some give orders and others take orders. The notion that the game could be "co-designed" and the play determined "just-in-time" rather than prescribed, occurs as irresponsible in a finite game, if it occurs at all. In some situations where the outcome must be the same each time (for example drug efficacy or manufacturing interchangeable parts), prescriptive play is a responsible approach. However, most change integration requires unique approaches and therefore the rules for engagement are different each time. This means that we are not talking about the same game played differently; what we are talking about is a different game each time. This different game is co-designed, just in time, against a background of clear intentions and objectives. Play has a minimum of rules, and design and execution are "just-in-time" events. When this approach is used, a totally unforeseeable structural resonance emerges between the elements that make up the socio-economic whole of Organization and new possibilities and results emerge. In the aftermath, it's often called organizational transformation.

These four attributes of the organizational field, *framework*, *discipline*, *intention*, and *articulation*, are basic constraints for Organization and as such they are the pillars of its existence. We will now take a look into the field of Organization and explore its more complex nature.

The four constraints form two pairs; one pair is *discipline and framework* the other pair *intention and articulation*. Each pair's members are correspondents, one to the other. Each arises as a function of the other—discipline as a function of framework (and vice versa) and articulation as a function of intention (and vice versa).

One way to understand the idea of correspondents is to look at your hand, as we mentioned earlier. Notice, it has a front and back. Each, front and back, is distinct and yet they are also related—they come together—you cannot have one without the other. They present themselves at the same time, in the same place, and as a unified whole comprised of distinct elements.

As you read through the rest of this chapter, we invite you to use this organizational taxonomy as a guide to think about your organization and your breakthrough project. Here are some questions you and your team might explore:

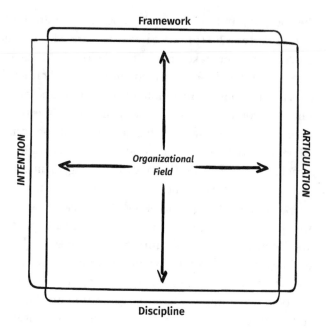

Figure 13.1 Organizational Field

1. What is our framework for this breakthrough project—i.e. what support structures exist, and what support structures will need to be developed? What resources exist, and what resources will need to be developed?

2. What disciplines or branches of learning will we need in order to initiate this breakthrough project? What expertise do we already have? Examples of disciplines for breakthrough might include engineering, organizational development, or software development.

3. What is our intention for generating new order and prospects for the organization's future as we engage in this breakthrough project? What organizational state-of-mind do we need to hold in order to create this breakthrough? What intention will generate the purposeful, creative energy needed to drive the desired outcomes?

4. How do we articulate what we are up to in this breakthrough project. What processes and practices of participating in this breakthrough project need creating, identifying, and naming?

In our model, as outlined in the rest of this chapter, framework and discipline make up the vertical dimension of the field while intention and articulation make up the horizontal dimension. The vertical axis and the horizontal axis form a two-dimensional Cartesian grid, which is the basis for building our organizational taxonomy. The following principles will apply as we build this taxonomy:

- Everything that exists has a correspondent.
- Correspondents serve as extremes for a unifying theme (a spectrum).
- Correspondents are not opposites, but rather, they are interdependent competing influences.
- Correspondents are mutually arising – one comes with and is a requisite of the other.

For example, People and Organization are correspondents. Now test this statement against our four principles. The first principle may require a little more thought than the others, but if you think of Organization in the broadest of terms, it will hold. You can't have an organization without people, and where there are people, organization will arise.

Let's look at the correspondents of the vertical axis of framework and discipline, and the correspondents of the horizontal axis of intention and articulation. Since these correspondents are a spectrum, your breakthrough team can discuss where you are along each spectrum. Different team members may have different perceptions about this which can lead to rich and valuable dialogue about your engagement in the breakthrough process. This analysis of where you are on each spectrum should be revisited at different stages of the breakthrough project. There is no right or wrong. It's just important to know "What's so" for your team members.

The Three Correspondents of Discipline and Framework

Leadership, Development, and Management along with their less apparent, but not less important correspondents; Possibility, Efficacy, and Stewardship form the vertical dimensions of Organization.

These dimensions are foundational to Organization and without a clear understanding of each; most large-scale changes will fail to fully integrate, and it is also unlikely that they will meet performance expectations.

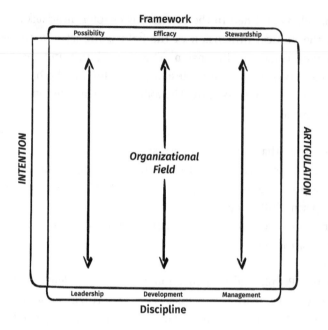

Figure 13.2 The 3 Correspondents of Discipline and Framework

The Three Correspondents of Intention and Articulation

Design, Application, and Execution along with three foundational correspondents—Context, Process, and Content—form the horizontal dimensions of Organization. Substitute Strategic, Objective, and Tactical for Context, Process, and Content as we work through the taxonomy. These terms are commonly understood and have more practical meaning. The substitutes are three of many possibilities that can serve you in your analysis and application. The horizontal dimensions, like the vertical, are also foundational and it is important to understand them for the same reasons.

The Six Fields of Leverage in Organization

The three vertical and three horizontal organizational correspondents form six spectrums and each spectrum is the foundation for a field of leverage. Leverage is defined as the place where there is the potential for the greatest effect. There are six fields of leverage in Organization: (1) Creativity, (2) Innovation, (3) Reality, (4) Potential, (5) Capacity, and (6) Capability. Each of these fields of leverage are described below. And each is an important point for exploration for your breakthrough team.

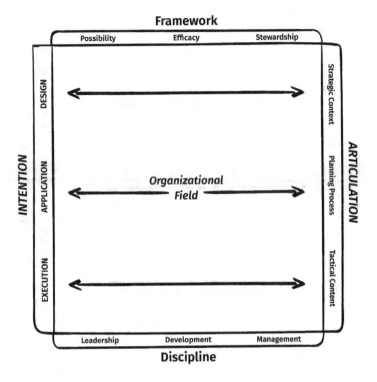

Figure 13.3 The 3 Correspondents of Intention and Articulation

We can see that *design* and *strategy* form a horizontal spectrum on which a field of *creativity* can arise. *Application* and *objective* can give rise to *innovation*. *Execution* and *tactics* can give rise to a new, generated *reality*.

We also have three vertical correspondents and their three potential fields of leverage. We can see that *leadership* and *possibility* form a vertical spectrum for realizing *potential*. *Development* and *efficacy* give rise to creating *capacity*. *Management* and *stewardship* can give rise to building *capability*.

A spectrum does not insure the presence of a field of leverage. The spectrum is only the foundation on which the field can arise. It takes intermediation (the intentional creation of discontinuities) to realize the field.

Before we move on, spending some time on the use of terms *spectrum*, *mediation*, and *intermediation* will be helpful.

Spectrum is used in many ways and its application has evolved over the years. In most modern usages there is a unifying theme. Early examples of unifying themes are optics and light intensity. The first unifying use of spectrum, *optics*, referred to the range of colors observed when white light passed through a prism. Soon after the term was used to refer to the

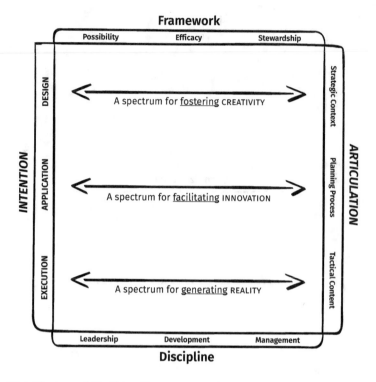

Figure 13.4 Horizontal Unifying Themes

frequency or wavelength of light ... light intensity is the unifying theme. In our usage for organization there are unification themes. For example, *creativity* is the unifying theme for the extremes *design* and *strategy*.

Early application of the term spectrum did not emphasize unification themes. An examination of early usage would have us think of the ends of a spectrum as being extreme interdependent-opposites. Some examples are: good and bad, up and down, and soft and hard. In our usage this will not be the case. The extremes of an organizational spectrum do not have to be opposites, they just have to be interdependent—that is, one requires the other in order to exist. Polarity Management (Johnson 1992) is one helpful model in understanding the relationships between interdependent extremes on a continuum. His key point is that polarities are to be managed (or "inter-mediated" in our language), not problems to be solved.

It the case of opposites interdependency is inherent—it is fixed—it is given by the circumstances. When there is no opposition, then, interdependency is a function of creation—it is given as fixed rather than that fixed as given as is the case with circumstance.

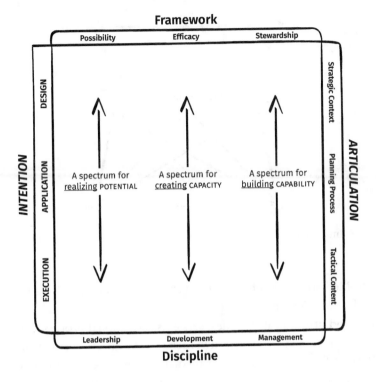

Figure 13.5 Vertical Unifying Themes

The preceding notion is important because extreme interdependent-opposites can be mediated with decisions made to favor one side and foreclose on the other. Get rid of "bad" and keep "good!" When spectrums are comprised of extreme interdependents but not opposites, intermediation is needed. This is because the process of intermediation recognizes the value of both ends of the spectrum. Intermediation is a "both and" process while mediation is and "either or" process. Let's take a closer look at mediation and intermediation.

Mediation, in its broadest sense, is the rational process of reconciling mutually interdependent, opposites. With mediation there are three possibilities: 1) A perfect stasis between X and Y—almost impossible in a changing world, 2) A choice in favor of X and against Y, or a choice in favor of Y and against X. Mediation is a bi-directional process. It is a way of "coming to the point" or "setting the direction"—that is, a point or direction on the spectrum. Mediators lead conversations to "fixed decisions" based in compromise or consensus—very useful for some matters and not for other

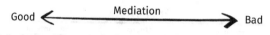

Figure 13.6 Mediation

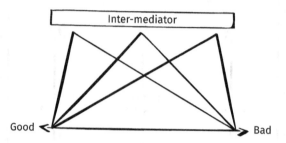

Figure 13.7 Intermediation

matters. Mediation is useful where "facts" must dominate. This is a very tactical form of decision-making.

Intermediation, in its broadest sense, is the rational process of providing biases (informed views) through inclusion of extremes rather than reconciliation of opposites. With intermediation there are an infinite number of possible good decisions—some more right than others but more right only in their time. Intermediation is a tri-directional process. It is a way of "coming to *many points*." To do this, the inter-mediator works above the spectrum, not on it, to lead conversations in ongoing decision-making. Intermediation is useful where "facts" are present but, by the nature of the undertaking, they are always insufficient. This is a very strategic form of decision-making.

Done well, intermediation includes some humor. Like the comic operatic interlude of an intermezzo, a skillful intermediating-leader will insert between the scenes of decision-making the kind of comic relief and contrast that seems to help us endure high drama. We certainly do not mean to imply that decision-making processes in your company resemble operatic performances with its attendant wailing, leaping, thrashing, pirouetting, falling on swords and all of that stuff!

Creativity in Organization

When it comes to *creativity in Organization* what we can say is: 1) It is not definable, 2) It is not well understood, and 3), we know it when we see it.

In spite of this, there is a useful way to think about creativity as it relates to organization that is useful.

Creativity in organization arises through divergent and cross-disciplinary engagement. It is seen as having originality that is appropriate to need, and that can manifest into reality. Creativity arises on a field made by the dynamic tension of *design* and *strategy*.

To create means to generate new ideas and concepts, or new associations between existing ideas and concepts. Seemingly a simple phenomenon, creativity is in fact quite complex and not well understood. Scores of definitions exist in psychological literature alone and creativity has been a subject of study not only in behavioral and social psychology, psychometrics, cognitive science, philosophy, history, economics, design research, business, and management, among others. For all the study, there is no single, authoritative perspective or definition of creativity and there is no standardized measurement technique.

Attempts to develop a creativity quotient similar to the Intelligence Quotient (IQ) have all failed because the process depends on the personal judgment of an observer. The ambiguity and multi-dimensional nature of creativity has led to the development of entire industries that pursue creative ideas and the development of creativity techniques, all of which represent a series of creative acts.

Linus Pauling is widely attributed to have said, when asked how he created scientific theories, "one must endeavor to come up with many ideas— then discard the useless ones" (cf., Ivancevic and Ivancevic 2007: 28). It is that field arising between design and strategy that winnows the ideas found in design and grounds them is well-bounded strategies.

Potential in Organization

Potential is a liminal field found between creativity and innovation. The liminal field is one of ambiguity, openness, and indeterminacy. On this field, organizations become highly malleable and people feel disoriented. Liminal fields are transitional and require organizational norms and limits to be relaxed in order to open the way to change and things that are new.

Leveraging potential is about optimizing energy, which is the same as optimizing work, which is not the same as being more efficient. Efficiency is about elimination of unnecessary work. This is a process with diminishing returns. Leverage is a process with exponential returns. It is about working through systems, as contrasted with working directly. When we work through systems it is possible to realize more results with less work. Both approaches are about energy optimization. In the first example we sell-short by conserving energy and in the second we buy-long by generating energy.

In a Newtonian, linear world-at-work each unit of work added produces the same level of results as the preceding unit did and therefore work and results are directly correlated. In a leveraged, non-linear world-at-work each unit of work added leads to more results than the preceding unit and therefore work and results have an inverse relationship—one that leads to increasing results and decreasing work.

Here is a direct application of work. You have an arrow and you have a target to hit with the arrow. The target is 500 yards away, and a quick test shows you can physically throw the arrow ten yards. You throw the arrow ten yards and then walk to where the arrow lays and throw it again another 10 yards. About 50 shots are needed to reach the target. Allowing ten seconds per shot means reaching the target will take 500 seconds or 8 minutes and 20 seconds. Next, we figure out how many "arrow throwers" we need to hire in order to have a thousand arrows hit the target each day. While this example may seem silly, a lot of work is applied through this kind of thinking.

Now let's take a different approach and use a crossbow to put the arrow in the target. We get the same result in a fraction of the time and energy. The crossbow is another way to visualize the transformation of potential energy into kinetic energy (leverage). Here the crossbow is the system. Cocking the crossbow is the work that creates potential. Pulling the trigger drives the arrow through the air by transforming stored potential into kinetic energy.

There is no possibility for potential energy unless we work using a system. Leverage begins in Organization with the work of design and strategy to create a system that provides leverage. Think of design as a way to get at "the what" and strategy as an expression of "the intent" behind the design. It begins by sketching out an idea—much like Leonardo da Vinci did when he conceived the possibility of a giant double crossbow that could sling stones (Gelb 2000). A breakthrough idea! Previously crossbows were designed to sling arrows and da Vinci took this application to a whole new level. This is what thinking outside the box looks like ... or maybe we can say it's thinking outside the bow?

When strategy is over-designed or too prescriptive it will almost certainly foreclose on innovation. To leverage potential using a system, we must also come up with applications for the idea. It is in envisioning possible applications that innovation happens. To innovate we must be free to speculate. We must be prepared to be wrong and also be prepared to be responsible for something that goes beyond what we could have previously imagined. Early-stage speculative thinking is how we get the game in play. This is where we might pilot some of the more promising applications—the ones that indicate the most efficacy and feasibility. For da Vinci's idea, building a scale model of the giant crossbow would be an example of a pilot.

Effective execution requires increased articulation. As new applications are introduced, there is a corresponding need to raise skill levels of people in the organization. Think about the earlier example of putting arrows in a target. Throwing an arrow at the target is a very low-skill process when compared with firing an arrow using a crossbow. The skill level needed to hit the target is much higher when using a crossbow. In this example we are using the crossbow and the skill required to use it as a proxy for leveraging work through a system. The greater the efficacy in application and the more refined the skill, the greater the leverage.

The process of changing something that is well established by introducing something new is a classic definition of innovation. It is one thing to come up with a compelling idea, like da Vinci's giant crossbow for hurling stones, and quite another to integrate that idea into an established system.

Innovation

Innovation in Organization is defined by the presence of something new and substantially different in the way work is performed and what the organization has to work with. Evidence for innovation includes things like a material increase in shareholder value, customer value, or product value. Innovation makes the organization better off, and ongoing innovation grows both the business and the organization.

Creativity and innovation are often used interchangeably, but in fact they are distinct. Put simply, creativity is about coming up with ideas that can be expressed as possibilities (design). Innovation is about turning those ideas into useful realities through application and technology. Creativity, no matter how compelling, will not drive innovation. It will allow for it, but that's not the same thing as providing the energy and space to innovate.

Innovation goes beyond the incremental change achieved through problem solving. Innovation is about establishing new organizational realities that are discontinuous. Innovation drives the organizational economy. As leaders, we need to focus on sourcing innovation. Sourcing innovation includes taking into account that when something new is established, even in its early stages, it will interrupt and disrupt what has been previously established. Just because value is being added does not mean innovation won't have a negative or destructive effect as new developments impinge on existing organizational norms and practices.

Innovation can impact existing organizational norms and practices in two ways—preservative innovation and disruptive innovation.

Preservative innovation will support and reinforce established norms and practices (how markets are approached, how capital projects are gated, and so on). This kind of innovation is evolutionary step-change, moving forward along an existing trajectory with a high probability of success and low uncertainty for outcomes.

Disruptive innovation, even before its full implementation, will have the opposite effect. It will at least threaten, and more likely displace, established norms. The integration of new applications and technology can be very disturbing, even when thoughtfully managed. Disruptive innovation involves leaps of faith in the face of insufficient advance knowledge and understanding. Calculating the chance of success is almost impossible if the criteria-for-success is too rigid. Early-stage innovation requires an act of existential faith.

A Closer Look at Organizational Taxonomy

The balance of this chapter is devoted to examining what is inside the organizational four boundaries that were discussed previously—*framework, discipline, intention,* and *articulation.*

Grounding Possibility—Leveraging Potential

Potential is about the realization of possibility—the possibility of things that do not yet exist, but that could. Realizing possibility takes a critical mass of people to ground the possibility. Typically, at the start, this is a very small, aligned group. These are the few in the beginning who see that a possibility could become a reality. The existence of such a group means that potential has been established. Leveraging this potential is a discipline of Leadership and the fulcrum is the role of Leading.

Realizing Potential—Leveraging Capacity

Here we are concerned with two things. The first is capacity itself and the second is the utilization of capacity. We must also take into account that some capacity will be fixed—such as a manufacturing line—and some will be variable—such as human systems. In the first instance, fixed capacity, we can be fairly accurate in our calculations. In the second—variable capacity—we can only estimate. With human systems the variable is potential energy, which as previously stated, is a function of the use of systems (crossbow vs. chucking arrows). Leveraging capacity is a discipline of Development and its fulcrum is the role of Piloting.

Achieving Productivity—Leveraging Capability

This is the endgame for leverage. For our purposes, capability is skills-based translation of potential and capacity into productivity. Leveraging capability is a discipline of Management and the fulcrum is Supervising.

A Model for Leverage in Organization

Now that we have delineated the three correspondents of Discipline and Framework (Leadership, Development, and Management), and the three correspondents of Intention and Articulation (Design, Application, and Execution), we can integrate these correspondents with the six fields of leverage in Organization (Creativity, Potential, Innovation, Capacity, Reality, and Capability) into a model that helps us to frame the nine key roles in Organization for integrating change.

A useful approach to framing organizational roles is represented in Figure 13.8. The model for leverage in Organization presupposes that when people organize—come together in Organization—that a field of energy is created—one that can be leveraged.

The model is built on a few basic ideas, which includes 12 competing influences, nine roles, and six unifying themes or spectrums.

Framework

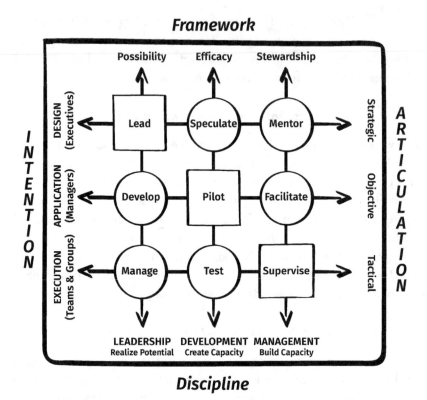

Figure 13.8 A Model for Leverage in Organization

A closer examination of the three vertical and three horizontal unifying themes in the model above (see Figures 13.4 and 13.5) will begin to reveal an organizational source code—a code that when understood provides access to *creativity, innovation, reality, potential, capacity,* and *capability.*

While this discussion may appear and feel abstract thus far, this next section will pull things together out of our exploration of constraints, competing influences, continua, and unifying themes.

In a five-decade long examination of Organization, from the perspective of what people do and how they work, as contrasted with what people are told to do and how they are told to work, we have uncovered nine roles that are part of most jobs that include managing others. The roles became apparent in our study of six unifying themes. As each role is described, we encourage you to think about these roles in terms of your breakthrough project and how these roles are being filled by various team members. It is also important to notice if any roles are not being fulfilled and what the implications for that might be.

Framework

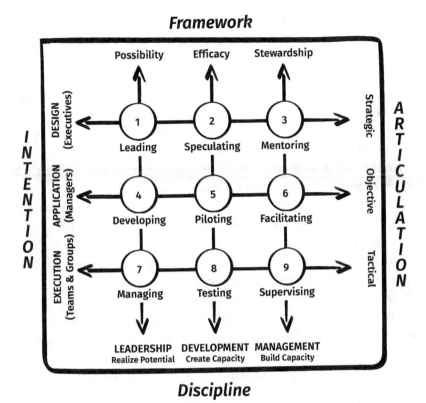

Figure 13.9 Overview of Organizational Dimensions and the Nine Roles in Organization

The graph above in Figure 13.9 emerged as we saw that Design, Application, and Execution are transcendent elements of Leadership, Development, and Management. The converse also seems to be the case. This insight revealed the possibility of nine intersections at which generic organizational roles for integrating change emerge. We think of these intersections and their related roles as attractors around which patterns of responsibility and practice emerge.

People use the terms role and position all the time as if they are the same thing. For this examination, role and position are not equivalents. For example, CEO and COO are positions, formal positions, not roles. From any position, be it team leader, director, VP, Division President, or CEO; many roles must be played out. Sometimes we lead a strategic conversation—at other times we facilitate a group in formulation, next we might mentor one of our direct reports, then manage a work group that needs direction and in between all this, we pilot a new possibility to determine its efficacy and feasibility. The commitments we make, the initiatives we launch, the projects we start, and circumstances determine role emphasis and frequency.

Think of the roles we play as individual practice areas. Consider that each area has the potential for professional development as well as personal development. Noticing which role(s) the job-at-hand calls for allows us to better articulate our work and, at the same time, learn and grow personally and professionally. Most of our work requires interaction with others. When we are aware of the role we are working from and what the role calls for, then we can be a good listener. It is almost impossible to interact with another human being and not learn something.

The question is not "Can I learn from another?" The question is "Am I positioned for learning?" What would it take to position ourselves in ways where we learn from another? As we begin to understand the design of Organization, we will see how to position ourselves for learning and how to increase our effectiveness and that of others.

Let's take a closer look at the nine individual practice areas and the implications of their horizontal and vertical groupings. We'll begin with the three vertical groupings—Leadership, Development, and Management.

Realizing Potential Through Leadership

Leadership is an organizational scale discipline that provides the opening for ever-expanding potential. It is *shaped by wisdom*—a thoughtful and statesmanship-like knowledge based in experience and enlightenment. Here we *commit to breakthrough*—creating fields that argue for discontinuous results and major achievements of lasting value. Here we *work through deduction*—deriving conclusions by reason, inference, assumption, and interpretations that go beyond those explicit in what can be directly observed.

Leadership is *framed in possibility* while perceiving subtle recurring unique patterns with recognizable designs (fractals) occurring at every scale. The possibility arises from an *informed exploration* through the use of creative thought, supposition, conjecture, theory, imagination, and vision. A pattern-based expression of the potential for favorable outcomes is both informed by the past and yet unfettered by the past. In Leadership there are three roles:

Leading
Developing
Managing.

These roles arise at the intersection of possibility with design, application, and execution.

Responsibilities and practices for the three LEADERSHIP roles are outlined in the boxes.

In your breakthrough team, here are some questions you can ask yourselves regarding the Leadership role in the context of your breakthrough initiative:

1. Do we understand what it means to lead, develop and manage for possibility? If so, how well are we doing? What can we do better?
2. How well are we fulfilling the responsibilities of the leadership role, such as providing meaning for the work, insuring that possibility becomes reality, and managing for predictability?

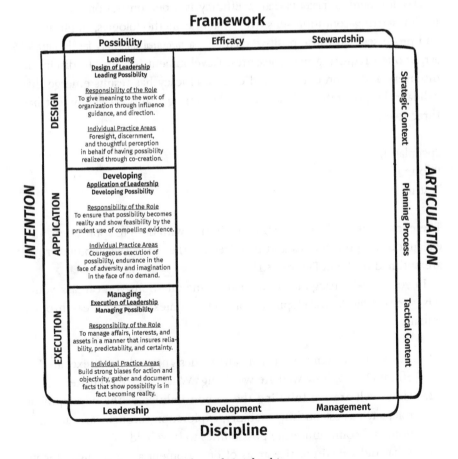

Figure 13.10 Realizing Potential Through Leadership

3. What individual practice areas of leadership are a strength for us and what can be improved?

Creating Capacity Through Development

Development is an organizational scale discipline that provides will, volition, and determination for ever-expanding capacity. It is *shaped by exploitation*—a skillful and intentional use of what emerges to greatest possible advantage. Here we *commit to existence*—bringing certainty to the transformation of possibility into previously un-thought realities. Here we *work through conduction*—recording and transmitting intermediate outcomes that are demonstrations of feasibility.

Development is *framed in efficacy*. Efficacy is a demonstration of suitability for starting-condition-sensitive, systemic methodologies, applications and processes that cause positive change—a *measured suitability for the intended purpose* often requiring new measures. Development is a way to discipline discovery and to produce desired effects. Efficacy has results emerge that validate the possibility of the change becoming reality. Development has three roles:

Speculating
Piloting
Testing.

These roles arise at the intersection of efficacy with design, application, and execution. Responsibilities and practices for the three Development roles are outlined in the in Figure 13.11.

In your breakthrough team, here are some questions you can ask yourselves regarding the Development role in the context of your breakthrough initiative:

1. Do we understand what it means to design, apply, and execute for efficacy? If so, how well are we doing? What can we do better?
2. How well are we fulfilling the responsibilities of the development role, such as establishing viability, exploration through early application, and communicating possibilities to stakeholders?
3. What individual practice areas of development are a strength for us and what can be improved?

Framework

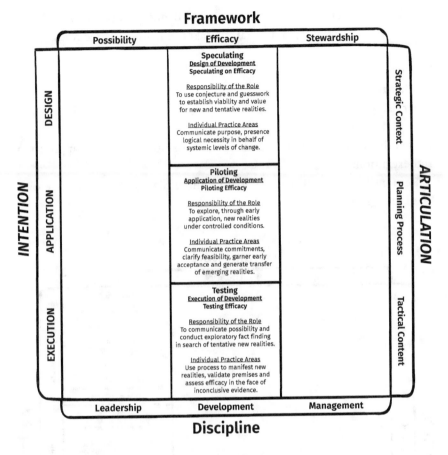

Figure 13.11 Creating Capacity Through Development

Building Capability Through Management

Management is an organizational scale discipline that provides the determination to build capability. It is *shaped by reality*, by objective views based in deterministic beliefs where outcomes are explained by preceding events. Here we commit to demonstrating improvement through the "cause-and-effect" building on what exists. The results validate empirical views and real causes, accumulating knowledge and skill to build core competencies. Here we work through induction—drawing conclusions about validity based on facts and events, and explaining anomalies as logical derivations of general principles.

Management is framed by stewardship. Stewardship means taking responsibility for improvement in performance using authority and careful exercise of influence to integrate proven processes with emergent processes to foster reliability, predictability, and certainty. Management has three roles:

Mentoring
Facilitating
Supervising.

These roles arise at the intersection of stewardship with design, application and execution.

Responsibilities and practices for the three Management roles are outlined in Figure 13.12.

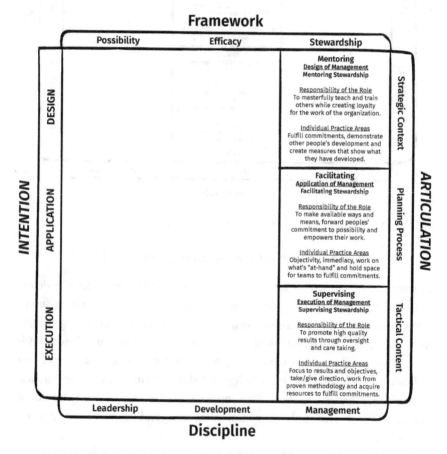

Figure 13.12 Building Capability Through Management

Here are some questions you and your breakthrough team can ask yourselves regarding the Management role in the context of your breakthrough initiative:

1. Do we understand what it means to mentor, facilitate, and supervise for stewardship? If so, how well are we doing? What can we do better?
2. How well are we fulfilling the responsibilities of the management role, such as teaching and training others, creating loyalty, providing the ways and means for breakthrough, and promoting high quality results?
3. What individual practice areas of management are a strength for us and what can be improved?

Your dialogue and discussion of these questions about responsibilities and practices for Leading, Developing, and Managing can provide you and your breakthrough team with a realistic picture of where you are and where you want to go in your processes of integrating change.

Next, we will examine the horizontal dimensions of this organizational taxonomy: Strategy-Design, Planning-Application, and Tactical Execution.

Strategic Design: Integrating the Context for Change

Strategic Design is not the same thing as "designing strategy," though it can be applied to that. It is an approach to design that is strategic—directional, but not prescriptive—flexible, not rigid. Strategic Design allows for timely mid-course corrections. It is here that we work in possibility to fashion overarching frameworks using conjecture and the mentoring of new ideas. Sub-structures (divisions, departments, etc.) are engaged to evolve resonant strategies that are consistent with corporate needs but also meet unique local needs.

Strategic Design communicates potential expressed in "scenarios" that point to one or more possible realities. The work is to enroll others in the possibility of those potential realities.

Strategic Design has three roles:

Leading
Speculating
Mentoring.

These roles arise at the intersection of design with possibility, efficacy, and stewardship.

Responsibilities and practices for the three design roles are outlined in Figure 13.13.

Here are some questions you and your breakthrough team can ask yourselves regarding the Management role in the context of your breakthrough initiative:

1.   Do we understand what it means to design for possibility, efficacy, and stewardship? If so, how well are we doing? What can we do better?
2.   How well are we fulfilling the responsibilities of the design role, such as giving meaning to the work, using conjecture and guessing to establish viability of the breakthrough project, and teaching others?

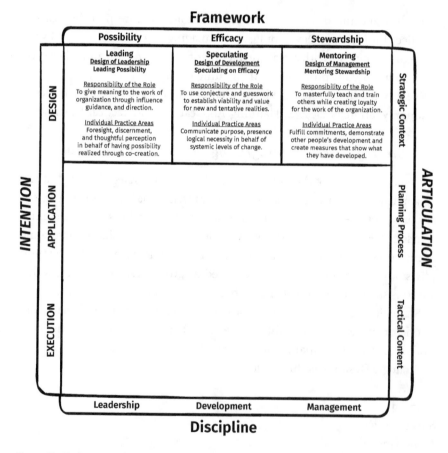

Figure 13.13 Strategic Design: Integrating the Context for Change

3. What individual practice areas of design are a strength for us and what can be improved?

Objective Application: Integrating Processes for Change

Objective application has intended outcomes as a primary focus and process as a secondary derivative of intention. The test for efficacy of Objective Application is the effectiveness of process not efficiency. Early applications of new processes are likely to be effective (i.e., produce intended outcomes), but inefficient (i.e., wasting resources). The first concern is focusing the process on objective results and once the objective is served then efficiency can be addressed. This approach moves possibility along a spectrum of feasibility toward reality. Along the way, intent and purpose are clarified, and change-amenable methods, procedures, and techniques are devised that integrate emergent knowledge and practices.

Objective Application engages the organization in discovery—it's about finding the means of transforming possibility into useful realities. Objective Application has three roles:

Developing
Piloting
Facilitating.

These roles arise at the intersection of application with possibility, efficacy, and stewardship.

Responsibilities and practices for the three Objective Application roles are outlined in Figure 13.14.

We offer these sample questions for you and your breakthrough team to consider as you explore and apply the roles of Objective Application with the shared focus on intention.

1. Do we understand what it means to have Objective Application of leadership for possibility, development for efficacy, and management for stewardship? If so, how well are we doing? What can we do better?
2. How well are we fulfilling the responsibilities of the application role, such as insuring that possibility becomes reality, exploring new realities through early application, and providing ways and means for breakthrough?

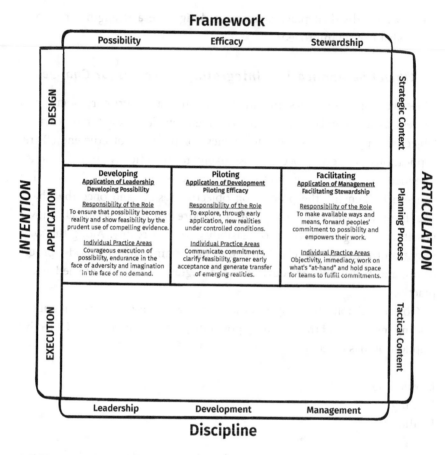

Figure 13.14 Objective Application: Integrating Processes for Change

3. What individual practice areas of application are a strength for us and what can be improved?

Tactical Execution: Integrating the Content for Change

Tactical Execution is focused on bringing resolution to processes to ensure repeatable results, minimize deviations from target norms, and to teach and transfer operational skills. The work is with teams and groups on producing results that become the evidence for the new reality. The teams work to bring about new levels of efficiency and ensure results that are consistent with originating intentions. Processes include measuring systems that track against plan.

Tactical Execution is about creating processes that can be repeated in ways that bring reliability, predictability, and certainty to the day-to-day running of the business. Processes are documented and best practices are identified.

Tactical Execution has three roles:

Managing
Testing
Supervising.

The roles arise at the intersection of application with possibility, efficacy, and stewardship.

Responsibilities and practice for the three Tactical Execution roles are outlined in the Figure 13.15.

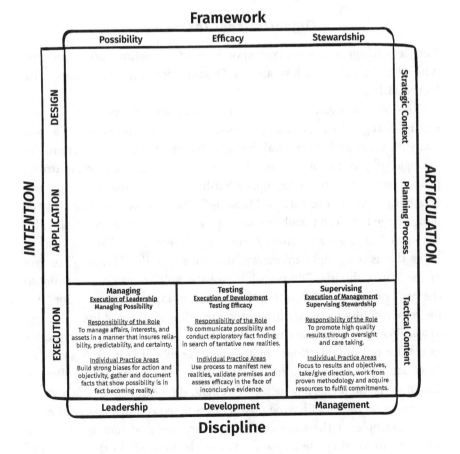

Figure 13.15 Tactical Execution: Integrating the Content for Change

In your breakthrough team, here are some questions you can ask yourselves regarding the Tactical Execution roles in the context of your breakthrough initiative:

1. Do we understand what it means to execute through managing possibilities, testing for efficacy, and supervising for stewardship? If so, how well are we doing? What can we do better?
2. How well are we fulfilling the responsibilities of the execution role, such as managing affairs, interests, and assets for predictability, communicating possibilities through exploratory fact-finding, and promoting high quality results?
3. What individual practice areas of execution are a strength for us and what can be improved?

Organizational Taxonomy

Now let's integrate the six correspondents of Discipline and Framework with the six fields of leverage in Organization into one chart. (See Figure 13.16.)

Consider this organizational taxonomy as a map of the territory for integrating change. There are many ways to work with this taxonomy as you and your team undertake breakthrough change in your organization. For example, if you are in the very beginning stages of your breakthrough project, you can turn to the upper left-hand intersection of Design and Possibility. This is the role of "Leading." The role of "Leading" in the design stage is to lead possibility (as opposed to managing for stability, for example). Leading for possibility requires a different mind-set and way of being that is open and exploratory. You can see in this "Leading" section of the Matrix that the "Responsibility of the Role" is to give meaning to the work of Organization through influence, guidance, and direction. It is the responsibility of Leadership in the early design stages of breakthrough to ask "Why are we doing this?" "What makes this project meaningful for us and for our organization?" In addition, the role of Leading has specific "individual practice areas" that are appropriate and useful in this effort to design for possibility. They include foresight, discernment, and thoughtful perception on behalf of having possibility realized through co-creation.

For example, at the time of this writing, Mel and Judi are working with a team to co-create a new field of academic study in the domain of

Framework

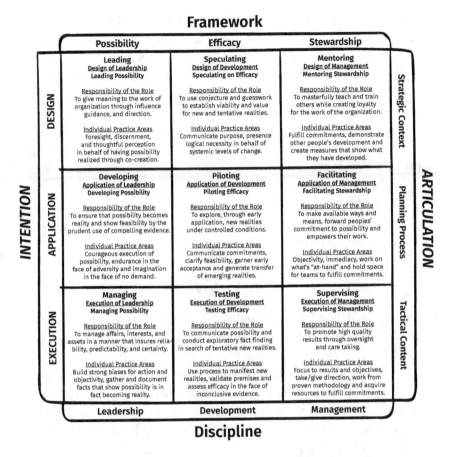

	Possibility	Efficacy	Stewardship	
DESIGN	**Leading** **Design of Leadership** **Leading Possibility** Responsibility of the Role To give meaning to the work of organization through influence guidance, and direction. Individual Practice Areas Foresight, discernment, and thoughtful perception in behalf of having possibility realized through co-creation.	**Speculating** **Design of Development** **Speculating on Efficacy** Responsibility of the Role To use conjecture and guesswork to establish viability and value for new and tentative realities. Individual Practice Areas Communicate purpose, presence logical necessity in behalf of systemic levels of change.	**Mentoring** **Design of Management** **Mentoring Stewardship** Responsibility of the Role To masterfully teach and train others while creating loyalty for the work of the organization. Individual Practice Areas Fulfill commitments, demonstrate other people's development and create measures that show what they have developed.	**Strategic Context**
APPLICATION	**Developing** **Application of Leadership** **Developing Possibility** Responsibility of the Role To ensure that possibility becomes reality and show feasibility by the prudent use of compelling evidence. Individual Practice Areas Courageous execution of possibility, endurance in the face of adversity and imagination in the face of no demand.	**Piloting** **Application of Development** **Piloting Efficacy** Responsibility of the Role To explore, through early application, new realities under controlled conditions. Individual Practice Areas Communicate commitments, clarify feasibility, garner early acceptance and generate transfer of emerging realities.	**Facilitating** **Application of Management** **Facilitating Stewardship** Responsibility of the Role To make available ways and means, forward peoples' commitment to possibility and empowers their work. Individual Practice Areas Objectivity, immediacy, work on what's "at-hand" and hold space for teams to fulfill commitments.	**Planning Process**
EXECUTION	**Managing** **Execution of Leadership** **Managing Possibility** Responsibility of the Role To manage affairs, interests, and assets in a manner that insures reliability, predictability, and certainty. Individual Practice Areas Build strong biases for action and objectivity, gather and document facts that show possibility is in fact becoming reality.	**Testing** **Execution of Development** **Testing Efficacy** Responsibility of the Role To communicate possibility and conduct exploratory fact finding in search of tentative new realities. Individual Practice Areas Use process to manifest new realities, validate premises and assess efficacy in the face of inconclusive evidence.	**Supervising** **Execution of Management** **Supervising Stewardship** Responsibility of the Role To promote high quality results through oversight and care taking. Individual Practice Areas Focus to results and objectives, take/give direction, work from proven methodology and acquire resources to fulfill commitments.	**Tactical Content**
	Leadership	Development	Management	

INTENTION (left side)   **ARTICULATION** (right side)

Discipline

Figure 13.16 Organizational Taxonomy

global consciousness. Currently there are no university courses, programs, degrees, or academic publications in this domain, but the team feels that there is great value in developing these elements of an academic field of study. We are in the very early stages of design and are exploring possibilities through inviting each team member to share their unique expertise and experience in the field. As we listen to what each member brings to the conversation, we practice *foresight* as we look for what could exist, *discernment* of what belongs in the field we are defining and what does not, and *thoughtful perception* of what each person brings that could lead to our co-creation.

If the breakthrough project you have undertaken is in its earliest stages, you need to have a primary emphasis on Design. You can work across the top row in the matrix from "Design of Leadership" to "Design of Development," to "Design of Management," understanding and delineating the various responsibilities and individual practice areas. This analysis will allow you to name and amplify the areas that are strengths for your design team, and to identify what responsibilities and practice areas need to be brought in or developed.

If your breakthrough project is at a mature and fully developed stage, you are in the discipline of management and your framework for the project is stewardship. This places you in the third column in Figure 13.16, working from top to bottom through strategic design, planning for application, and finally undertaking Tactical Execution. Your team can assess the responsibilities and the practice areas for each of the three roles of stewardship: mentoring, facilitating, supervising.

Summary

While this model and our description of it may appear linear, in application it is not linear. There is no step one, step two, and so forth. Each breakthrough project is unique and it requires all nine roles to be activated at different times and in different situations. The benefit of using this model in your analysis of where you are and where you want to go is that it overcomes our natural tendency to reside in the roles of management and execution. Many of these nine roles are underutilized in most change initiatives, and these underutilized roles are exactly what are needed if you want to create something that has never been created before. Working through each of these roles assures that you are not skipping or overlooking important responsibilities and practices that experience has shown are essential for sustainable change in Organization.

Different forces can impact which roles should be dominant at different times. While there is an overall movement from the early stage of design, through piloting different applications, to execution of the change, and there is an overall focus that typically begins at the higher levels in the organization with strategy, through the middle levels of planning, to the lower levels of the hierarchy with tactics, other things can interrupt this natural flow. Anything from a new CEO, to an emergency in production, to changing governmental regulation can interrupt the flow of your breakthrough project. When (not if) something like this happens, this organizational taxonomy provides a structured way to look at "What's so" right now, and what responsibilities and practice areas ought to be emphasized until you have gotten to a more stable place with a new organizational norm.

We encourage you to regularly revisit this organizational matrix as a way to check where you are on your breakthrough project and what roles, responsibilities, and practices can move you forward to full realization of your original intentions for the project. We hope that you now have a much better sense of when and how to activate each role in your change integration efforts.

Conclusion

We congratulate you for delving into this complex field of change integration and for getting to the end of this book. The journey is not over. If this is your first time reading this book, the journey is only beginning. Friends and colleagues who read early versions of the manuscript for this book were already familiar with the Integrating Change model but they told us that a second or even third reading deepened their understanding and their ability to execute the models and ideas presented here.

The first reading is like a vocabulary lesson when you learn a new language, and we consider this a new language for how to think about the higher level essence of Organization. At first, much of the vocabulary is strange, or the words are familiar but are used in unfamiliar ways. But hopefully there are glimmers of new ways to communicate and think about how organizations work and how they can be changed for greater effectiveness and impact.

The second reading is similar to re-reading the chemistry textbook in order to prepare for the final exam and to conduct the assigned laboratory experiments. As a reader, you gain a bit more understanding of the key concepts and how they are applied. If you study the chemistry text in a study group, you are able to share perspectives and insights, and it makes it easier to work together to prepare for the lab experiments. So it is with this book, especially if you took us up on our invitation to take on a Breakthrough Initiative, which by definition must be done in a team. If each member of your team has read this book and is working together on a project that is designed to make a difference beyond expectations, your discussions and decisions are where the real learning takes place.

If you are so brave as to undertake a third reading, you are likely motivated to do so because you want to share what you've learned about integrating change with others. Perhaps your organizational Breakthrough Initiative was so successful that it is time to expand this approach and this thinking throughout other parts of the system and you are called to lead that effort. Perhaps you are working with emerging leaders in either an academic or an organizational context and you want to help them think and perform in ways that are beyond what they originally thought was possible.

We are here to support your integrating change journey in whatever way we can. We hope you will contact us with your questions, your challenges, your suggestions, and your successes. We have created an online space for the Integrating Change community to support each other at www.integrating-change.com, so please stay in touch and let us know of your interest.

As we conclude, we want to underscore a few important principles in leading the integration of change (with a special nod to Peter McGaugh for inspiration):

1. People at work are fundamentally committed to contributing and making a difference. They want to know that what they do makes a difference.

2. You can't manage change, but you can integrate it through aligning the human and business systems.

3. A leader's primary job is to initiate change. Change must first be initiated, then integrated, and only then can it be managed.

4. Generative listening—listening for possibility—is one of the most important practice areas for leadership. It requires an open mind, the humility to know you don't have all the answers, and immense curiosity.

5. This curiosity creates the space for others and for you as the leader to speak with honesty, authenticity, and integrity.

6. An environment where people can speak with honesty, authenticity, and integrity is an environment of granted trust, which is essential to impactful positive systemic change.

7. It takes courage to stand in and commit to a declared future that is uncertain. There is a trust that what is required next will emerge because of your shared intention, your framework for change, the disciplines you call upon, and your articulation of what's needed.

8. It's important to honor that which you sense but cannot yet see, and to honor what others can sense but not yet see.
9. As a leader, and leadership resides in each of us, you always have a choice. Choose wisely.

References

Buerkli, D. (2019) "What Gets Measured Gets Managed" – It's Wrong and Drucker Never Said it. *Medium.com*. Retrieved from https://medium.com/centre-for-public-impact/what-gets-measured-gets-managed-its-wrong-and-drucker-never-said-it-fe95886d3df6 on November 27, 2020.

Capra, F. (1996) *The Web of Life: A New Scientific Understanding of Living Systems*. New York: Anchor Books.

Carse, J. (2011) *Finite and Infinite Games: A Vision of Life as Play and Possibility*. New York: Free Press,

Gelb, M. (2000) *How to Think like Leonardo da Vinci: Seven Steps to Genius Every Day*. New York: Dell Publishing.

Johnson, B. (1992) *Polarity Management: Identifying and Managing Unsolvable Problems*. Amherst, MA: HRD Press.

Ivancevic, V. and Ivancevic, T. (2007) *Computational Mind: A Complex Dynamics Perspective*. Heidelberg, Germany: Springer-Verlag.

Lorenz, E. (1972) Does the Flap of a Butterfly's Wings in Brazil Set Off a Tornado in Texas? *American Association for the Advancement of Sciences, 139th meeting*. Washington, D.C.

Radin, D. (2006) *Entangled Minds: Extrasensory Experiences in a Quantum Reality*. New York: Paraview.

GLOSSARY

Note: Italicized words are cross-referenced in this document.

Actions for Integration There are four actions: (1) *disintermediate resource*, which includes *disintermediate by circumstance* and through *facilitated intervention*, (2) *intermediate possibility* (also see *triage*), (3) *mediate differences*, and (4) *remediate problems*.

Adapt (1) Organizational *capability* (mechanism) that promotes continuity for survival. (2) Learn from experience to eliminate surprise and preserve value. One of the four *capacities* for integration.

Agreement The shared perspective that an action is "right," meaning it will produce the intended results based on past evidence. Agreement resolves issues and maps processes through negotiation all before taking action. It is useful for situations where certainty and predictability are required from the start.

Alignment The shared perspective that a proposed action is good enough to put "the game in play" or forward the play and further a cause in which group members have common, communicated commitments.

Amplitude The maximum extension of a vibration or oscillation, measured from the position of equilibrium.

Art Originally a verb meaning the process of "putting things together." In organization, one of the *domains*.

Art of Leadership One of the three domains of Organization. When leading, the challenge is to create new possibilities for the business, to focus on what does not yet exist, to lead business growth through new products, new services and new categories.

Articulation   The balancing factor for the four attributes that establish Organization's perimeters; *framework, discipline, intention, and articulation*. The creation, identification, and naming of processes and practices of participation.

Attractor Model   A three-circle model useful for distinguishing any number of individual and organizational relationships including, for example, leadership, management, and development (the basis systems of Organization), and context, process, and content (creating new realities).

Belief   An idea one holds to be true regardless of evidence. Holding firm on a belief, be it validated or not, is one way to create conditions for *circumstantial breakthrough*.

Breakdown   (1) An outcome inconsistent with what has been intended or committed to. Breakdowns have outcomes that are significantly short of what was intended. Breakdowns may be caused by *circumstance* or by *intention*. (2) A gap between what we have and what we're committed to. (3) A gap between current and future state that needs to be created.

Breakthrough   Any outcome that exceeds, by a notable margin, highest expectations that would be remotely predictable as a function of past performance. Breakthroughs may be caused by *circumstance* or by *intention*. A breakthrough is always a positive discontinuity.

Business Systems   One of three systems comprising organization; the other two are *human systems* and *integration systems*. Business systems is the focus of *management*. Business systems are concerned with reliability, predictability, certainty, and repeatability—the *science* of organization.

Business-centric Integration   Business by principles of *management science*: developing business, doing business, and running the business. Developing business is the work done today to increase the business the company does in the future: opening new locations, entering new markets, increasing product lines. Doing business is the day-to-day transactional work of selling goods and services. Running the business focuses on fulfilling on the business the company is already doing.

Capacity   As applied to leadership, an unexplored potential ability to develop leadership arts. As applied to organization, ability ("headroom") to absorb change. Also, one of four abilities to integrate change: *create, innovate, adapt,* and *react.*

Catalyst   In chemistry, a substance to start a reaction that becomes discarded waste once it creates a transformation or speeds up a process. In organizations, the four catalysts to create change integration are to *educate, develop, train,* and *instruct/drill.*

Categories of Integration   *Organizational integration* encompasses *intra-organizational integration* and *inter-organizational integration. Individual integration* encompasses *intra-personal integration* and *interpersonal integration.*

Change   Change is the process by which the future invades our lives.

Change Drivers   Nine forces behind global change in the marketplace, identified in IBM Global CEO studies between 2004 and 2008.

Change Agent   Member of a breakthrough team. The individual acts on behalf of, and reports to, a *sponsor* during an *intra-organizational change integration.*

Change Integration   The "give and take" work done to align human systems and business systems around organizational transformation. Integration takes the changes that emerge from human systems and translates them into workable solutions for business systems. A highly effective means for organizations to mitigate risk and to increase certainty, particularly when organizations undertake large-scale change.

Chaos Theory   A branch of mathematics that studies the apparent randomness of chaotic, complex systems to discern underlying patterns, interconnectedness, and self-organization.

Circumstance   Happening by coincidence, unplanned. *Circumstantial cause,* as applied to *breakthrough,* is coincidental activity with consequences unforeseeable or unforeseen. Some circumstantial causes for breakthrough have been warfare, religion, environment, and *beliefs.*

Commitment   (1) Statement on behalf of a particular future that gives rise to a proactive interpretation; (2) An act between speaker and listener; (3) An individual speech act, only possible when there's a choice.

Communication   The medium for *content,* which establishes the value for results that people produce. It is one cornerstone of societal cohesion; the other two are *trust* and *relationship.* Communication among the three systems is the "life blood" of organizational change integration. Leaders are responsible for the *context* as well as *content* of their communications. Leaders must model frequent, low-amplitude communications and promote relational networks. Integration communicates between leadership and management.

Constraint(s)   Constraints are limits in a situation. Constraint is the intermediator between risk and uncertainty. Without constraint there is no creativity. Constraint can be circumstantial "in the broadest terms" or constraint can be applied intentionally during breakthrough change.

Content   A description of the facts of the current situation, without interpretation. The "What's so?" in designing "The Playing Field." Information and knowledge.

Context   Context is what leverages action. It is the source of meaning for work. Leadership's context is creative; management's is reactive. Aligned context is the responsibility of leaders. If you are interested in increased results or breakthrough level change, then alter the context.

Craft of Change Integration   One of the three domains of organization. When integrating, the challenge is to demonstrate feasibility and efficacy, to focus on what it takes to transform possibility into reality. To establish feasibility and efficacy requires concern not only for the reality of the marketplace, but also for the reality of an organization's capabilities and capacity (headspace available to create, innovate, adapt, and react).

Create (Creativity)   Invent; make something up that is held to be of value. Create is one of the four *capacities* for integration. Creativity involves acts of originality that add value. Creativity is within the *domain* of *leadership*. The quality of creativity in business is a direct reflection of the quality of education afforded its members. In organizations based upon hierarchies, creativity is diminished.

Creative Thinking   Holistic thinking governed by the right side of the brain—imagery, pattern recognition, intuition, synthesis; the thinking associated with *human systems* and *leadership*. (See *linear thinking*.)

Develop   Unfold and expand through application and testing. One of the *catalysts* for *integration*.

Dialectic   Approach to argue "against," rooted in dialogue between several parties who wish to persuade each other. Useful skill for integration when either/or choices arise.

Discipline   Branch of instruction or learning, such as science or economics. *Organizational discipline* forms the basic branches of organizational learning and it is therefore elemental to integrating change. Existence of *organizational-scale disciplines* depends upon (1) Presence of identifiable need and (2) Recognition that this need is relevant to the organization's future.

Discontinuous Change Change that is outside the normal boundaries of established norms, as is change driven by innovation.

Disintegration Collapse of all or part of an organization.

Disintermediate Resource One of four actions for integration. (1) Structural disassembly of established norms that may result in freeing up resources. *Disintermediation by circumstance* is unplanned and characterized by increasing disorder and ongoing degeneration of the organization. *Disintermediation through facilitated intervention* is disassembly of the organization with intention of generating new order and prospects for the future. (2) Reduction, reorganization or discontinuance of parts of a company.

Distinct Clearly differing from, within our understanding, easy to recognize or grasp meaning. In contrast, when some fact is in the background of our consciousness, it is *indistinct*.

Distinctions Easily recognized differences. Also, the "aha!" moments that change the way we think and act. In organization "collapsed distinctions" exist between management and leadership.

Domain Area of activity. In Organization the domain of leadership is *art*, of management is *science*, and of integration is *craft*.

Educate (education) Bring forth or draw out learning, beginning with observation and then through inquiry. One of the four *catalysts* for *integration*.

Effectiveness One approach to demonstrating *feasibility* and relative value to the organization; the other is *efficacy*. In breakthrough change integration, it is difficult to measure *quantitatively*, so it is best approached by using agreed-upon *qualitative* results such as achieving new goals or gaining learning.

Efficacy One approach to demonstrating *feasibility*; the other is *effectiveness*. Mainly a concern of *integration systems*, it involves repetitive acts measured by time and energy saved; for example, reduction in amount of work. "When integrating, the challenge is to demonstrate feasibility and efficacy."

Efficiency Mainly a concern of management, it concerns unique works measured *quantitatively* by degree to which a goal is achieved, such as cost reductions.

Ethics (1) Involves binary choice or best route in the face of repugnant options, weighted toward unique, individual acts. (2) Rules, values, or standards of right conduct for a particular group, especially for a profession.

Existence   The occurring world, both physical and non-physical. The state of existence for business systems is authoritative hierarchy, for human systems is relational network, and for development systems is dynamic matrix.

Feasibility   (1) One requirement for a successful breakthrough change integration. When integrating, the challenge is to demonstrate feasibility and efficacy. (2) Capability of being done, effected, or accomplished.

Field   An area of the world where some things are more likely to happen and/ or others are less likely to happen. Organizational Systems are the field in which business systems, human systems, and development systems exist.

Fractal   The same pattern of wholeness is found at every scale, the repetition of patterns at all scales from micro to macro. (See *holographic*.)

Framework   A support structure in which other support structures can be developed and organized. Frameworks facilitate organizational development and running the day-to-day business.

Framing Integration (art)   The work of creating a basic structure to organize complex issues in a conceptual frame of reference. The work is generative, emphasizing intermediate process and the triage of possibility to improve the odds of breakthrough that will provide new and lasting value for the organization. Considerations are best use of resources, greatest need, and probability of success. Intermediated decisions are arrived at through alignment of various viewpoints.

Generalist   Individual in organization who sees relationships and relevance of a range of viewpoints. Useful communication skill for integrators.

Generate Breakthrough   Condition in which one breakthrough leads to recursive breakthroughs. See list of ten points to consider for generating breakthrough.

Globalizers   CEOs who took a globally oriented strategy to change, as identified in IBM Global CEO studies.

Goal   Within *intentional cause, goals* with unexpected results can open doors to breakthroughs. Breakthroughs can sometimes be given the misnomers of stretch goals or incremental results.

Holographic   Existing simultaneously at every scale of organization.

Homeostasis   Maintenance of the same state. Within organizations, the tendency to maintain stable, balanced energy and resist change.

Horizontal Integration   Traditionally a structure used in marketing to sell a product in numerous markets. *Horizontal change integration* establishes new norms beyond continuous improvement across vertical spans of control within the same company or across vertically integrated companies. Also see *vertical integration*.

Human Systems   One of three systems comprising Organization; the other two are *integration systems* and *business systems*. Human systems is the focus of *leadership*. Humans systems is concerned with relationships, ideas, and energy (possibility and unrealized potential)—and the art of leadership.

Hypothesis Suggested   explanation of a phenomenon or a reasoned proposal suggesting a possible correlation between multiple phenomena. During *operationalizing integration*, operationalizing the hypothesis is the *process* of creating the proposal, developing a measurement tool for data, collecting data, then testing the hypothesis. It involves research and analysis.

Informs Management   informs integration; integration informs leadership.

Innovate   Find new applications for existing technology and add value. One of the four *capacities* for integration.

Innovation   A form of change that is the product of *intention*. We innovate by taking something that has been established and applying it in a new way for a different purpose.

Instruct/Drill   Practice and condition a defined set of skills by using rigorous repetition. One of four *catalysts* for organizational change integration.

Integration   To bring together and incorporate parts into a whole. This is the *meta-discipline* whose principal domain is *craft*. Often described as the "missing link" between *art* and *science*. Integration's challenge is to demonstrate feasibility and efficacy, and to transform possibility into reality.

Integration Systems   One of three systems comprising Organization; the other two are *human systems* and *business systems*. Integration systems is the focus of change agents. *Efficacy* and *effectiveness* are its concerns.

Intention (intent)   Purposeful creative energy that drives outcomes. An "organizational state-of-mind"—one that increases the potential for particular results—as can be seen in the collective intention of an organization.

Intentional Cause   Purposeful action with consequences unforeseeable or unforeseen. Context shifts and goals with unexpected results are notable intentional causes of breakthrough.

Intentionality   A state-of-mind that increases the potential for an intended reality.

Intermediate Possibility   One of four *actions for integration*. Generate possibility and break through established norms. The process of "triaging possibilities" to identify and evaluate those with highest probability of success.

Intermediation   The action of integrating discontinuity to generate possibilities and break through established norms.

Internalizing Integration (craft)   The work of gaining acceptance for a pending shift in norm, that violates established deviations to the current norm. The work processes are investigation, communication, participation, and instruction. (See *operationalizing integration* and *framing integration*.)

Jurisdiction Power,   authority, or control over an area, department, or discipline. It is the denominator for *disintegration* in an organization. For example: "Risk can be measured quantitatively and as such is the jurisdiction of business systems."

Language   Symbolic medium for *meaning*. The initial existence of *meaning* arises as a creation in language. The meaning in language is unique to the individual.

Lead   An act of existential courage on behalf of something not yet in existence. An art form. The principal domain of leading is art (creativity).

Leader   One who designs an organization's future, using the art of *leadership*. An ordinary human being with the commitment to produce a result whose realization would be extraordinary given the perceived current circumstances. A leader has the integrity to see this commitment through to its realization.

Leadership   *Meta-discipline* whose principal *domain* is *art* (creativity and innovation). Leadership's challenge is to create new possibilities for organization. It is about *form* and *forming*. Leadership is not about authority; it's about standing for something.

Learning   Information transfer or discovery; an internal change motivated by self that involves resolution of dissonance. Knowledge, information, and understanding as a foundation for learning are no longer sufficient. Leaders must learn to see into complexity in ways that will distinguish the basic patterns out of which organizational complexity arises in the first place.

Leverage   Potential for greatest effect. People make the positive leverage that is the source of results or the negative leverage that leads to breakdowns.

Lexicon   Language and terms unique to a *specialization*.

Liminal Space   Space of flux where state change occurs, the liminal space between the current prevailing norm or organization and the desired future state.

Linear Thinking   Sequential thinking and focused, reductionist logic controlled by the left side of the brain; the thinking associated with *business systems* and *management*. (*In contrast, see creative thinking.*)

Local Realism   The idea that any part of the organization is a "private reality" and exists without material effect elsewhere.

Machine Tool   A tool that builds other tools, such as the Attractor Model.

Management   *Meta-discipline* whose principal *domain* is *science*. Management's challenge is to provide reliability, predictability, and certainty to the organization. Its work is grounded in authoritative hierarchies.

Management Sciences   Specialized *capabilities* for maintaining day-to-day operations, decision analysis, and problem solving of an organization, based upon *scientific method*. (See *method*.)

Meaning   It is not enough that *language* might serve as a symbolic medium for meaning. The initial existence of meaning arises as a creation in language. The two are a mutually arising phenomenon.

Mediate differences   One of four *actions* for integration. Assess for higher or lower certainty of success; neutral assessment of strengths and weaknesses between competing influences, choices or paths to follow in the effort to turn a possibility into a reality.

Mediation   Action to reduce deviations from the norm with the intention of increasing predictability, reliability, certainty, and repeatability. Within the realm of continuous improvement, mediated change requires committed neutrality, while assessing strengths and weaknesses among competing influences. To arrive at mediated decisions, the organization might engage an authority or rely upon agreement between several parties to set standards.

Meta-discipline   Any of the three overarching organizational *disciplines*— *management, integration,* or *leadership*.

Methodology   Collection, study, and critique of individual *methods* in each of the *management sciences* applied to running business.

Myth   Form of story that leads to reshaping reality. One substitution for truth and facts; the other is *superstition*.

Norms   Part of the work of integration is to discover and communicate existing norms, thus preparing the organization for impending shifts in norms. Many existing norms are so deeply imbedded and so pervasive that they go unnoticed and therefore unquestioned.

Operationalizing Integration (science)   The work of defining a concept and related variables, so they can be measured and expressed quantitatively. The work processes of this empirical approach are research and analysis. (See *internalizing integration* and *framing integration*.)

Organization (Dictionary)   A network of conversations between individuals. People, business, and organization are one. There can be no organization without people. Organizations have all the key attributes of societal formations and are therefore subject to the variability and unexpected changes that come with human interaction. The three primary systems that are essential to Organization are *human systems*, *business systems*, and *integration systems*.

Organization (Our Revision)   A complex system of mutually dependent structures that form into subsystems. The subsystems manifest fractal-like patterns at all scales: individual, team, group, and organization. The actions and interactions of subsystems, within scale, and across scales and perspectives, produce incalculable permutations of overlapping interests that serve complementary and conflicting purposes.

Perspective   Viewpoint held by people or by an organization. Perspective is influenced by one's position in organization. The perspectives of leadership, management, and integration can often differ.

Playing Field   The playing field is designed using the Attractor Model to lay the foundations for a Breakthrough Initiative. It consists of three questions: "What's so," "What's possible?" and

"What are our next actions?"

Private Reality   Reality in isolation that exists without material effect elsewhere. See "Local Reality."

Problem-solution Model   Narrowly defined, *linear thinking* associated with scientific method and mostly useful for management.

Process   Simultaneous ongoing activities; activities that don't stop before other activities can begin. Process is the *context* when we "put things together" for *breakthrough change integration*. The ways and means to get something accomplished.

Qualitative   Able to be measured by setting agreed-upon terms dealing with effectiveness, efficacy, and feasibility. Generally, able to be measured descriptively in terms of relative value. Qualitative research is often used in surveys. For breakthrough change integration, registers for accomplishment might be employed.

Quantitative   Able to be measured numerically, monetarily, or in units or percentages of time. Quantitative measurement falls into two broad categories: discrete data that measures attributes and continuous data that measures variables. Discrete data includes binomial data (such as yes/no, pass/fail), category data (types), and probability.

Quantum Organization   An organization where continuous organizational learning and adaptation take place as a result of the effective integration of *human* and *business systems*.

React   (1) Organizational *capability* (mechanism) that promotes continuity for survival. (2) Respond to unwanted surprises and minimize loss of value. One of the four *capacities* for integration. "Reacting to adversity usually requires repair, recovery and reestablishing work so it falls within acceptable boundaries of performance norms." The work is concerned with remedial process (see *remediate problems*).

Realization   Change that achieves expected return on the investment.

Recursion   Successive, overlapping steps in a chain. Lead, integrate, and manage are recursions of activities, and breakthroughs are often recursive. With each recursion the rate of breakthrough outcomes often accelerates.

Relationship   The medium for *process*, which shapes the action people take. One cornerstone of societal cohesion; the other two are *communication* and *trust*.

Remediate Problems   One of four *actions* for *integration*. Repair, refurbish, reestablish, and/or recover all or portions of preexisting norms. The focus is to restore or maintain order to reduce *risk* and increase certainty.

Remediation   Fixing a preexisting condition that has lost integrity.

Risk   Potential for loss of something already possessed. In organization, a financial term associated with loss of money. Risk can be measured quantitatively.

Scale (verb)   To raise or lower in relative importance in organization. Both disciplines and specializations can be scaled. (noun) A certain relative size, extent, or importance, as in "integration at the scale of organization."

Scientific Management   Machine-Age approach to business that trains workers for repetition and reliability in the interests of organizational stability.

Source Creative   individual(s) who can stand for the possibility of a break-through. They are curious, proactively promote a simple notion, have tenacious belief in a possibility they see, are willing to "stand in the face of no agreement," and to communicate their ideas.

Specialization   Subset of a *discipline* in organization, often with an associated title. Specialists are experts in particular fields.

Spectrum   A unifying theme.

Sponsor   Lead member of a breakthrough team during an *intra-organizational change integration. Change agents* act on behalf of, and report to, the *sponsor.*

Standing in the Face of no Agreement   You take a stand for what you see, even if no one agrees with you. It's the dilemma of the leader in the process of creating something that has never existed before. Remaining committed until it takes on a life of its own.

Superstition   One substitution for truth and facts; the other is *myth.*

System   In Toomey's Laws for Change Integration, see "the longer a system exists the less amenable it is to change" and other descriptions of how a system operates. (See *business systems, human systems, integration systems.*)

System Complexity   A function of the number of specializations and their interrelatedness.

Systems Perspective   Viewpoint that organization is similar to an organism, where all the subsystems are interrelated.

Teaching   Transfer of knowledge or of things that work and are repeated. Teaching approaches the student as a passive receptacle of knowledge. (See *training.*)

Tool Broadly   an instrument that you can leverage to do work. For example, *dialectic* is a tool for integration, and measurement instruments are tools of management. Too often executive management perceives "the corpo-ration" as a Machine-Age set of tools that can be re-machined for change and they forget that the organization is people.

Train   Transfer skills and knowledge through teaching.

Transformation   A new condition created with no new material added except a catalyst, which is discarded in the process.

Translation   Ability to interpret business information and goals so employees understand. One job for integration systems is to translate the changes that come from human systems into workable solutions for business systems.

Triage Allocation of scarce resources in ways that derive the most benefit. (See *intermediate possibility*.)

Trust The medium for context, which provides meaning to the work people do. One cornerstone of societal cohesion; the other two are *communication* and *relationship*.

Uncertainty A state of ambivalence or indefinite outcome regarding what you don't yet have but intend to acquire or achieve. Uncertainty cannot be measured quantitatively in breakthrough change integration. (See *risk*.)

Value To hold in high regard; a function of intention and commitment. In Organization, "value" has traditionally meant "shareholder value" but the four capacities for integration—create, innovate, adapt, and react—are all concerned with value to the whole organization. Instruments can be designed to measure value either qualitatively or quantitatively.

Vertical Integration Traditionally a structure that unites companies through a hierarchy, usually leading to common ownership. Vertical integrations can exist within leadership and management within hierarchical spans of control, going unrecognized by leaders.

Vertical Change Integration The establishment of new norms beyond continuous improvement, within a span of control within the same company. Also see *horizontal integration*.

Vicious Cycle Negative feedback loops that create breakdowns in the organization.

Virtuous Cycle Positive feedback loops that benefit the organization.

Workability (1) The bridge between integrity and value creation. In designing for breakthrough change, demonstrate early workability. (2) The state of being practical or feasible, able to be worked.

INDEX

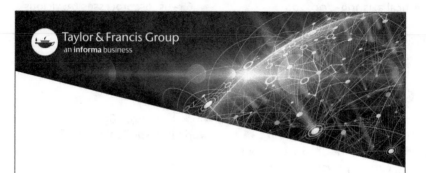